T. Flynn

MORAL OBLIGATION

AND

DUTY AND INTEREST

ESSAYS AND LECTURES

BY

H. A. PRICHARD

WITH AN INTRODUCTION BY
J. O. URMSON

OXFORD UNIVERSITY PRESS
LONDON OXFORD NEW YORK

Oxford University Press

OXFORD LONDON NEW YORK
GLASGOW TORONTO MELBOURNE WELLINGTON
CAPE TOWN SALISBURY IBADAN NAIROBI LUSAKA ADDIS ABABA
BOMBAY CALCUTTA MADRAS KARACHI LAHORE DACCA
KUALA LUMPUR HONG KONG TOKYO

Duty and Interest first published by the Clarendon Press 1929
Moral Obligation first published by the Clarendon Press 1949
First issued together as an Oxford University Press paperback 1968

REPRINTED LITHOGRAPHICALLY IN GREAT BRITAIN
AT THE UNIVERSITY PRESS, OXFORD
BY VIVIAN RIDLER
PRINTER TO THE UNIVERSITY

NOTE TO THE ORIGINAL EDITION

IT has long been a matter of regret to those who knew Harold Prichard that he published so little of the fruits of his many years of concentrated thought about philosophical problems. On moral philosophy, which was his main subject for the last half of his life, he published no more than two articles and two lectures. But he was known to have written a good deal more, even if his persistent self-criticism had led him to tear up many drafts which he had come to think unsatisfactory. When I was given the opportunity of going through what he had left behind him I found that he had made considerable progress with a book on moral obligation, although he had, apparently, added little to it later than 1937. There were also a certain number of short (in some cases very short) papers dealing with particular ethical questions. Finally, it seemed well to republish the two articles on ethical subjects which had appeared, one in *Mind* for 1912 and one in *Philosophy* for 1935, and his British Academy lecture on Duty and Ignorance of Fact. His inaugural lecture, as White's Professor of Moral Philosophy, on Duty and Interest, is not republished, because much of it is used in the long essay on Moral Obligation.[1] The papers have been arranged in their probable chronological order.

An admirable memoir of Prichard by Professor H. H. Price has appeared in the papers of the British Academy, and there is no need to add to this preface a second account of Prichard's views; the essays will speak for themselves. I believe no one can read them without feeling that in him we had one of the very finest philosophical minds of the whole generation to which he belonged.

W. D. ROSS

3 *October* 1949

---

[1] The inaugural lecture is included in this reprint.

CONTENTS

INTRODUCTION

THIS book contains H. A. Prichard's writings on moral philosophy. Some were published in his lifetime, others were selected from his literary remains by W. D. Ross; and they were assembled in the volume *Moral Obligation*, first published in 1949 and here reprinted with the addition of 'Duty and Interest', Prichard's inaugural lecture as White's Professor of Moral Philosophy. Though much of that lecture is incorporated in the long essay entitled 'Moral Obligation', also printed here, its historical importance makes it desirable that it should be readily available in its original form.

Like Ross in his note to the original edition of this book, I draw the attention of readers anxious to know more of the man and his work to H. H. Price's obituary notice of Prichard in Volume XXXIII (1947) of the *Proceedings of the British Academy*. As a member of the very last generation of undergraduates to attend Prichard's lectures and informal instruction, I learnt to admire his patience as a teacher, his philosophical acuity and, above all, his quite exceptional intellectual honesty and independence, before I studied his writings. But some hint of these qualities can be discovered in the writings. I echo the words of Ross: 'I believe no one can read them without feeling that in him we had one of the very finest philosophical minds of the whole generation to which he belonged'.

But, no doubt, if one is sufficiently selective in marshalling facts and arguments, it is not difficult to make a plausible case for the opinion that the philosophical views of Prichard can now be quietly put aside. Certainly it must be conceded that his influence in his lifetime was great, particularly in his own university of Oxford; but this may be counted a misfortune. Did he not constantly overbear his opponents with dogmatic assertion? 'If we reflect, we become forced to admit ....', he would say, and further discussion would be fruitless. If his lectures commanded a faithful audience, were they not, dogmatism aside, mainly a destructive criticism of his selected targets? Outside moral philosophy, he was a champion of such lost causes as the synthetic *a priori* truth of Euclidian geometry; within moral philosophy, the intuitionism which he expounded has disappeared, except to be perfunctorily refuted in the first or second chapter of ethical textbooks. For it was an irrational dogmatism—either one saw by inspection the moral truths which Prichard saw or one was morally blind, and nothing more was to be said. Further, what can a generation of philosophers with a respect for idiom find of value in a philosopher who perpetrated such barbarisms as 'I shall be oughting to do a'? And if we think that philosophy should concern itself with real moral issues, what are we to make of a man whose puzzles are about exchanging a banana for an apple, an obligation to go to bed, or what one should do if a man's life depended on the correct guess of the fall of a die?

This unfavourable judgement of Prichard, while overstated, is not without justice. But it is not merely overstated, it is highly selective. Thus it must be owned that he did maintain his views, once formed, with vehemence, and would brush aside most criticism as shallow and ill-conceived. But these views were arrived at by the most careful and honest thinking, and, outside the dialectical forum, he continually reconsidered them. Views earlier accepted and later abandoned were attacked with the same vigour as those which he had always rejected. Moreover those philosophers whom he attacked most frequently and most vigorously were those he most respected. Thus he dismissed without argument the logical positivism of the thirties as being unworthy of a reply his sustained attacks on Hume's moral philosophy and Green's political philosophy, on the other hand, were based on careful reading and combined with great respect for his antagonists. When Prichard thought that he had found a fatal flaw in the argument of a Hume, a Green, or a Sidgwick, he concentrated on it and remorselessly exposed it, allowing himself to be sidetracked by no subsidiary issues. But he said of Green in 'Duty and Interest' that 'the more you study any particular sentence, the more you are convinced that every word of it has been weighed and that, whether or not it is true, it expresses exactly what he meant to say'. This is why he thought it worth while to attack Green's views.

Again, it is true that Prichard often employs an odd, or even bizarre, idiom. But he could also employ a powerful and simple prose, and always avoided the facile, thought-saving jargon of philosophy. Still more important, he often showed a very remarkable sensitivity and respect for the features of ordinary language. Anyone who reads 'The Obligation to Keep a Promise' will see that Prichard, at least, did not need to be told that a promise was performative, a kind of action, rather than constative. Or, again, Austin's 'Ifs and Cans' is rightly celebrated for its subtle demonstration of the idiosyncratic character of the expression 'I can, if I choose'; he showed differences between this and typical conditional statements which philosophers had to admit that they had overlooked until Austin pointed them out. But the basic point had been seen and made by Prichard in 1932. In 'Duty and Ignorance of Fact', considering the statement 'Well, at least I can do the action, e.g. shout, *if* I choose', he remarks: 'Such a statement, however, as we see when we reflect, is very odd. It cannot be meant literally, and can at best be only an idiom. For while it is sense to say: "If I choose to make a loud noise, I shall in fact make it," it cannot be sense to say: "If I choose to make it, I *can* make it." And no one would maintain that our *ability* to do something, as distinct from our *doing* it, can depend on our choosing to do it.' His own view is that 'I can do X if I choose' is a brachylogical way of saying 'Since I can choose to do X, I can do X'; which may or may not be satisfactory. But here again, Prichard's reflection had led him to a degree of clarity denied to his contemporaries.

Much of what is found least acceptable by many in Prichard's philosophy arises from his unwillingness to falsify what seemed to him to be the basic facts. As he makes clear in the penultimate paragraph of 'Duty and Ignorance of Fact', it was clear to him that any philosophical theory must be tested by reference to the less general facts that we know to be the case. To do otherwise is to prefer simplicity to truth. It is from this consideration, not from natural dogmatism, that his intuitionism stems. This intuitionism is the doctrine that there are many distinct obligations, such as truth-telling and promise-keeping, which must be recognized as ultimate and which cannot be argued to or treated as special cases of some more general obligation.

Now it seemed obvious to Prichard that on particular occasions, when explaining why we have a duty to perform some action, we do give such answers as that we had promised to do it, that gratitude required it, that it would be deceitful not to do it, that it would relieve suffering, and the like. Therefore any general ethical theory must make *this* intelligible, not substitute something else for it. Prichard has no objection to our looking for some unifying theory; indeed, he says in the essay 'Moral

Obligation' that 'it is almost bound to occur to us that acts of different sorts cannot all be duties unless they possess some common character, the possession of which renders them duties'. But one's zeal for an answer to this inquiry must not be allowed to make one forget or falsify the basic facts to be explained. What Prichard claimed was that a careful examination of attempts to discover such a common characteristic always failed, either by unintelligibility or by falsification of the basic data. If, for example, one claimed that promotion of welfare was the common character of all kinds of duties, Prichard's answer was that, when faced with the performance of an action which one had promised to do, one could not represent the manifest duty of performance as one of promoting welfare without destroying the data one's theory was supposed to explain. If we are tempted by such theories 'the only remedy lies in actually getting into a situation which occasions the obligation, or—if our imagination be strong enough—in imagining ourselves in that situation, and then letting our moral capacities of thinking do their work'.

Whether Prichard succeeded in showing, as he claimed, that all teleological ethical theories must inevitably fail may be doubtful. Many would claim that there are more subtle teleological theories which escape his net. But we do well to heed Prichard's arguments and learn to imitate his scrupulous respect for the facts. It was this, not dogmatism, which led, or misled, him to his celebrated view that moral philosophy, in looking for the common character, rested on a mistake.

Similarly we shall find an unwavering regard for the facts to be the clue to his careful and deflationary examination of the attempts of Green and others to explain the duty of political obedience. On this occasion, perhaps, his views will attract more sympathy from the philosophers of the present day. His lectures on Green's views on political obligations are a model of careful criticism. He ends by asking whether the question about the ground of political obedience has in fact any single correct answer. 'We are apt', he tells us, 'to assume that the questions "Ought an Englishman to obey the Crown and Parliament, an Italian to obey Mussolini, a German to obey Hitler?" are instances of the same question. But is this really so— because the thing called a state may in each case be different, and if there are kinds of state, the duty to obey may depend on the kind?' For candid good sense, expressed in plain and simple

English, these lectures have few rivals. When Prichard has
compared the question 'Why ought a subject to obey his
ruler?' to the question 'Why ought we to read books?', the false
assumptions of classical political theory quickly lose their plausibility.

It would be unwise for us, then, to put aside the writings of
Prichard. An attentive reader will always learn from them. But
no doubt we should read them with the same wary scrutiny that
Prichard gave to the works of Green. I myself find Prichard's
criticism of Plato and Aristotle surprisingly imperceptive. In
'Does Moral Philosophy Rest on a Mistake?' Prichard speaks
of his 'extreme sense of dissatisfaction produced by a close
reading of Aristotle's *Ethics*', a work I regard as being still the
greatest in its field. When I read his paper 'The Meaning of
ἀγαθόν in the *Ethics* of Aristotle' I can conclude only that Prichard's
dissatisfaction arose from profound misunderstanding. The
frequently repeated criticism of Plato also, for trying to found
duty on interest, while of great non-historical interest as philosophical argument, seems to lack sympathetic understanding
of Plato.

But, though we are all likely to be at times puzzled and
repelled by Prichard's views and arguments, a mind so subtle,
so candid and so honest as Prichard's, informed by such respect
for facts and helped by frequent acuity of ear for linguistic
usage, inevitably produced much which we cannot safely ignore.
Only the dullest and least teachable of his readers can fail to
learn from him.

                                                      J. O. URMSON

March 1968

1

DOES MORAL PHILOSOPHY REST ON A MISTAKE?[1]

PROBABLY to most students of Moral Philosophy there comes a time when they feel a vague sense of dissatisfaction with the whole subject. And the sense of dissatisfaction tends to grow rather than to diminish. It is not so much that the positions, and still more the arguments, of particular thinkers seem unconvincing, though this is true. It is rather that the aim of the subject becomes increasingly obscure. 'What', it is asked, 'are we really going to learn by Moral Philosophy?' 'What are books on Moral Philosophy really trying to show, and when their aim is clear, why are they so unconvincing and artificial?' And again: 'Why is it so difficult to substitute anything better?' Personally, I have been led by growing dissatisfaction of this kind to wonder whether the reason may not be that the subject, at any rate as usually understood, consists in the attempt to answer an improper question. And in this article I shall venture to contend that the existence of the whole subject, as usually understood, rests on a mistake, and on a mistake parallel to that on which rests, as I think, the subject usually called the Theory of Knowledge.

If we reflect on our own mental history or on the history of the subject, we feel no doubt about the nature of the demand which originates the subject. Any one who, stimulated by education, has come to feel the force of the various obligations in life, at some time or other comes to feel the irksomeness of carrying them out, and to recognize the sacrifice of interest involved; and, if thoughtful, he inevitably puts to himself the question: 'Is there really a reason why I should act in the ways in which hitherto I have thought I ought to act? May I not have been all the time under an illusion in so thinking? Should not I really be justified in simply trying to have a good time?' Yet, like Glaucon, feeling that somehow he ought after all to act in these ways, he asks for a *proof* that this feeling is justified. In other words, he asks '*Why* should I do these things?', and his and other people's moral philosophizing is an attempt to supply the answer, i.e. to supply by a process of reflection a proof of the truth of what he and they have prior to

[1] From *Mind*, vol. xxi, no. 81, Jan. 1912.

reflection believed immediately or without proof. This frame of mind seems to present a close parallel to the frame of mind which originates the Theory of Knowledge. Just as the recognition that the doing of our duty often vitally interferes with the satisfaction of our inclinations leads us to wonder whether we really ought to do what we usually call our duty, so the recognition that we and others are liable to mistakes in knowledge generally leads us, as it did Descartes, to wonder whether hitherto we may not have been always mistaken. And just as we try to find a proof, based on the general consideration of action and of human life, that we ought to act in the ways usually called moral, so we, like Descartes, propose by a process of reflection on our thinking to find a test of knowledge, i.e. a principle by applying which we can show that a certain condition of mind was really knowledge, a condition which *ex hypothesi* existed independently of the process of reflection.

Now, how has the moral question been answered? So far as I can see, the answers all fall, and fall from the necessities of the case, into one of two species. *Either* they state that we ought to do so and so, because, as we see when we fully apprehend the facts, doing so will be for our good, i.e. really, as I would rather say, for our advantage, or, better still, for our happiness; *or* they state that we ought to do so and so, because something realized either in or by the action is good. In other words, the reason 'why' is stated in terms either of the agent's happiness or of the goodness of something involved in the action.

To see the prevalence of the former species of answer, we have only to consider the history of Moral Philosophy. To take obvious instances, Plato, Butler, Hutcheson, Paley, Mill, each in his own way seeks at bottom to convince the individual that he ought to act in so-called moral ways by showing that to do so will really be for his happiness. Plato is perhaps the most significant instance, because of all philosophers he is the one to whom we are least willing to ascribe a mistake on such matters, and a mistake on his part would be evidence of the deep-rootedness of the tendency to make it. To show that Plato really justifies morality by its profitableness, it is only necessary to point out (1) that the very formulation of the thesis to be met, viz. that justice is ἀλλότριον ἀγαθόν, implies that any refutation must consist in showing that justice is οἰκεῖον ἀγαθόν, i.e. really, as the context shows, one's own advantage, and (2) that the term λυσιτελεῖν supplies the key not only to the problem but also to its solution.

The tendency to justify acting on moral rules in this way is natural. For if, as often happens, we put to ourselves the question 'Why should we do so and so?', we are satisfied by being convinced either that the doing so will lead to something which we want (e.g. that taking certain medicine will heal our disease), or that the doing so itself, as we see when we appreciate its nature, is something that we want or should like, e.g. playing golf. The formulation of the question implies a state of unwillingness or indifference towards the action, and we are brought into a condition of willingness by the answer. And this process seems to be precisely what we desire when we ask, e.g., 'Why should we keep our engagements to our own loss?'; for it is just the fact that the keeping of our engagements runs counter to the satisfaction of our desires which produced the question.

The answer is, of course, not an answer, for it fails to convince us that we ought to keep our engagements; even if successful on its own lines, it only makes us *want* to keep them. And Kant was really only pointing out this fact when he distinguished hypothetical and categorical imperatives, even though he obscured the nature of the fact by wrongly describing his so-called 'hypothetical imperatives' as imperatives. But if this answer be no answer, what other can be offered? Only, it seems, an answer which bases the obligation to do something on the *goodness* either of something to which the act leads or of the act itself. Suppose, when wondering whether we really ought to act in the ways usually called moral, we are told as a means of resolving our doubt that those acts are right which produce happiness. We at once ask: 'Whose happiness?' If we are told 'Our own happiness', then, though we shall lose our hesitation to act in these ways, we shall not recover our sense that we ought to do so. But how can this result be avoided? Apparently, only by being told one of two things; *either* that anyone's happiness is a thing good in itself, and that *therefore* we ought to do whatever will produce it, *or* that working for happiness is itself good, and that the intrinsic goodness of such an action is the reason why we ought to do it. The advantage of this appeal to the goodness of something consists in the fact that it avoids reference to desire, and, instead, refers to something impersonal and objective. In this way it seems possible to avoid the resolution of obligation into inclination. But just for this reason it is of the essence of the answer, that to be effective it must neither include nor involve the view that the apprehension of the goodness of anything necessarily arouses the desire for it. Otherwise the answer resolves itself into a form of the former answer by substituting desire or inclination for the sense of obligation, and in this way it loses what seems its special advantage.

Now it seems to me that both forms of this answer break down, though each for a different reason.

Consider the first form. It is what may be called Utilitarianism in the generic sense, in which what is good is not limited to pleasure. It takes its stand upon the distinction between something which is not itself an action, but which can be produced by an action, and the action which will produce it, and contends that if something which is not an action is good, then we *ought* to undertake the action which will, directly or indirectly, originate it.[1]

But this argument, if it is to restore the sense of obligation to act, must presuppose an intermediate link, viz. the further thesis that what is good ought to be.[2] The necessity of this link is obvious. An 'ought,' if it is to be derived at all, can only be derived from another 'ought'. Moreover, this link tacitly presupposes another, viz. that the apprehension that something good which is not an action ought to be involves just the feeling of imperativeness or obligation which is to be aroused by the thought of the action which will originate it. Otherwise the argument will not lead us to feel the obligation to produce it by the action. And, surely, both this link and its implication are false.[3] The word 'ought' refers to actions and to actions alone. The proper language is never 'So and so ought to be', but 'I ought to do so and so'. Even if we are sometimes moved to say that the world or something in it is not what it ought to be, what we really mean is that God or some human being has not made something what he ought to have made it. And it is merely stating another side of this fact to urge that we can only feel the imperativeness upon us of something which is in our power ; for it is actions and actions alone which, directly at least, are in our power.

Perhaps, however, the best way to see the failure of this view is to see its failure to correspond to our actual moral convictions. Suppose we ask ourselves whether our sense that we ought to pay our debts or to tell the truth arises from our recognition that in doing so we should be originating something good, e.g. material

---

[1] Cf. Dr. Rashdall's *Theory of Good and Evil*, vol. i, p. 138.

[2] Dr. Rashdall, if I understand him rightly, supplies this link (cf. ibid., pp. 135–6).

[3] When we speak of anything, e.g. of some emotion or of some quality of a human being, as good, we never dream in our ordinary consciousness of going on to say that therefore it ought to be.

comfort in *A* or true belief in *B*, i.e. suppose we ask ourselves whether it is this aspect of the action which leads to our recognition that we ought to do it. We at once and without hesitation answer 'No'. Again, if we take as our illustration our sense that we ought to act justly as between two parties, we have, if possible, even less hesitation in giving a similar answer; for the balance of resulting good may be, and often is, not on the side of justice.

At best it can only be maintained that there is this element of truth in the Utilitarian view, that unless we recognized that something which an act will originate is good, we should not recognize that we ought to do the action. Unless we thought knowledge a good thing, it may be urged, we should not think that we ought to tell the truth; unless we thought pain a bad thing, we should not think the infliction of it, without special reason, wrong. But this is not to imply that the badness of error is the reason why it is wrong to lie, or the badness of pain the reason why we ought not to inflict it without special cause.[1]

It is, I think, just because this form of the view is so plainly at variance with our moral consciousness that we are driven to adopt the other form of the view, viz. that the act is good in itself and that its intrinsic goodness is the reason why it ought to be done. It is this form which has always made the most serious appeal; for the goodness of the act itself seems more closely related to the obligation to do it than that of its mere consequences or results, and therefore, if obligation is to be based on the goodness of something, it would seem that this goodness should be that of the act itself. Moreover, the view gains plausibility from the fact that moral actions are most conspicuously those to which the term 'intrinsically good' is applicable.

Nevertheless this view, though perhaps less superficial, is equally untenable. For it leads to precisely the dilemma which faces everyone who tries to solve the problem raised by Kant's theory of the good will. To see this, we need only consider the nature of the acts to which we apply the term 'intrinsically good'.

There is, of course, no doubt that we approve and even admire certain actions, and also that we should describe them as good, and as good in themselves. But it is, I think, equally unquestionable

---

[1] It may be noted that if the badness of pain were the reason why we ought not to inflict pain on another, it would equally be a reason why we ought not to inflict pain on ourselves; yet, though we should allow the wanton infliction of pain on ourselves to be foolish, we should not think of describing it as wrong.

that our approval and our use of the term 'good' is always in respect of the motive and refers to actions which have been actually done and of which we think we know the motive. Further, the actions of which we approve and which we should describe as intrinsically good are of two and only two kinds. They are either actions in which the agent did what he did because he thought he ought to do it, or actions of which the motive was a desire prompted by some good emotion, such as gratitude, affection, family feeling, or public spirit, the most prominent of such desires in books on Moral Philosophy being that ascribed to what is vaguely called benevolence. For the sake of simplicity I omit the case of actions done partly from some such desire and partly from a sense of duty; for even if all good actions are done from a combination of these motives, the argument will not be affected. The dilemma is this. If the motive in respect of which we think an action good is the sense of obligation, then so far from the sense that we ought to do it being derived from our apprehension of its goodness, our apprehension of its goodness will presuppose the sense that we ought to do it. In other words, in this case the recognition that the act is good will plainly *presuppose* the recognition that the act is right, whereas the view under consideration is that the recognition of the goodness of the act *gives rise* to the recognition of its rightness. On the other hand, if the motive in respect of which we think an action good is some intrinsically good desire, such as the desire to help a friend, the recognition of the goodness of the act will equally fail to give rise to the sense of obligation to do it. For we cannot feel that we ought to do that the doing of which is *ex hypothesi* prompted solely by the desire to do it.[1]

The fallacy underlying the view is that while to base the rightness of an act upon its intrinsic goodness implies that the goodness in question is that of the motive, in reality the rightness or wrongness of an act has nothing to do with any question of motives at all. For, as any instance will show, the rightness of an action concerns an action not in the fuller sense of the term in which we include the motive in the action, but in the narrower and commoner sense in which we distinguish an action from its motive and mean by an action merely the conscious origination of something, an origination which on different occasions or in different people may be prompted by different motives. The question 'Ought I to pay my

[1] It is, I think, on this latter horn of the dilemma that Martineau's view falls; cf. *Types of Ethical Theory*, part ii, book i.

bills?' really means simply 'Ought I to bring about my trades-men's possession of what by my previous acts I explicitly or im-plicitly promised them?' There is, and can be, no question of whether I ought to pay my debts from a particular motive. No doubt we know that if we pay our bills we shall pay them with a motive, but in considering whether we ought to pay them we inevitably think of the act in abstraction from the motive. Even if we knew what our motive would be if we did the act, we should not be any nearer an answer to the question.

Moreover, if we eventually pay our bills from fear of the county court, we shall still have done *what* we ought, even though we shall not have done it *as* we ought. The attempt to bring in the motive involves a mistake similar to that involved in supposing that we can will to will. To feel that I ought to pay my bills is to be *moved towards* paying them. But what I can be moved towards must always be an action and not an action in which I am moved in a particular way, i.e. an action from a particular motive; otherwise I should be moved towards being moved, which is impossible. Yet the view under consideration involves this impossibility, for it really resolves the sense that I ought to do so and so, into the sense that I ought to be moved to do it in a particular way.[1]

So far my contentions have been mainly negative, but they form, I think, a useful, if not a necessary, introduction to what I take to be the truth. This I will now endeavour to state, first formu-lating what, as I think, is the real nature of our apprehension or appreciation of moral obligations, and then applying the result to elucidate the question of the existence of Moral Philosophy.

The sense of obligation to do, or of the rightness of, an action of a particular kind is absolutely underivative or immediate. The rightness of an action consists in its being the origination of some-thing of a certain kind A in a situation of a certain kind, a situation consisting in a certain relation B of the agent to others or to his own nature. To appreciate its rightness two preliminaries may be necessary. We may have to follow out the consequences of the proposed action more fully than we have hitherto done, in order to realize that in the action we should originate A. Thus we may not appreciate the wrongness of telling a certain story until we realize that we should thereby be hurting the feelings of one of our

---

[1] It is of course not denied here that an action done from a particular motive may be *good*; it is only denied that the *rightness* of an action depends on its being done with a particular motive.

audience. Again, we may have to take into account the relation B involved in the situation, which we had hitherto failed to notice. For instance, we may not appreciate the obligation to give X a present, until we remember that he has done us an act of kindness. But, given that by a process which is, of course, merely a process of general and not of moral thinking we come to recognize that the proposed act is one by which we shall originate A in a relation B, then we appreciate the obligation immediately or directly, the appreciation being an activity of *moral* thinking. We recognize, for instance, that this performance of a service to X, who has done us a service, just in virtue of its being the performance of a service to one who has rendered a service to the would-be agent, ought to be done by us. This apprehension is immediate, in precisely the sense in which a mathematical apprehension is immediate, e.g. the apprehension that this three-sided figure, in virtue of its being three-sided, must have three angles. Both apprehensions are immediate in the sense that in both insight into the nature of the subject directly leads us to recognize its possession of the predicate; and it is only stating this fact from the other side to say that in both cases the fact apprehended is self-evident.

The plausibility of the view that obligations are not self-evident but need proof lies in the fact that an act which is referred to as an obligation may be incompletely stated, what I have called the preliminaries to appreciating the obligation being incomplete. If, e.g., we refer to the act of repaying X by a present merely as giving X a present, it appears, and indeed is, necessary to give a reason. In other words, wherever a moral act is regarded in this incomplete way the question '*Why* should I do it?' is perfectly legitimate. This fact suggests, but suggests wrongly, that even if the nature of the act is completely stated, it is still necessary to give a reason, or, in other words, to supply a proof.

The relations involved in obligations of various kinds are, of course, very different. The relation in certain cases is a relation to others due to a past act of theirs or ours. The obligation to repay a benefit involves a relation due to a past act of the benefactor. The obligation to pay a bill involves a relation due to a past act of ours in which we have either said or implied that we would make a certain return for something which we have asked for and received. On the other hand, the obligation to speak the truth implies no such definite act; it involves a relation consisting in the fact that others are trusting us to speak the truth, a relation the apprehension of which gives rise to the sense that communication of the truth is something owing by us to them. Again, the obligation not to hurt the feelings of another involves no special relation of us to that other, i.e. no relation other than that involved in our both being men, and men in one and the same world. Moreover, it seems that the relation involved in an obligation need not be a relation to another at all. Thus we should admit that there is an obligation to overcome our natural timidity or greediness, and that this involves no relations to others. Still there is a relation involved, viz. a relation to our own disposition. It is simply because we can and because others cannot directly modify our disposition that it is our business to improve it, and that it is not theirs, or, at least, not theirs to the same extent.

The negative side of all this is, of course, that we do not come to appreciate an obligation by an *argument*, i.e. by a process of non-moral thinking, and that, in particular, we do not do so by an argument of which a premiss is the ethical but not moral activity of appreciating the goodness either of the act or of a consequence of the act; i.e. that our sense of the rightness of an act is not a conclusion from our appreciation of the goodness either of it or of anything else.

It will probably be urged that on this view our various obligations form, like Aristotle's categories, an unrelated chaos in which it is impossible to acquiesce. For, according to it, the obligation to repay a benefit, or to pay a debt, or to keep a promise, presupposes a previous act of another; whereas the obligation to speak the truth or not to harm another does not; and, again, the obligation to remove our timidity involves no relations to others at all. Yet, at any rate, an effective *argumentum ad hominem* is at hand in the fact that the various qualities which we recognize as good are equally unrelated; e.g. courage, humility, and interest in knowledge. If, as is plainly the case, ἀγαθά differ ᾗ ἀγαθά, why should not obligations equally differ *qua* their obligatoriness? Moreover, if this were not so there could in the end be only one obligation, which is palpably contrary to fact.[1]

---

[1] Two other objections may be anticipated: (1) that obligations cannot be self-evident, since many actions regarded as obligations by some are not so regarded by others, and (2) that if obligations are self-evident, the problem of how we ought to act in the presence of conflicting obligations is insoluble.

To the first I should reply:

(*a*) That the appreciation of an obligation is, of course, only possible for a developed moral being, and that different degrees of development are possible.

(*b*) That the failure to recognize some particular obligation is usually due to the

Certain observations will help to make the view clearer.

In the first place, it may seem that the view, being—as it is—avowedly put forward in opposition to the view that what is right is derived from what is good, must itself involve the opposite of this, viz. the Kantian position that what is good is based upon what is right, i.e. that an act, if it be good, is good because it is right. But this is not so. For, on the view put forward, the rightness of a right action lies solely in the origination in which the act consists, whereas the intrinsic goodness of an action lies solely in its motive; and this implies that a morally good action is morally good not simply because it is a right action but because it is a right action done because it is right, i.e. from a sense of obligation. And this implication, it may be remarked incidentally, seems plainly true.

In the second place, the view involves that when, or rather so far as, we act from a sense of obligation, we have no purpose or end. By a 'purpose' or 'end' we really mean something the existence of which we desire, and desire of the existence of which leads us to act. Usually our purpose is something which the act will originate, as when we turn round in order to look at a picture. But it may be the action itself, i.e. the origination of something, as when we hit a golf-ball into a hole or kill someone out of revenge.[1] Now if by a purpose we mean something the existence of which we desire and desire for which leads us to act, then plainly, so far as we act from a sense of obligation, we have no purpose, consisting either in the action or in anything which it will produce. This is so obvious that it scarcely seems worth pointing out. But I do so for two reasons. (1) If we fail to scrutinize the meaning of the terms 'end' and 'purpose', we are apt to assume uncritically that all deliberate action, i.e. action proper, must have a purpose; we then become puzzled both when we look for the purpose of an action

fact that, owing to a lack of thoughtfulness, what I have called the preliminaries to this recognition are incomplete.

(c) That the view put forward is consistent with the admission that, owing to a lack of thoughtfulness, even the best men are blind to many of their obligations, and that in the end our obligations are seen to be co-extensive with almost the whole of our life.

To the second objection I should reply that obligation admits of degrees, and that where obligations conflict, the decision of what we ought to do turns not on the question 'Which of the alternative courses of action will originate the greater good?' but on the question 'Which is the greater obligation?'

[1] It is no objection to urge that an action cannot be its own purpose, since the purpose of something cannot be the thing itself. For, speaking strictly, the purpose is not the *action's* purpose but *our* purpose, and there is no contradiction in holding that our purpose in acting may be the action.

done from a sense of obligation, and also when we try to apply to such an action the distinction of means and end, the truth all the time being that since there is no end, there is no means either. (2) The attempt to base the sense of obligation on the recognition of the goodness of something is really an attempt to find a purpose in a moral action in the shape of something good which, as good, we want. And the expectation that the goodness of something underlies an obligation disappears as soon as we cease to look for a purpose.

The thesis, however, that, so far as we act from a sense of obligation, we have no purpose must not be misunderstood. It must not be taken either to mean or to imply that so far as we so act we have no *motive*. No doubt in ordinary speech the words 'motive' and 'purpose' are usually treated as correlatives, 'motive' standing for the desire which induces us to act, and 'purpose' standing for the object of this desire. But this is only because, when we are looking for the motive of the action, say, of some crime, we are usually pre-supposing that the act in question is prompted by a desire and not by the sense of obligation. At bottom, however, we mean by a motive what moves us to act; a sense of obligation does sometimes move us to act; and in our ordinary consciousness we should not hesitate to allow that the action we were considering might have had as its motive a sense of obligation. Desire and the sense of obligation are co-ordinate forms or species of motive.

In the third place, if the view put forward be right, we must sharply distinguish morality and virtue as independent, though related, species of goodness, neither being an aspect of something of which the other is an aspect, nor again a form or species of the other, nor again something deducible from the other; and we must at the same time allow that it is possible to do the same act either virtuously or morally or in both ways at once. And surely this is true. An act, to be virtuous, must, as Aristotle saw, be done willingly or with pleasure; as such it is just not done from a sense of obligation but from some desire which is intrinsically good, as arising from some intrinsically good emotion. Thus, in an act of generosity the motive is the desire to help another arising from sympathy with that other; in an act which is courageous and no more, i.e. in an act which is not at the same time an act of public spirit or family affection or the like, we prevent ourselves from being dominated by a feeling of terror, desiring to do so from a sense of shame at being terrified. The goodness of such an act is different from the goodness of an act to which we apply the term moral in the strict and narrow sense, viz. an act done from a sense of obligation. Its goodness lies in the intrinsic goodness of the emotion and of the consequent desire under which we act, the goodness of this motive being different from the goodness of the moral motive proper, viz. the sense of duty or obligation. Nevertheless, at any rate in certain cases, an act can be done either virtuously or morally or in both ways at once. It is possible to repay a benefit either from desire to repay it, or from the feeling that we ought to do so, or from both motives combined. A doctor may tend his patients either from a desire arising out of interest in his patients or in the exercise of skill, or from a sense of duty, or from a desire and a sense of duty combined. Further, although we recognize that in each case the act possesses an intrinsic goodness, we regard that action as the best in which both motives are combined; in other words, we regard as the really best man the man in whom virtue and morality are united.

It may be objected that the distinction between the two kinds of motive is untenable, on the ground that the *desire* to repay a benefit, for example, is only the manifestation of that which manifests itself as the *sense of obligation* to repay whenever we think of something in the action which is other than the repayment and which we should not like, such as the loss or pain involved. Yet the distinction can, I think, easily be shown to be tenable. For, in the analogous case of revenge, the desire to return the injury and the sense that we ought not to do so, leading, as they do, in opposite directions, are plainly distinct; and the obviousness of the distinction here seems to remove any difficulty in admitting the existence of a parallel distinction between the desire to return a benefit and the sense that we ought to return it.[1]

Further, the view implies that an obligation can no more be based on or derived from a virtue than a virtue can be derived from an obligation, in which latter case a virtue would consist in carrying out an obligation. And the implication is surely true and

[1] This sharp distinction of virtue and morality as co-ordinate and independent forms of goodness will explain a fact which otherwise it is difficult to account for. If we turn from books on Moral Philosophy to any vivid account of human life and action such as we find in Shakespeare, nothing strikes us more than the comparative remoteness of the discussions of Moral Philosophy from the facts of actual life. Is not this largely because, while Moral Philosophy has, quite rightly, concentrated its attention on the fact of obligation, in the case of many of those whom we admire most and whose lives are of the greatest interest, the sense of obligation, though it may be an important, is not a dominating factor in their lives?

important. Take the case of courage. It is untrue to urge that, since courage is a virtue, we ought to act courageously. It is and must be untrue, because, as we see in the end, to feel an obligation to act courageously would involve a contradiction. For, as I have urged before, we can only feel an obligation to *act*; we cannot feel an obligation to *act from a certain desire*, in this case the desire to conquer one's feelings of terror arising from the sense of shame which they arouse. Moreover, if the sense of obligation to act in a particular way leads to an action, the action will be an action done from a sense of obligation, and therefore not, if the above analysis of virtue be right, an act of courage.

The mistake of supposing that there can be an obligation to act courageously seems to arise from two causes. In the first place, there is often an obligation to do that which involves the conquering or controlling of our fear in the doing of it, e.g. the obligation to walk along the side of a precipice to fetch a doctor for a member of our family. Here the acting on the obligation is externally, though only externally, the same as an act of courage proper. In the second place there is an obligation to acquire courage, i.e. to do such things as will enable us afterwards to act courageously, and this may be mistaken for an obligation to act courageously. The same considerations can, of course, be applied, *mutatis mutandis*, to the other virtues.

The fact, if it be a fact, that virtue is no basis for morality will explain what otherwise it is difficult to account for, viz. the extreme sense of dissatisfaction produced by a close reading of Aristotle's *Ethics*. Why is the *Ethics* so disappointing? Not, I think, because it really answers two radically different questions as if they were one: (1) 'What is the happy life?', (2) 'What is the virtuous life?' It is, rather, because Aristotle does not do what we as moral philosophers want him to do, viz. to convince us that we really ought to do what in our non-reflective consciousness we have hitherto believed we ought to do, or if not, to tell us what, if any, are the other things which we really ought to do, and to prove to us that he is right. Now, if what I have just been contending is true, a systematic account of the virtuous character cannot possibly satisfy this demand. At best it can only make clear to us the details of one of our obligations, viz. the obligation to make ourselves better men; but the achievement of this does not help us to discover what we ought to do in life as a whole, and why; to think that it did would be to think that our only business in life was self-improvement.

Hence it is not surprising that Aristotle's account of the good man strikes us as almost wholly of academic value, with little relation to our real demand, which is formulated in Plato's words: οὐ γὰρ περὶ τοῦ ἐπιτυχόντος ὁ λόγος, ἀλλὰ περὶ τοῦ ὄντινα τρόπον χρὴ ζῆν.

I am not, of course, *criticizing* Aristotle for failing to satisfy this demand, except so far as here and there he leads us to think that he intends to satisfy it. For my main contention is that the demand cannot be satisfied, and cannot be satisfied because it is illegitimate. Thus we are brought to the question: 'Is there really such a thing as Moral Philosophy, and, if there is, in what sense?'

We should first consider the parallel case—as it appears to be—of the Theory of Knowledge. As I urged before, at some time or other in the history of all of us, if we are thoughtful, the frequency of our own and of others' mistakes is bound to lead to the reflection that possibly we and others have *always* been mistaken in consequence of some radical defect of our faculties. In consequence, certain things which previously we should have said without hesitation that we *knew*, as e.g. that $4 \times 7 = 28$, become subject to doubt; we become able only to say that we thought we knew these things. We inevitably go on to look for some general procedure by which we can ascertain that a given condition of mind is really one of knowledge. And this involves the search for a criterion of knowledge, i.e. for a principle by applying which we can settle that a given state of mind is really knowledge. The search for this criterion and the application of it, when found, is what is called the Theory of Knowledge. The search implies that instead of its being the fact that the knowledge that A is B is obtained directly by consideration of the nature of A and B, the knowledge that A is B, in the full or complete sense, can only be obtained by first knowing that A is B, and then knowing that we knew it by applying a criterion, such as Descartes's principle that what we clearly and distinctly conceive is true.

Now it is easy to show that the doubt whether A is B, based on this speculative or general ground, could, if genuine, never be set at rest. For if, in order really to know that A is B, we must first know that we knew it, then really, to know that we knew it, we must first know that we knew that we knew it. But—what is more important—it is also easy to show that this doubt is not a genuine doubt but rests on a confusion the exposure of which removes the doubt. For when we *say* we doubt whether our previous condition was one of knowledge, what we *mean*, if we mean anything at all, is that we doubt whether our previous *belief* was *true*, a belief which we should express as the *thinking* that A is B. For in order to doubt whether our previous condition was one of knowledge, we have to think of it not as knowledge but as only belief, and our only question can be 'Was this belief true?' But as soon as we see that we are thinking of our previous condition as only one of belief, we see that what we are now doubting is not what we first *said* we were doubting, viz. whether a previous condition of knowledge was really knowledge. Hence, to remove the doubt, it is only necessary to appreciate the real nature of our consciousness in apprehending, e.g. that $7 \times 4 = 28$, and thereby see that it was no mere condition of believing but a condition of knowing, and then to notice that in our subsequent doubt what we are really doubting is not whether this consciousness was really knowledge, but whether a consciousness of another kind, viz. a belief that $7 \times 4 = 28$, was true. We thereby see that though a doubt based on speculative grounds is possible, it is not a doubt concerning what we believed the doubt concerned, and that a doubt concerning this latter is impossible.

Two results follow. In the first place, if, as is usually the case, we mean by the 'Theory of Knowledge' the knowledge which supplies the answer to the question 'Is what we have hitherto thought knowledge really knowledge?', there is and can be no such thing, and the supposition that there can is simply due to a confusion. There can be no answer to an illegitimate question, except that the question is illegitimate. Nevertheless the question is one which we continue to put until we realize the inevitable immediacy of knowledge. And it is positive knowledge that knowledge is immediate and neither can be, nor needs to be, improved or vindicated by the further knowledge that it was knowledge. This positive knowledge sets at rest the inevitable doubt, and, so far as by the 'Theory of Knowledge' is meant this knowledge, then even though this knowledge be the knowledge that there is no Theory of Knowledge in the former sense, to that extent the Theory of Knowledge exists.

In the second place, suppose we come genuinely to doubt whether, e.g., $7 \times 4 = 28$ owing to a genuine doubt whether we were right in believing yesterday that $7 \times 4 = 28$, a doubt which can in fact only arise if we have lost our hold of, i.e. no longer remember, the real nature of our consciousness of yesterday, and so think of it as consisting in believing. Plainly, the only remedy is to do the sum again. Or, to put the matter generally, if we do come to doubt whether it is true that A is B, as we once thought, the remedy lies not in any process of reflection but in such a reconsideration of the nature of A and B as leads to the knowledge that A is B.

With these considerations in mind, consider the parallel which, as it seems to me, is presented—though with certain differences—by Moral Philosophy. The sense that we ought to do certain things arises in our unreflective consciousness, being an activity of moral thinking occasioned by the various situations in which we find ourselves. At this stage our attitude to these obligations is one of unquestioning confidence. But inevitably the appreciation of the degree to which the execution of these obligations is contrary to our interest raises the doubt whether after all these obligations are really obligatory, i.e. whether our sense that we ought not to do certain things is not illusion. We then want to have it *proved* to us that we ought to do so, i.e. to be convinced of this by a process which, as an argument, is different in kind from our original and unreflective appreciation of it. This demand is, as I have argued, illegitimate.

Hence, in the first place, if, as is almost universally the case, by Moral Philosophy is meant the knowledge which would satisfy this demand, there is no such knowledge, and all attempts to attain it are doomed to failure because they rest on a mistake, the mistake of supposing the possibility of proving what can only be apprehended directly by an act of moral thinking. Nevertheless the demand, though illegitimate, is inevitable until we have carried the process of reflection far enough to realize the self-evidence of our obligations, i.e. the immediacy of our apprehension of them. This realization of their self-evidence is positive knowledge, and so far, and so far only, as the term Moral Philosophy is confined to this knowledge and to the knowledge of the parallel immediacy of the apprehension of the goodness of the various virtues and of good dispositions generally, is there such a thing as Moral Philosophy. But since this knowledge may allay doubts which often affect the whole conduct of life, it is, though not extensive, important and even vitally important.

In the second place, suppose we come genuinely to doubt whether we ought, for example, to pay our debts, owing to a genuine doubt whether our previous conviction that we ought to do so is true, a doubt which can, in fact, only arise if we fail to remember the real nature of what we now call our past conviction. The only remedy lies in actually getting into a situation which

occasions the obligation, or—if our imagination be strong enough
—in imagining ourselves in that situation, and then letting our
moral capacities of thinking do their work. Or, to put the matter
generally, if we do doubt whether there is really an obligation to
originate A in a situation B, the remedy lies not in any process of
general thinking, but in getting face to face with a particular
instance of the situation B, and then directly appreciating the
obligation to originate A in that situation.

2

DUTY AND IGNORANCE OF FACT[1]

THE question which I propose to consider is essentially dull and tiresome; it worries us little, if at all, in practical life; and it is apt to be ignored or, at least, only casually treated by those whose business is theory. Nevertheless, at any rate for theory, it is important.

As it first presents itself the question is: 'If a man has an obligation, i.e. a duty, to do some action, does the obligation depend on certain characteristics of the situation in which he is, or on certain characteristics of his thought about the situation?' The question is vague because of the vagueness of the term 'thought', but at the outset this does not matter. Consideration of it, however, will force us to consider another question, viz.: 'Can an obligation really be an obligation to do some *action*, and, if not, what should be substituted for the term "action"?' And, should a substitute prove necessary, the main question will have to be modified accordingly.

To appreciate the importance, and even the meaning, of the question, we have first to see how it arises.

We have all from time to time thought that we ought, and again that we ought not, to do certain actions. And, if we were asked to give a general account of these actions, we should be inclined to say that, though not all of one sort, yet they all fall under one or other of a limited number of kinds of action which are set out in current moral rules, i.e. current general statements each stating that a man ought or ought not to do an action of a certain kind. Further, at any rate until certain difficulties have occurred to us, we think these rules true. We think, for instance, that a man ought to speak the truth, to carry out the orders of his government, not to steal, and not to hurt the feelings of another. And this is not surprising, since these rules are simply the result of an attempt to formulate those various general characteristics of the particular acts we have thought duties, which have led us to think them duties.

Elucidation, however, is needed of the general character of the meaning of a moral rule, and therefore also of the thought which it is used to express.

[1] Annual Philosophical Lecture, Henriette Hertz Trust, British Academy, 1932.

It is, no doubt, not easy to say what we mean by 'an action' or by 'doing something'. Yet we have in the end to allow that we mean by it originating, causing, or bringing about the existence of something, viz. some new state of an existing thing or substance, or, more shortly, causing a change of state of some existing thing. This is shown by the meaning of our phrases for various particular actions. For by 'moving our hand' we mean causing a change of place of our hand; by 'posting a letter' we mean bringing about that a letter is in a pillar-box; and so on. We may be tempted to go farther, and say that we mean by 'an action' the *conscious* origination of something, i.e. the originating something knowing that we are doing so. But this will not do; for no one, for instance, thinks himself to be denying that he has hurt a man's feelings when he says that he did not know that he was hurting them and, indeed, thought he was not. Correspondingly, we mean by 'doing an action of a certain kind' bringing about something of a certain kind, viz. a state of a certain kind, of a thing of a certain kind. Consequently the meaning of a moral rule can be stated in the form: 'A man ought, or ought not, to bring about a thing of a certain kind.' Thus by 'A man ought to honour his parents' we mean: 'A man ought to bring about in his parents the knowledge that he holds them in honour.'

But this is not all. We ordinarily think that in doing certain actions we bring about the things which we do directly, while in doing certain others we do so indirectly, i.e. by directly bringing about other things which in turn cause them. Thus we think that in moving our head we bring about a change of place of our head directly, whereas in giving a friend the family news we bring about his receipt of the news indirectly, i.e. by bringing about directly certain other changes which in turn cause it. No doubt on reflection we may find it difficult to defend the thought that, e.g., in moving our head we directly cause our head to change its place; and we may be reduced to thinking that, in moving our head, what we bring about directly is some new state of certain cells of our brain of which we are wholly unaware in doing the action. But such a reflection does not conflict with our thought that we bring about certain things indirectly. Nor does it lead us to deny the distinction between bringing something about directly and bringing something about indirectly, since, so long as we think that we bring about certain things indirectly, we inevitably imply that there are certain things which we bring about directly, even if we do not know what they are. It is as impossible for all bringing about to be indirect as for all knowledge to be indirect. And, if we now turn to the phrase for the act of a certain kind referred to in some moral rule, we find that in every case it stands for bringing about something of a certain kind indirectly. We mean, for instance, by 'honouring a parent' causing a parent to find himself held in honour by causing something else to cause it; we mean by 'speaking the truth' causing another to know our thought by causing certain sounds which cause him to have this knowledge; and so on. We can therefore say generally that the meaning of a moral rule has the form: 'A man ought, or ought not, to bring about a thing of a certain kind indirectly.'

To bring about something indirectly is, however, to bring it about in a less strict sense than that of bringing it about directly. For, where we bring about something by causing something to cause it, the result is not wholly due to us. And, where we bring about something X indirectly, what we bring about in the strict sense is the thing which causes X. Correspondingly, we use the term 'action' both in a strict sense in which it means bringing about something directly, and also in a looser sense in which it means bringing about something whether directly or indirectly. And where, e.g., some action of ours is referred to as giving some relation the family news, we must allow that our action in the strict sense is some such act as transferring certain ink to certain places on a piece of paper; and in support of this admission we might point out that, in the strict sense of 'action', our action must cease with the cessation of our activity. We have, therefore, to allow that if a moral rule is stated in terms of 'doing something' and of 'bringing about something' in the strict sense, its meaning will be of the form: 'A man ought to do such an act or acts, i.e. bring about such a thing or things, as will cause a thing of the kind A to assume a state of the kind X.'

Further, in stating some moral rule, we are plainly in two respects speaking elliptically. Thus, in asserting that a man ought to support his indigent parents, we clearly do not mean that a man ought at *any* time to support his indigent parents. We are thinking, and expect to be understood as asserting, that the duty exists only when two conditions are satisfied. The first is, of course, that the man has parents who are indigent and willing to receive the means of support; and the second is that he is able to support them. For we never think that an action can be a man's duty unless he is able to do it. But since to support parents is to bring about something indirectly, the realization of the second condition involves the existence of a certain combination of things capable of having certain changes of state effected in them, such that, on the one hand, the man can produce the changes directly, and also such that, on the other hand, if these changes are produced, they will result in the parents' having the means of support. In asserting a moral rule, however, we take for granted that a man has permanently the capacity of bringing about certain things directly, and therefore we think of the realization of the second condition as consisting simply in the fact that the situation in which the man is is such that some one, or some group, of the things which he can bring about directly would, if produced, effect his parents' possession of the means of subsistence. Consequently, to generalize, we can say that any moral rule, when modified to express fully the thought which it is used to express, will be of the following form: 'When the situation in which a man is contains a thing of the kind A capable of having a state of the kind X effected in it, and when also it is such that some state or combination of states Y which the man can bring about directly would, if brought about, cause a state of the kind X in A, the man ought to bring about that state or combination of states.'

Again, once the thought is expressed in this form, it becomes obvious that, in having the thought, we are implying that when a man has an obligation to do some act in the strict sense, corresponding to the rule, what renders him bound to do the action is the special character of the situation in which he is, in the two respects just indicated, this being what gives rise to the fact that, if he were to do the action, he would indirectly be causing a state of the kind in question. Plainly, therefore, if we were to put forward a particular set of rules as exhaustive, we should be implying that the question whether we are bound to do some particular action, in the strict sense, will turn on whether the existing situation contains any of the various pairs of conditions which would bring the act under one or other of the rules. Clearly also, even if we did not think such rules as we could offer exhaustive, we should still think that the question could only be settled in the same kind of way, although we could not settle it.

Now when we reflect on this general idea or thought underlying our assertion of a set of moral rules, viz. that where we have an obligation to do some action in the strict sense, it depends on certain characteristics of the situation, we find it in two related respects very attractive. For, first, being the thought that any obligation depends solely on certain characteristics of the situation, it is on its negative side the thought that the obligation is wholly independent of our knowledge and thought about the situation. And we welcome this negative side, since we do not like to think that the question whether some action is a duty turns not on the nature of the situation but on that of our attitude towards it in respect of knowledge and thought. Moreover, the thought seems implied in much of our procedure in actual life. For frequently when in doubt, as we often are, whether some action in the narrow sense is a duty, our doubt seems to arise from doubt about the actual facts. Thus when I see someone who shows symptoms of having fainted and it occurs to me that, if I shouted, I might revive him, I may doubt whether I am bound to shout; and, when I do, my doubt sometimes seems to arise partly from doubt whether he has really fainted, and partly from doubt whether shouting would revive him. And if I try to resolve my doubt about the duty by resolving my doubt about the facts, I at least seem to be implying that the question whether I am bound to shout turns on what the facts really are. Second, the thought implies that if some action is a duty, it would bring about some state referred to in a moral rule, such as the recovery of a sick man, and would not be merely an act which we think would be likely to do so; and we welcome this implication because we should like to think that, if we have done some duty, we have achieved some change to which a moral rule refers, e.g. that we have helped a man out of trouble, and not merely done something which we thought would do this but which possibly has in fact damaged a man who was in no trouble at all.

Yet there is no denying that if we try to defend this thought we become involved in very awkward consequences. There are various admissions which we shall have to make which we thoroughly dislike when we come to reflect on them.

The most awkward of these emerges as soon as we ask: 'How am I to *know* that some moral rule is applicable to me here and now?' The rule being of the form recently stated, the question becomes: 'How am I to *know* that the situation satisfies the two conditions necessary for the application of the rule, viz. first, that it contains a particular thing of the kind A capable of having a state of the kind X effected in it, and, second, that it is such that some act or acts which I can do would cause this A to assume a state of the kind X?' And as regards the first condition, we shall have to admit that the situation may often satisfy it, without my knowing, or even being able to discover, that it does so. We may perhaps insist that sometimes I know that there is someone to whom I have made a promise, or again that I have parents who are in difficulties; but we cannot deny that sometimes I am uncertain whether there is someone to whom I have made a promise, or whether my parents are in difficulties, or again whether a man whom I meet is ill, at any rate with an illness which anything I can do would be likely to diminish. And we shall have to allow that in most of these latter cases I have no means of resolving my doubt. We shall therefore have to admit that for this reason alone I may often have a duty without knowing, or even being able to discover, that I have. Again, as regards the second condition, there are, undeniably, absolutely no occasions on which, where some particular state Y which I can bring about directly would cause an effect of the kind X, I either *know*, or can even come to *know*, that it would, although of course I may have a strong opinion about the matter. For plainly I never either do or can *know* that any particular action which I can do in the narrow sense would have a certain effect. Thus, unquestionably, I neither do nor can know that giving a man a certain drug would cause his recovery; and if in fact I give him the drug, and afterwards find that he has recovered, even then I cannot *know* that I have cured him, though I may think it very likely. Again, I never *know* that by uttering certain sounds I shall cause a man to know what I think; and I know that however much I may try to speak the truth, I may fail. Consideration, then, of the second condition forces us to admit that there is absolutely no occasion on which a moral rule applies to me on which I can know that I have the duty in question. In fact, reflection on these conditions compels us to admit that no moral rule can express knowledge, and that, to express knowledge, we must substitute a hypothetical statement in which we replace the word 'when' of a moral rule by 'if'. To express knowledge, its form will have to be: '*If* the situation in which a man is contains a thing of the kind A capable of having a state of the kind X produced in it, and *if* also it be such that one of the things which he can bring about directly will, if he brings it about, cause A to assume such a state, then he ought to bring about that thing.' The need of this substitution is obvious, since for the reasons given an individual is sometimes uncertain whether the first, and always uncertain whether the second, condition is realized. Indeed, on this view that an obligation, if there be one, depends on certain features of the situation, we are driven to the extreme conclusion that, although we may have duties, we cannot know but can only believe that we have; and therefore we are even rendered uncertain whether we, or anyone else, has ever had, or will ever have, a duty.

Here we may note the answer which this view requires us to give to a question which is often raised. Obviously at different times opposite views have been taken of the rightness or wrongness of certain kinds of action, in consequence of different views concerning matters of fact. Thus while some men must in the past have been sincerely convinced that it was a duty to torture heretics, most men are now equally convinced that a man ought not to do so; and the explanation obviously lies in a difference of opinion about the effects of torture. And the question is often asked: 'Where there is such a difference of view concerning the rightness or wrongness of a certain kind of action, which party is right?' To this question, on the view we are considering, the answer can only be: 'We do not know; no one knows; and no one ever will know. Even those, e.g., who considered it a duty to torture heretics may have been right.'

That we can never know that we have a duty is not, however, the only conclusion to which we are driven on this view. There are others related to it. One is that, though we may have duties, we can never, strictly speaking, do a duty, if we have one, *because* it is a duty, i.e. really in consequence of *knowing* it to be a duty. And the reason is, of course, simply that we can never have the knowledge. At best, if we have a duty, we may do it because we think without question, or else believe, or again think it possible, that the act is a duty. Another conclusion is that some past act of mine may have been a duty although in doing it I believed that the act was one which I ought not to do. Thus my shouting on seeing a man may have been in fact a duty, because he was faint and shouting would revive him, and yet I may have shouted to satisfy a grudge, believing that he was asleep and that my shouting would disturb him. A third is that I may do some act which is in fact a duty, although in doing it I do not even suspect that it will have the effect which renders it a duty. This would happen, e.g., if I shouted simply to attract the attention of the passers-by and without noticing the man's condition at all. Similar conclusions, too, have

to be drawn with regard to acts of the kinds which we think we
ought not to do.

These conclusions being all unwelcome, we naturally want to
discover what modification of the form of a moral rule would
enable us to escape them, and then to consider how we fare if we
accept it. Now what the conclusions all followed from was the
thought underlying the assertion of a set of moral rules, that if
some particular action is a duty, the obligation depends on certain
facts of the situation. And to this thought there is only one alternative, viz. the thought that the obligation depends on our being in
a certain attitude of mind towards the situation in respect of knowledge, thought, or opinion. This thought can be described as the
subjective view of the basis of an obligation, not in the sense that
no acts are really right or really wrong, but in the sense of the
view that the ground of an obligation lies in some state of the man's
own mind. And in contrast the opposed view can be designated the
objective view.

The question, therefore, at once arises: 'What have we to
represent this state or attitude as being, if we are to render this
alternative view at least plausible?' The most obvious suggestion
is, of course, to represent it as our thinking certain things likely or
probable, and to represent the alternative view as being that if,
e.g., I am bound to shout, it is because I think it likely that the
man in front of me has fainted and that, if he has fainted shouting
would cure him, i.e. have his revival as an effect. But, when we
come to consider this view, we find that we do not like it either.

It seems to have, no doubt, at least one definite advantage over
the view which it is to replace. It seems not to preclude us from
thinking that it is possible to *discover* our duties, since, when we
think something likely, we either know, or at least by reflecting can
discover, that we do. The question whether I am thinking something likely is no more one about which I can be mistaken than is
the question whether I have a certain pain. Consequently, also,
the view does not preclude us from thinking that it is sometimes
possible for us to do some action, knowing that we ought to do it.
For the same reason it saves us from having to allow that we are,
and must always remain, uncertain whether we have or shall ever
have a duty.

On the other hand, it of course inevitably implies that any obligation I may have depends not on the fact that the action would
have a certain character, if I were to do it—that of producing

a certain effect—but on my thinking it likely that it would. It implies, e.g., that where I am bound to shout, my obligation depends not on the fact that if I were to shout I should be reviving a man who has fainted, but on my thinking it likely that I should. And a paradox involved comes to light if we imagine ourselves omniscient beings, who in consequence knew the circumstances. For if we were such beings, the analogous view would be that, if we were bound to shout, what would render us bound to shout would not be the fact that shouting would cure the man, but our knowing that it would; and it would therefore imply that this knowledge, so far from being the knowledge of the ground of the obligation, was itself the ground of the obligation, and that our knowledge of the ground of the obligation consisted in our knowing that we knew that shouting would cure the man.

Again, to defend the view, we shall have to modify it at least to the extent of maintaining that if, for instance, I am bound to shout, what renders me so bound is not simply my thinking it likely but my thinking it at least in a certain degree likely that shouting would cure the man. For no one would maintain that I am bound to shout if I think the likelihood remote beyond a certain degree. But then we are faced by the question: 'What degree is necessary?' And we have to answer that we can formulate it only within certain limits which differ in different cases according to the degree of benefit to the other man which I think likely to accrue from my shouting. We shall, therefore, also have to allow that I shall not always be able to discover whether I ought to shout, since there will be borderline cases in which I shall be unable to discover whether the degree to which I think the act likely to confer a certain benefit is sufficient to render it a duty. And therefore we shall have to allow that even on this view I may have a duty without being able to discover that I have it.

Again, the view, at any rate unless further modified, implies not only that in similar circumstances it may be one man's duty but not another's to do some action, owing to some difference in their thought about the facts, but also that the same thing is true of a single individual at different moments. For I may at first think it just, but only just, possible that shouting would cure a man, and then on further consideration think that there is a very good chance that it will; and, if so, while at first I shall not be bound to shout, afterwards I shall. And, again, the converse may happen.

Also, we have to distinguish from 'thinking likely' what for lack of a better phrase we may call 'thinking without question'. For on seeing a man who has fainted, instead of thinking it likely, I may from lack of reflection think without question that shouting would cure him, not being uncertain that it would, and therefore not 'thinking it likely', but at the same time not being certain. And on the view in question, unless it be modified, we shall have to hold that when this happens I am not bound to shout, in spite of thinking without question that shouting would cure him, since I am not thinking it likely.

It will, however, probably occur to us that these last two difficulties can be met by a further modification. This is to maintain (1) that I am bound to shout only if I think it likely that shouting would effect a cure, *after* having considered the circumstances fully, i.e. after having considered as fully as I can whether he is ill and whether shouting would cure him if he is, and so having obtained the best opinion I can about the circumstances, and (2) that whenever I have not done this I am bound to do something else, viz. to consider the circumstances fully.

This modification, it must be allowed, does remove the difficulties. Nevertheless, the idea that, where we have not done so, we ought to consider the circumstances fully, is itself not free from difficulty. This becomes obvious as soon as we ask: '*Why*, for instance, when it first strikes me that shouting might cure the man, am I bound to consider fully whether it would?' For the answer which we are first inclined to give is: 'Because, if I were to consider the matter fully, I might come to think shouting in a certain degree likely to cure him, and, if I did, I should then be bound to shout.' And yet this answer cannot be right. For plainly the duty of doing one action cannot possibly depend on the possibility of the duty of doing another the duty of doing which cannot arise unless the former action has actually been done. Moreover, if the answer were right, I could always escape a duty to shout merely by abstaining from considering the circumstances, and yet no one thinks this possible. The truth is that our having a duty to consider the circumstances cannot be based on the possibility of our having a future duty of another kind if we were to consider them. Rather, to vindicate such a duty, we must represent the two so-called duties as respectively an element and a possible element in a *single* duty, viz. to consider the circumstances, and then *if*, but only if, as a result, we reach a certain opinion, to do a certain future action. And if we do this we can explain the need of this complicated and partially hypothetical phrase for what is, after all, a single duty by the fact that the duty is one of the full nature of which we are at the time inevitably ignorant owing to our ignorance of the facts.

Again, if the view is to correspond with what we ordinarily think, still further modifications may seem necessary for various reasons, of which one is that we ordinarily think, for instance, that before it can be a duty for me to shout I must also have considered what is likely to be the effect of shouting on anyone else who may be within range.

But, in order to consider the main issue, we need not inquire what, if any, further modifications are needed. For, even if they are needed, the fundamental issue will remain the same, viz.: 'If I have an obligation, does it depend on the existence of certain facts of the situation or on my having certain thoughts about certain facts of the situation?'

Here it may be noted that the issue is not avoided by those who would deny the truth of any set of moral rules on the ground that, if we think them true, we are involved in the absurdity of admitting that we may at any moment have conflicting duties, i.e. two or more duties only one of which we can carry out. For, in order to avoid this admission, they have to maintain that where some action is a duty it is because it would possess some such character as that of producing something good in a greater degree than any other of the acts which the man is able to do. And, in maintaining this, they will be faced with the same question in a slightly different form, viz.: 'Does the obligation depend on the fact that the action would possess this character in a greater degree than any other, or does it depend on the fact that the man, after full consideration, thinks it likely that it would?'

The issue, then, being as stated, the first thing to do appears to consist in ascertaining which of the alternative views better corresponds with the thought of our ordinary life.

There are two ways in which this thought appears to imply the objective view. First, we frequently think without question both that the situation contains some thing in a certain state, and also that some action which we could do would produce a change in it of a certain kind, and then think without question that we ought to do the action. Thus, when we do not reflect, we frequently think without question that a man whom we meet has some malady and that giving him some drug would relieve it, and, where we do, we think without question that we ought to give the drug. And here we seem to imply that what renders us bound to do the act is just the fact that the situation is of a certain sort, together with the fact that the act would have a certain effect in that situation. Secondly, we often seek to change the mind of someone else about a duty by trying to convince him that he is mistaken about the facts; and, in doing so, we seem to imply that the question whether he has the duty depends on the nature of the facts. Thus, where A thinks he ought to vote for X rather than Y, B may try to convince A that he ought to vote for Y by arguing that X and Y will, if elected, act otherwise than as A expects. Again, we may argue with a friend that he ought to send his child to school M rather than school N, which he considers the better, on the ground that M is really the better. And if someone were to maintain that he ought to torture a certain heretic, as the only way of saving his soul, we should presumably try to convince him that he was mistaken by convincing him that torture would not have this effect.

On the other hand, at any rate a large portion of our ordinary thought is in direct conflict with the objective view. Consider, e.g., our attitude to the question: 'Ought we to stop, or at least slow down, in a car, before entering a main road?' If the objective view be right, (1) there will be a duty to slow down only if in fact there is traffic; (2) we shall be entitled only to think it likely—in varying degrees on different occasions—that we are bound to slow down; and (3) if afterwards we find no traffic, we ought to conclude that our opinion that we were bound to slow down was mistaken. Yet, provided that after consideration we think that there is even a small chance of traffic, we, in fact, think that there is definitely a duty to slow down, and that the subsequent discovery that there was no traffic would not prove us mistaken. Again, imagine that we are watching a car approaching along a road which we know forks, and of which one fork has, we know, just suffered a landslide, and that we have no idea which road the driver is intending to take, or whether he knows about the landslide.[1] The objective view would require us to think that there is a duty to stop the car only if it is going to destruction, so that, if we are anxious to do what we ought, we can only insure ourselves against the possibility of failure to do what we ought by stopping the car, knowing that, after all, we may be doing something we are not bound to do. Yet plainly we in fact think without any doubt whatever that we are bound to stop the car, unless we have reason for being quite

[1] I owe the illustration to Mr. R. G. Collingwood.

confident that the car is about to take the safe fork. Again, no nurse thinks that she is bound to light a fire in her patient's room only if in fact there will be a frost next morning. She thinks she is bound to do so, unless she thinks there is practically no chance of a frost. Indeed, the objective view is in direct conflict with all the numerous cases in which we think without question that we ought to do something which we are thinking of as of the nature of *an insurance* in the interest of someone else.

Moreover, the extent to which our ordinary thought involves the subjective view is usually obscured for us by our tendency to think that the terms 'likely' and 'probable' refer to facts in nature. For we are apt, for instance, to express our thought that someone has probably fainted, and that shouting would probably revive him, by the statements 'He has probably fainted' and 'Shouting would probably revive him'. We are then apt to think that these statements state the existence of certain facts in nature called probabilities, in the spirit which leads some physicists to regard electron-waves as waves of probability;[1] and we are then apt to think that an obligation to shout arises from these probabilities. It needs, however, but little reflection to realize that there are no such things as probabilities in nature. There cannot, e.g., be such a thing as the probability that someone has fainted, since either he has fainted or he has not. No doubt it is extremely difficult to formulate the precise nature of the fact which we express, for instance, by the statement: 'X has probably fainted.' But at least we must allow that, whatever its precise nature may be, the fact must consist in our mind's being in a certain state or condition. And, once this is realized, it becomes obvious that most of our ordinary thought involves the subjective view.

Again, even when we try to change someone else's mind about a duty, we do not really imply the objective view. This is shown by our thinking that when our attempt to change his opinion about the facts is over, then, whether we have or have not succeeded, the question whether he is bound to do the action will turn on the nature of *his opinion* about the facts. Thus we think that, provided the would-be torturer remained, in spite of all we have said, in a very high degree confident that torturing, and torturing only, would save the heretic, he would be bound to inflict the torture. No doubt we also think that we should take steps to prevent him; but here there is no inconsistency. And, in fact, we not infre-

[1] Cf. *The Mysterious Universe*, p. 122 (Sir James Jeans).

quently think ourselves bound to do some action which will prevent someone else doing something which he is bound to do. Indeed, if this were not so, few would fight conscientiously for their country.

Undoubtedly, then, the subjective view better corresponds with our ordinary thought. Yet, as should now be obvious, it is exposed to various difficulties. Of these the chief are two. The first is that on this view knowledge of the existence of borderline cases precludes us from thinking that we can always discover our duties. Still in this respect it is more satisfactory than the objective view, since the latter implies that we can never discover a duty. The second and more fundamental difficulty is that it represents the duty of doing some action as depending not on the fact that the action would have a certain character if we were to do it, but on our thinking it likely that it would. And to maintain this seems impossible.

We thus seem to have reached an impasse. For both the alternative views lead to fundamental difficulties, and yet there is no third course.

Before, however, we consider the matter further, we ought to consider a difficulty which is common to both views, and which, if it proves well founded, will force us to modify both.

In considering the problem, we have throughout been taking for granted that an obligation is necessarily an obligation to do some *action*, and, strictly speaking, an action in the strict sense. But we ought at least to ask ourselves whether this assumption, obvious though it seems, is true.

Unquestionably an obligation must be an obligation to perform some *activity*. An obligation can be an obligation only to be *active*, and not to be *affected*, in a particular way. And to say that an obligation is always an obligation to do some *action*, in the strict sense, e.g. to move my arms, is really to say that the activity which an obligation is an obligation to perform consists in *doing* something, as distinct from an activity of some other kind, such as thinking or imagining. But, as was said earlier, by 'doing something' in the strict sense, we mean bringing about something directly, i.e. bringing about something in the strict sense. Therefore to assert that an obligation is an obligation to do something is really to assert that the activity of the kind which an obligation is an obligation to perform consists in bringing about something. And in making this assertion we are implying that there is a special *kind* of activity, and indeed a special kind of *mental* activity, for which the proper phrase is 'bringing about something'. For if we thought that what we call 'bringing about X' really consists in performing an activity of some other kind of which X will be an effect, we should have to allow that what we call the obligation to bring about X is really the obligation to perform some particular activity of this other kind of which X would be an effect, and that, therefore, an obligation, so far from being an obligation to do something, is always an obligation to perform an activity of this other kind. In asserting, then, that an obligation is an obligation to *do* something, we are implying that there is a special kind of activity consisting in doing something, i.e. bringing about something.

On reflection, however, we become forced to admit that, though on certain occasions we do bring certain things about, yet there is no kind of activity consisting in bringing about something. We can realize this in the following way. It will, of course, be allowed that where we think of some past action of ours as one in which we indirectly brought about some particular thing, as where we think of ourselves as having cured someone's illness, we think it fair to ask: '*How* did we do the action?' We take the question to have the intelligible meaning: 'What was that by the direct production of which we indirectly produced what we did?'; and we can give some sort of answer. But we can also ask a question verbally similar, where we think of some past action as one in which we directly brought about something. Where, e.g., I think of myself as having moved my hand, I can ask: '*How* did I move it?' In such a case, of course, the question cannot be of the same kind, because *ex hypothesi* I am not thinking of the action as one in which I caused some particular thing by causing something else, and so I cannot be asking: 'By directly causing what, did I cause what I did?' The legitimate question is: 'What was the activity by performing which I caused my hand to move?', and an answer would be 'Willing the existence of the movement'. And in so answering I should be implying that what I called moving my hand really consisted in setting myself to move it, and that I referred to this activity as moving my hand because I thought that this activity had a change of place of my hand as an effect. Again, in another case my answer might be: 'By setting myself to move my other hand,' the case being one in which I set myself to move one hand and in fact moved the other. And here also I should be implying that what I called 'moving my hand' really consisted in a particular activity of another sort of which the change of place of my hand was an effect. The general moral can be stated thus: In no case whatever, where we think of ourselves as having brought about something directly, do we think that our activity was that of bringing about that something. On the contrary, we think of the activity as having been of another sort, and mean, by saying that we brought about directly what we did, that this activity of another sort had the change in question as a direct effect.

The same·conclusion can be reached by considering what we really mean by saying, 'I can do so and so', when we use 'do' in the strict sense. It may first be noticed that if in ordinary life we are asked whether we can do some action in the strict sense, we cannot always give a definite answer. No doubt if we were asked: 'Can we make a noise identical in pitch with the highest C of the piano?' we should unhesitatingly answer 'No'; and if we were asked: 'Can we make a loud noise?' we should unhesitatingly answer 'Yes.' But if we were asked: 'Can we make a noise similar in pitch to the middle C of the piano?' we should have to answer 'I don't know', though we might possibly add 'But I *think* I can.' It may next be noticed that even where we unhesitatingly answer 'Yes' we are, if pressed, inclined to hedge to the extent of saying: 'Well, at least I can do the action, e.g. shout, *if* I choose.' Such a statement, however, as we see when we reflect, is very odd. It cannot be meant literally, and can at best be only an idiom. For while it is sense to say: 'If I choose to make a loud noise, I shall in fact make it,' it cannot be sense to say: 'If I choose to make it, I *can* make it.' And no one would maintain that our *ability* to do something, as distinct from our *doing* it, can depend on our choosing to do it. Indeed, the statement really presupposes the thought that I *can* choose to make a loud noise, and is in fact only a brachylogical way of saying: 'Since I can choose to make a loud noise, and since choosing to make it would in fact have a loud noise as an effect, I can make it.' At the same time 'choose' cannot be an accurate phrase for what we mean, since 'choose' means choose between alternatives, and in fact we have no alternatives in mind. 'Will', the verb corresponding to 'volition', might perhaps be suggested as the proper substitute; but the term would be merely artificial. What seems wanted is one or other of the two phrases which have already been used, viz. 'setting myself to', or 'exerting myself to', so that 'choosing to make a loud noise' becomes 'setting or exerting myself to make a loud noise'. And, if this is right, what is in our minds when we say 'I can make a loud noise' is not the thought that there is a special kind of activity of which I am capable consisting in bringing about a loud noise, but rather the thought that a special kind of activity of which I am capable, consisting in setting myself to bring about a loud noise, would have a loud noise as an effect.

Two conclusions are at once obvious. (1) The first is that the true answer to any question of the form 'Can I do so and so?' must be 'I don't know.' This is, of course, clear in certain cases. Plainly we never *know* that if we were to set ourselves to thread a needle, we should thread it; or that if we were to set ourselves to draw a line through a point on a piece of paper, we should succeed. But in the last resort this is the only answer ever possible, since we never *know* that we have not become paralysed. Even in the case of moving our arms or making a noise we do not *know* that, if we were to set ourselves to do it, we should do anything, though, of course, we may think it very likely both that we should do something, and also that we should move our arms, or make a noise, in particular. (2) The second conclusion is that whatever we are setting ourselves to do, we never in so setting ourselves *know* that we shall be doing what we are setting ourselves to do, bringing about what we are setting ourselves to bring about, or indeed that we are doing anything at all. In other words, it follows that where we are setting ourselves to do something, we never *know* what we shall be doing, and at best can only find out afterwards what we have done. And for this reason alone we cannot sustain the view to which reference was made earlier that 'doing something' means not simply bringing about something, but bringing about something knowing that we are doing so. For, apart from other objections, if it did, we in using the phrase should be implying that there is a special kind of activity consisting in bringing about something, of the special nature of which we are aware in performing the activity; and we do not think this. At the same time, the view has an underlying element of truth; for though bringing about something is *not*, setting ourselves to bring about something *is*, a special kind of activity of the special nature of which we are aware in performing it; and therefore the idea underlying the view is sound, though misapplied.

As regards an obligation, the moral is obvious. It is simply that, contrary to the implication of ordinary language and of moral rules in particular, an obligation must be an obligation, not to *do* something, but to perform an activity of a totally different kind, that of setting or exerting ourselves to do something, i.e. to bring something about.

It may be objected that, if an obligation were an obligation to perform a mental activity of a special kind other than that of bringing something about, the nature of that activity would have to be describable by itself, and not solely by reference to something else, as it is implied to be if we describe it as setting ourselves to bring something about. But to this two replies can be given. The first is that we find no difficulty in allowing the appropriateness of this procedure in analogous cases. Thus we have no difficulty in allowing the existence of such a kind of thing as desire, although we are perfectly aware that to desire is necessarily to desire something, e.g. the eating of an apple or the prosperity of our country, so that no desire can be described simply in terms of a certain state of mind. Again, we readily allow that there is such a thing as a state of wondering, or, again, of being angry, although we are quite aware that to wonder is to wonder, for instance, whether rain is coming, and to be angry is to be angry with someone for what he has done. The second reply is simply that if we try to describe the nature of the activity which we perform when we think we are bringing about something, without reference to bringing about something, we find that we totally fail.

If, however, we allow, as we now must, that an obligation must be an obligation not to do something but to set ourselves to do something, we have to modify accordingly not only the original question but also both the alternative views of the basis of an obligation.

The effect, however, as regards the relation between the alternatives is simply to intensify their difference. For, given the modification, on either view an obligation will be an obligation not to bring about something directly but to set ourselves to do so. And if there be an obligation to set ourselves to bring about some particular thing Y directly, then, on the objective view, the obligation will depend on an additional fact the existence of which we shall be unable to discover, viz. that setting ourselves to bring about Y would bring it about directly, while on the subjective view it will depend in part on an additional thinking something likely, viz. our thinking that setting ourselves to bring about Y would be likely to bring it about.

The question therefore arises whether this modification renders it any easier to decide between the alternatives. And the answer appears to be that in one respect it does. For once it has become common ground that the kind of activity which an obligation is an obligation to perform is one which may bring about nothing at all, viz. setting ourselves to bring about something, we are less inclined to think that, for there to be an obligation to perform some particular activity, it must have a certain indirect effect. To this extent the modification diminishes the force of the objective view without in any way impairing that of its rival. Yet undoubtedly it does nothing to remove what is, after all, the outstanding difficulty of the subjective view—a difficulty compared with which the others are only difficulties of detail, i.e. difficulties concerning its precise nature. This difficulty of the view in its original form lies in its representing the obligation to do some action as depending not on the fact that the action would have a certain character, if we were to do it, but on our thinking it likely that it would. This dependence seems impossible. For an obligation to do some action seems to be a character of the action; and therefore, it would seem, it must depend on the fact that the action would have a certain characteristic, if it were done, and not on our thinking it likely that it would. And if here we substitute for 'do some action' 'set ourselves to do some action', there is a difficulty of precisely the same kind.

It is, however, worth considering whether, after all, this difficulty is insuperable, and whether it may not simply arise from a mistake. We are apt to think of an obligation to do some action as if it were, like its goodness or badness, a sort of quality or character of the action. Just as we think that when we say of some action which we could do that it would be good, or, again, bad, we are stating that, in a wide sense of the term 'character', it would have a certain character, so we are apt to think that when we say of it that we are bound, or bound not, to do it, we are stating that it would have a certain character, for which the proper term would be 'ought-to-be-doneness' or 'ought-not-to-be-doneness'. And this tendency is fostered by our habit of using the terms 'right' and 'wrong' as equivalents for 'ought' and 'ought not'. For when we express our thought that we ought, or ought not, to do some action by saying that the act would be right, or wrong, our language inevitably implies that the obligation or disobligation is a certain character which the act would have if we were to do it, a character for which the only existing words are 'rightness' in the one case and 'wrongness' in the other. And when we think this, we in-

evitably go on to think that the obligation or disobligation must
depend on some character which the act would have. But, as we
recognize when we reflect, there are no such characteristics of
an action as ought-to-be-doneness and ought-not-to-be-doneness.
This is obvious; for, since the existence of an obligation to do some
action cannot possibly depend on actual performance of the action,
the obligation cannot itself be a property which the action would
have, if it were done. What does exist is the fact that you, or that I,
ought, or ought not, to do a certain action, or rather to set ourselves to do a certain action. And when we make an assertion containing the term 'ought' or 'ought not', that to which we are
attributing a certain character is not a certain activity but a
certain man. If our being bound to set ourselves to do some action
were a character which the activity would have, its existence
would, no doubt, have to depend on the fact that the activity
would have a certain character, and it could not depend on our
thinking that it would. Yet since, in fact, it is a character of ourselves, there is nothing to prevent its existence depending on our
having certain thoughts about the situation and, therefore, about
the nature of the activity in respect of its effects. Indeed, for this
reason, its existence must depend on some fact about ourselves.
And while the truth could not be expressed by saying: '*My setting
myself to do so-and-so* would *be* right, because *I think* that it would
have a certain effect'—a statement which would be as vicious in
principle as the statement '*Doing so-and-so* would *be* right because
I think it would be right'—there is nothing to prevent its being ex-
pressible in the form '*I* ought to set myself to do so-and-so, because
I think that it would have a certain effect'. We are therefore now
in a position to say that the fundamental difficulty presented by
the subjective view is simply the result of a mistake.

    This being so, there remains only one thing to do. This is to
consider, in some instance where we have considered the circumstances as fully as we can, whether we ought to perform some
particular activity, and then ask: 'Does the answer to this question
turn on the nature of our *thought* about the situation, and therefore
about the effect of the activity, or on the nature of the *situation* and
therefore on that of the effect of the activity?' This must be our
remaining task, once general difficulties have been cleared away.
For there is no way of discovering whether some general doctrine is
true except by discovering the general fact to which the problem
relates; and there is no way of discovering some general fact except

by apprehending particular instances of it. And here there is little that need be said. For we have only to carry out this procedure to find not that we are *inclined to think*, or even that we are of the opinion that, but that we are *certain*, i.e. *know*, that the answer turns not on the nature of the situation but on that of our thought about it. This certainty is attainable most readily if the instance taken is similar to those already considered in which our doubts about the nature of the situation are considerable. But it is attainable in any instance, provided that we really face the question.

We therefore cannot but allow that the subjective view is true, in spite of what at first seems its paradoxical character, and that, therefore, in order to defend any moral rule whatever, we must first modify its form accordingly.

P. 31, para. 5. The argument appears fallacious. For to say that an obligation is an obligation to do *some action* is consistent with holding that it is an obligation, e.g., to perform a particular activity of a certain sort which will have a certain particular effect. And we are only implying that there is a kind of activity which in certain cases has effects.

The concluding part seems to contain two mistakes:

(1) p. 33. It looks as though 'willing *X*' at any rate as used technically is a synonym for what I have called 'setting ourselves to bring about *X*'. This, however, does not affect the general argument. But the other mistake does;

(2) pp. 35–7. The difficulty put up for consideration is that the obligation to do some action must depend on some character that the action would have, and not on our thinking that it would have some character. And it is said to remain if we substitute for 'some action' (i.e. bringing about *X*) 'setting ourselves to do some action' (i.e. willing the existence of *X*). And it is resolved by denying that 'duty' is a property of an *action* as distinct from a person.

This resolution, except indirectly, does not affect the difficulty— which is that if we ought e.g. to will something *X*, it must be in virtue of a character which willing *X* would have and not in virtue of our thinking it would have it.

The proper resolution is to point out that if 'willing *X*' be substituted for 'bringing about *X*', then our thinking *X* likely to effect something else *Y* does enter into the character of the *activity* to which the 'ought' refers. For to will *X*, thinking it likely to produce *Y*, is one willing, and to will *X*, thinking it unlikely to produce *Y*, or to will *X*, not thinking of *Y* at all, is another. In other words, the *thinking* enters into the character of the *willing*.

P. 34, para. 2. The moral should be that if an obligation is to *do* some particular action, i.e. to will a change the willing of which would cause a certain change, we can never know that we ought to do a certain action.

P. 34, para. 2, sentence beginning 'And for this reason'. Fallacious, because this reason can't prevent our meaning this by 'doing something', but only shows that if we mean this by 'doing something' we are mistaken in thinking there is such a thing.

In the next sentence the 'if it did' statement is untrue.

H. A. P.

3

THE MEANING OF ᾿ΑΓΑΘΟΝ IN THE *ETHICS* OF ARISTOTLE[1]

I HAVE for some time found it increasingly difficult to resist a conclusion so heretical that the mere acceptance of it may seem a proof of lunacy. Yet the failure of a recent attempt to resist it has led me to want to confess the heresy. And at any rate a statement of my reasons may provoke a refutation.

The heresy, in brief, is that Aristotle (in the *Nicomachean Ethics*, except in the two discussions of pleasure—where ἀγαθόν is opposed to φαῦλον and μοχθηρόν) really meant by ἀγαθόν conducive to our happiness, and maintained that when a man does an action deliberately, as distinct from impulsively, he does it simply in order to, i.e. from the desire to, become happy, this being so even when he does what is virtuous or speculates. Of this heresy a corollary is the view that Aristotle, being anxious to persuade men first and foremost to practise speculation and secondarily to do what is virtuous, conceived that, to succeed, what he had to prove was that this was the action necessary to make a man happy. This corollary, however, which may seem only a further heresy, I propose to ignore. The heresy, in my opinion, is equally attributable to Plato, and for much the same reasons. But for simplicity's sake I propose to confine consideration to Aristotle, with, however, the suggestion that the same argument can be applied to Plato.

In attributing this view to Aristotle I do not mean to imply that he does not repeatedly make statements inconsistent with it. Nor do I mean to imply that the question of the consistency of these statements with the view simply escapes him; it seems to me that it does not, but that owing to a mistake he thought they were consistent with it. Nor do I mean to imply that his acceptance of this view appears on the surface; but rather that it becomes evident once we lay bare certain misleading elements in his account of the motive of deliberate action.

The first two chapters of the *Ethics*, and especially its opening sentence, are undoubtedly puzzling. Aristotle begins by saying: πᾶσα τέχνη καὶ πᾶσα μέθοδος, ὁμοίως δὲ πρᾶξίς τε καὶ προαίρεσις, ἀγαθοῦ τινὸς ἐφίεσθαι δοκεῖ· διὸ καλῶς ἀπεφήναντο τἀγαθόν οὗ πάντ᾽

ἐφιέται. 'Every art and every inquiry, and similarly every action and purpose, is thought to aim at some good; and for this reason the good has rightly been declared to be that at which all things aim.' Then after pointing out that certain aims or ends are subordinate to others, he contends that there must be one final end to which all others are subordinate, and that this will be τἀγαθόν, the good, and that, consequently, knowledge of this final end will have great influence on our lives, since if we have it, we shall have a definite mark or goal to aim at. And he goes on to say that, this being so, his object in the *Ethics* is to discover what this final end is.

Here, as the rest of the first book shows, Aristotle, in his first sentence, is not simply stating a common opinion, but stating it with approval and on the assumption that it is an opinion which his hearers will accept and so which can be used as a basis for his subsequent argument. And, so regarded, it is very sweeping.

Even if he had said that in every deliberate action we have an aim or are aiming at something, we should have regarded the statement, put forward as expressing a fact obvious to everyone, and so as needing neither elucidation nor discussion, as sufficiently sweeping. But what he does say is more sweeping. In effect, taking for granted that there is always something at which we are aiming, he commits himself to a general statement about its nature, stating that it is always ἀγαθόν τι, or, as we may translate the phrase, a good.

But besides being sweeping it is obscure. Even if Aristotle had said that in all action we are aiming at something, we should have felt that the statement needed elucidation. But saying as he does that we are aiming at something good, we have an additional puzzle. If, instead, he had said that we are always aiming at a pleasure, or at an honour, or at doing some good action, then we should have at least suspected we knew what he meant, whether or not we agreed. But the meaning of ἀγαθόν is not clear.

Consequently to discover his meaning we have to find out not only what he means when he speaks of us in a deliberate action as aiming at something (ἐφίεσθαί τινος) or as having a τέλος or end, but also what he means by ἀγαθόν. And of these tasks, plainly the former has to be accomplished first.

The idea, which of course underlies the *Ethics*, that in all deliberate action we have an end or aim, is one the truth of which we are all likely to maintain when we first consider action, 'action' being a term which, for shortness' sake, I propose to use for deliberate action. The idea goes back to Plato; and Mill expresses it when he says that all action is for the sake of an end. We take for granted that in doing some action there must be some desire leading or moving us to do the action, i.e. forming what we call our motive, since, as we should say, otherwise we should not be doing the action; or, for this is only to express the same idea in other words, we take for granted that in doing the action we have a purpose, i.e. something the desire of which moves us to do the action. And, taking this for granted, we are apt to maintain that our purpose in doing the action always consists in something, other than the action, which we think the action likely to cause, directly or indirectly, such as an improvement in our health which we expect from taking a dose of medicine.

Further, taking this view of the motive of action, we are apt to express it metaphorically by saying that in any action we have an aim or that there is something at which we are aiming. For when we consider, e.g., taking a drug from the desire to become healthy, we are apt to think of the thing desired, viz. our health, as that by reference to which we have devised the action as what is likely to cause it, and so as similar to the target by reference to the position of which a shooter arranges his weapon before shooting. We are also apt to speak of our purpose metaphorically as our end, as being something which we think will come into existence at the end of the action. In either case, however, it is to be noticed that the terms 'end' and 'aim' are merely metaphorical expressions for our purpose, i.e. for that the desire of which is moving us to act. No doubt further consideration may afterwards lead us to abandon this view. For certain actions and notably acts of gratitude or revenge seem prompted by the desire to do the action we at least hope we are doing, such as the desire to inflict an injury on another equal to that to which he has done us. Yet we may not reflect sufficiently to notice this, or even if we do we may fail to notice that such actions require us to modify the view, or may even think, as Aristotle did, that the doctrine may be made to apply to them.

Plato, it may be noticed, expressly formulates this view in the *Gorgias*. In trying to show that orators and tyrants have the least power in States, he lays down generally[1] that a man in doing what he does wishes not for the action but for that for the sake of which he does it, this being implied to be some result of the action. And in support he urges that a man who takes a drug wishes not for

[1] *Gorgias*, p. 467.

taking the drug but for health, and that a man who takes a voyage wishes not for the sailing and the incurring of dangers but for the wealth for the sake of which he takes the voyage. He is, however, here obviously going too far in asserting that the man does not want to do the action itself, for if the man did not want to do the action, he would not be doing it. What Plato should have said and what would express the view accurately is this:

A man undoubtedly wants to do what he does, and this desire is moving him. But the desire is always derivative or dependent. His having it depends on his having another desire, viz. the desire of something to which he thinks the action will lead, and that is why this latter desire should be represented as what is moving him, since it is in consequence of having this latter desire that he has the desire to do the action.

The view, therefore, implies the idea that the desire to do some action is always a dependent desire, depending on the desire of something to which we think the action will lead. But, as we soon notice, this latter desire must either be itself an independent desire, i.e. a desire which does not depend on any other, or else imply such a desire, since otherwise, as Aristotle put it, desire would be empty and vain. We are therefore led to draw a distinction between an independent desire and a desire depending on a desire of something which we think the thing desired will cause. Aristotle, of course, recognized and even emphasized the distinction, but unfortunately he formulated it with a certain inaccuracy. He implies that it should be expressed as that between τὸ βούλεσθαί τι δι᾽ αὐτό, or καθ᾽ αὐτό, and τὸ βούλεσθαί τι δι᾽ ἕτερον. But the latter phrase must be short for τὸ βούλεσθαί τι διὰ τὸ βούλεσθαι ἕτερόν τι, and, this being so, the former phrase must be short for τὸ βούλεσθαί τι διὰ τὸ βούλεσθαι αὐτό, which, meaning wishing for something in consequence of wishing for itself, is not sense. The distinction should have been expressed as that between τὸ βούλεσθαί τι μὴ διὰ τὸ βούλεσθαι ἕτερόν τι and τὸ βούλεσθαί τι διὰ τὸ βούλεσθαι ἕτερόν τι or, to be more accurate, between desiring something not in consequence of desiring something else, and desiring something in consequence of desiring something else to which we think it will lead. And in this connexion it should be noticed that the English phrase for an independent desire, viz. the desire of something for its own sake, which is the equivalent of Aristotle's βούλεσθαί τι δι᾽ αὐτό, has really only the negative meaning of a desire which is not dependent on any other desire.

Further, having reached this distinction, we are soon led, as of course Aristotle was, to hold that in every action we must have some ultimate or final aim, consisting of the object of some independent desire, and to distinguish from this aims which we have but which are not ultimate.

Having drawn this distinction we do not ask: 'Of what sort or sorts are our non-ultimate aims?' since obviously anything may be such an aim. But we do raise the question: 'Of what sort or sorts is our ultimate aim in various actions?'

To this question Aristotle's answer is ἀγαθόν τι, since his opening statement covers ultimate as well as non-ultimate aims. And the most obvious way to ascertain what Aristotle considers our ultimate aim is, of course, simply to find out what he means by ἀγαθόν. But, as should now be obvious, there is also another way. Like ourselves, he must really mean by our ultimate or final aim that the independent desire of which, or, as he would put it, that the desire of which καθ' αὑτό, is moving us to act. Consequently, if he says of certain things that we desire and pursue, i.e. aim at, them καθ' αὑτά, we are entitled to conclude that he considers that in certain instances they are our ultimate aim. Now in Chapter 6 of Book I he maintains that there are certain kinds of things, viz. τιμή, φρόνησις, and ἡδονή, which are διωκόμενα καὶ ἀγαπώμενα καθ' αὑτά; and to these he adds in Chapter 7, § 5, νοῦς and πᾶσα ἀρετή, of which, together with τιμή and ἡδονή, he says that though we choose them for the sake of happiness, we also choose them δι' αὑτά, i.e. as being what they severally are, since we should choose them even if nothing resulted from them. And to say this is only to say in other words that in some instances our ultimate end is an honour, in others it is a pleasure, in others our being φρόνιμος, and so on. Consequently, if we hold him to this, the only possible conclusion for us to draw is that he considers (1) that in such cases our ultimate end is not ἀγαθόν τι, whatever he means by ἀγαθόν, and also (2) that our ultimate end is not always of the same sort, so that no single term could describe it. We thus reach the astonishing conclusion that Aristotle, in insisting as he does that we pursue these things for their own sake, is really ruling out the possibility of maintaining that our end is always ἀγαθόν τι, or indeed anything else, so that we are in a position to maintain that he has no right to assert that our ultimate end is always an ἀγαθόν, even before we have attempted to elucidate what he means by ἀγαθόν.

Further, if we next endeavour, as we obviously should, to do this, we get another surprise. Aristotle's nearest approach to an elucidation is to be found in Chapter 6, §§ 7–11, and Chapter 7, §§ 1–5. There he speaks of τὰ καθ᾽ αὑτὰ διωκόμενα καὶ ἀγαπώμενα as called ἀγαθά in one sense, and gives as illustrations τιμή, φρόνησις, and ἡδονή; and he speaks of τὰ ποιητικὰ τούτων ἢ φυλακτικά πως as called ἀγαθά in another sense, and he implies that these latter are διωκτὰ καὶ αἱρετὰ δι᾽ ἕτερον[1] and that πλοῦτος is an illustration.[2] Further, he appears to consider that the difference of meaning is elucidated by referring to the former as ἀγαθὰ καθ᾽ αὑτά and to the latter as ἀγαθὰ διὰ ταῦτα, i.e. ἀγαθὰ διὰ ἀγαθὰ καθ᾽ αὑτά. But this unfortunately is no elucidation, since to state a difference of reason for calling two things ἀγαθόν is not to state a difference of meaning of ἀγαθόν, and indeed is to imply that the meaning in both cases is the same. Nevertheless, these statements seem intended as an elucidation of the meaning of ἀγαθόν. And the cause for surprise lies in this, that if they are taken seriously as an elucidation, the conclusion can only be that ἀγαθόν includes 'being desired' in its meaning, and indeed simply means τέλος or end. For if they are so understood, Aristotle must be intending to say (1) that when we say of something that it is ἀγαθὸν καθ᾽ αὑτό what we *mean* is that it is διωκόμενον καὶ ἀγαπώμενον καθ᾽ αὑτό, i.e. simply that it is an ultimate end, and (2) that when we say of something that it is ἀγαθὸν δι᾽ ἕτερον, what we mean is that it is διωκόμενον καὶ ἀγαπώμενον δι᾽ ἕτερον, i.e. simply that it is a non-ultimate end. In other words, if here he is interpreted strictly, he is explaining that ἀγαθόν means τέλος, and by the distinction between an ἀγαθὸν καθ᾽ αὑτό and an ἀγαθὸν δι᾽ ἕτερον he means merely the distinction between an ultimate and a non-ultimate end. Yet if anything is certain, it is that when Aristotle says of something, e.g. πλοῦτος, that it is an ἀγαθόν he does not mean that it is a τέλος, i.e. that it is something at which someone is aiming, and that when he says of something, e.g. τιμή or φρόνησις, that it is an ἀγαθὸν καθ᾽ αὑτό, he does not mean that it is someone's ultimate end, i.e. what he speaks of in Book VI, 9, § 7 as τὸ τέλος τὸ ἁπλῶς. Apart from other considerations, if he did, then for him to say, as he in effect does, that we always aim at ἀγαθόν τι would be to say nothing, and for him to speak, as he does, of the object of βούλησις as τἀγαθόν would be absurd.

But this being so, what *does* Aristotle mean by ἀγαθόν? Here there is at least one statement which can be made with certainty. Aristotle unquestionably would have said that where we are

---

[1] *Ethics*, i. 7. 4.   [2] Ibid. i. 5. 8.

pursuing something of a certain kind, say, an honour, καθ' αὑτό, we are pursuing it ὡς ἀγαθόν, i.e. as a good. Otherwise there would not even have been verbal consistency between his statements, that we pursue, i.e. aim at, things of certain stated kinds, and that we always aim at ἀγαθόν τι. Again, unless we allow that he would have said this, we cannot make head or tail either of his puzzling statement in Book I, Chapter 2 that since, as there must be, there is some end which we desire for its own sake, this end must be τἀγαθόν, or, again, of its sequel in Chapter 7, where he proceeds to consider what that is to which the term τἀγαθόν is applicable by considering which of our various ends is a final end. For we are entitled to ask: '*Why* does Aristotle think that if we discover something to be desired and pursued for its own sake, we shall be entitled to say that it is τἀγαθόν?' And no answer is possible unless we allow that he thought that in desiring and pursuing something for its own sake we are desiring and pursuing it ὡς ἀγαθόν.

But Aristotle in saying, as he would have said, that in pursuing, e.g., an honour, we are pursuing it ὡς ἀγαθόν could only have meant that we are pursuing it in virtue of thinking that it would possess a certain character to which he refers by the term ἀγαθόν, so that by ἀγαθόν he must mean to indicate some character which certain things would have. Further, this being so, in implying as he does that in pursuing things of certain different kinds καθ' αὑτά we are pursuing them ὡς ἀγαθά, he must be implying that these things of different kinds have, nevertheless, a common character, viz. that indicated by the term ἀγαθόν. It will, of course, be objected that he expressly denies that they have a common character. For he says: τιμῆς δὲ καὶ φρονήσεως καὶ ἡδονῆς ἕτεροι καὶ διαφέροντες οἱ λόγοι ταύτῃ ᾗ ἀγαθά.[1] But the answer is simple; viz. that this is merely an inconsistency into which he is driven by his inability to find in these things the common character which his theory requires him to find, and that if he is to succeed in maintaining that we pursue these things of various kinds ὡς ἀγαθά, he *has* to maintain that in spite of appearances to the contrary they have a common character.

Nevertheless, though we have to insist that Aristotle in fact holds that in pursuing any of these things καθ' αὑτό, i.e., as we should say, for its own sake, we are pursuing it ὡς ἀγαθόν, we cannot escape the admission that in doing so he is being inconsistent. For to maintain that in pursuing, e.g., an honour, we are pursuing it καθ'

---

[1] *Ethics*, i. 6. 11.

αὐτό, or, as we should say, for its own sake, is really to maintain
that the desire of an honour moving us is an independent desire,
i.e. a desire depending on no other. And, on the other hand, to
maintain that in pursuing an honour, we are pursuing it ὡς ἀγαθόν,
or as a good, is really to maintain that the desire of an honour
moving us is a dependent desire, viz. a desire depending on the
desire of something which will possess the character indicated by the
word ἀγαθόν, i.e. that we desire an honour only in consequence of
desiring something which will possess that character and of thinking
that an honour will possess it. It is, in fact, really to maintain that
in pursuing an honour, our ultimate aim, i.e. that the independent
desire of which is moving us, or what Aristotle would call that
which we are pursuing καθ' αὑτό, is not an honour but a good, i.e.
something having the character, whatever it may be, which is
indicated by the word ἀγαθόν, i.e. that we desire an honour only
in consequence of desiring a good. The principle involved will
become clearer, if we take a different illustration. In Chapter 6
Aristotle speaks of ὁρᾶν as one of the things which are pursued for
their own sake; and if he had said that we pursue ὁρᾶν ὡς αἰσθάνεσθαι he would in consistency have had to maintain that what we are
pursuing καθ' αὑτό is not ὁρᾶν but αἰσθάνεσθαι, and that the desire
of ὁρᾶν moving us is only a dependent desire depending on our
desiring something else which we think ὁρᾶν will be.

It will be objected that there is really no inconsistency, since
Aristotle conceives the characteristic referred to by ἀγαθόν as a
characteristic of an honour and of anything else which he would
say we pursue καθ' αὑτό, and that to speak of us as desiring something
in respect of some character which it would have is not to represent
our desire of it as dependent. In illustration it may be urged that
to speak of us as, in desiring to do a courageous action, desiring it
as a worthy or virtuous action is not to represent our desire to do
a courageous action as dependent. But the objection cannot be
sustained. For if we desire to do a courageous action, as something
which would be a virtuous action, i.e., really, a something which
we think would be a virtuous action, although our desire does not
depend on a desire of something which we think a courageous
action would *cause*, it does depend on the desire of something
which we think it would *be*. And as a proof of this dependence we
can point to the fact that if, while having this desire, we were to do
a good action, of another sort, e.g. a generous action, the desire
would disappear.

What is in the end plain is that Aristotle cannot succeed in maintaining that our ultimate end is always ἀγαθόν τι without abandoning his view that we pursue such things as τιμή and ἀρετή καθ' αὐτά, or, as we should say, for their own sake, and maintaining instead that we pursue them as things which we think will have the character to which the term ἀγαθόν refers. Nevertheless, in spite of having to allow that we are thereby attributing inconsistency to Aristotle, we have to admit that he, in fact, holds that in desiring and pursuing certain things for their own sakes we are desiring and pursuing them in respect of their having a certain character, viz. whatever it be to which he refers by the term ἀγαθόν.

So far the only clue reached to the meaning of ἀγαθόν is the idea that Aristotle used it to refer to a certain character possessed by certain things, the thought of the possession of which arouses desire for them, and indeed is the only thing which arouses desire for anything, except where our desire depends on another desire.

We have now to try to get to closer quarters with the question of its meaning. The question is really: 'What is the character which Aristotle considered we must think would be possessed by something if we are to desire it, independently of desiring something else to which we think it will lead, that character being what Aristotle used the word ἀγαθόν to refer to?'

Here it seems hardly necessary to point out that the answer cannot be 'goodness'. To rule out this answer it is only necessary to point out two things. First, if Aristotle had meant by ἀγαθόν good, he would have had to represent us as desiring for its own sake any good activity, whether ours or another's, whereas he always implies that a good activity which we desire is an activity of our own, and in addition he would have had to drop, as he never does, the idea of a connexion between a good activity and *our own* happiness. And second, Aristotle's term ἀγαθόν is always ἀγαθὸν τινί, as appears most obviously in the phrase ἀνθρώπινον ἀγαθόν and in the statement in Book IX, 8, § 8–9, where he says that reason always chooses what is best for itself—πᾶς γὰρ νοῦς αἱρεῖται τὸ βέλτιστον ἑαυτῷ—and goes on to add that the man who gives wealth to a friend assigns the greater good, the having done what is noble (τὸ κάλον), to himself. Once, however, we regard this answer as having to be excluded once for all, there seems to be no alternative to attributing to Aristotle a familiar turn of thought to which we are all very prone and which is exemplified in Mill and T. H. Green.

When we consider what we desire we soon come to the conclusion, as of course Aristotle did, that there are things of certain kinds which we desire, not in consequence of thinking that they will have an effect which we desire, but for themselves, such as seeing a beautiful landscape, being in a position of power, helping another, and doing a good action. We then are apt to ask, 'What is the condition of our desiring such things?' and if we do, we are apt to answer—and the tendency is almost irresistible—'It is impossible for us to desire any such thing unless we think of it as something which we should like, since, if we do not think of it thus, we remain simply indifferent to its realization.' Then, if asked what we mean by its being something we should like, we reply: 'Something which would give us enjoyment, or, alternatively, gratification, or, to use a term which will cover either, pleasure.' The tendency is one to which Mill gives expression when he says that desiring a thing and finding it pleasant are two parts of the same phenomenon; and Green exhibits it when he maintains, as in effect he does, that we can desire something only if we think of it as something which will give us satisfaction, i.e. gratification. In maintaining this we are really maintaining that the thing which we at first thought we desired for its own sake, such as seeing a beautiful landscape, or doing a good action, is really only being desired for the sake of a feeling of enjoyment or gratification, or, to put it generally, pleasure, which we think it will cause in us. And correspondingly, where we think of the desire as moving us to act, we are really maintaining that what we at first thought our ultimate end is really only our penultimate end or the proximate means, and that our ultimate end is really a pleasure which we think this will cause. We are, however, apt to think of a thing's giving us enjoyment, or alternatively gratification, as if it were a quality of the thing, just as we think of the loudness of a noise as a quality of the noise. And our tendency to do this is strengthened by the fact that the ordinary way of stating the fact that something X excites a feeling of pleasure, or of gratification, is to say that X is pleasant or gratifying, a way of speaking which suggests that what is in fact a property possessed by X of causing a certain feeling is a quality of X. The tendency is mistaken, since, as anyone must allow in the end, something's giving us enjoyment is *not* a quality of it, and when we say that something *is* pleasant, we are not attributing to it a certain quality but stating that it has a certain effect. Nevertheless, the tendency exists. And when it is operative in us, we state our original contention by saying that in desiring to see a beautiful landscape for its own sake, we desire it as something which will be pleasant, and that when we are acting on the desire, our ultimate end is the seeing a beautiful landscape as something which will be pleasant, thereby representing what on our view is really the proximate means to our end as our end.

This being the line of thought to which I referred, it remains for me to try to show that it was taken by Aristotle. Before we consider details we can find two general considerations which are in favour of thinking that he took it. In the first place, if we assume it to be indisputable that he thought that there are things of a certain sort which we desire for their own sake, but that in desiring them we desire them in respect of having a certain character to which he refers by the term ἀγαθόν, and then ask 'What can be the character of which he is thinking?' the only possible answer seems to be: 'That of exciting either enjoyment or gratification.' And in particular two things are in favour of this answer. First, it is easy, from lack of consideration, to think of exciting pleasure as a quality of the thing desired—as indeed Aristotle appears to do when he speaks of virtuous actions (αἱ κατ' ἀρετὴν πράξεις) as φύσει ἡδέα and as ἡδεῖαι καθ' αὑτάς,[1] i.e. as pleasant in virtue of their own nature; and second, the perplexity in which he finds himself in Chapter 6 when trying to elucidate the meaning of ἀγαθόν would be accounted for if what he was referring to was something which is not in fact a character common to the various things said to be ἀγαθά, although he tended to think of it as if it was. In the second place he applies the term ἀγαθόν not only to the things which we desire for themselves, but also to the things which produce or preserve them, and it is difficult to see how he can apply the term to the latter unless ἀγαθόν means productive of pleasure, whether directly or not. In fact, only given this meaning is it possible to understand how Aristotle can speak not merely of τιμή but also of πλοῦτος as an ἀγαθόν.

To pass, however, to special considerations, we seem to find evidence, and decisive evidence, in a quarter in which we at first should least expect it. At the beginning of Chapter 4 he directs his hearers' attention to the question: τί ⟨ἐστι⟩ τὸ πάντων ἀκρότατον τῶν πρακτῶν ἀγαθῶν, i.e. 'What is it that is the greatest of all achievable goods?' and he proceeds to say that while there is general agreement about the name for it, since both the many and

[1] *Ethics*, i. 8. 11.

the educated say that it is happiness, yet they differ about what happiness is, the many considering it something the nature of which is clear and obvious, such as pleasure, wealth, or honour, whereas, he implies, the educated consider it something else of which the nature is not obvious. Then in the next chapter he proceeds to state what, to judge from the three most prominent types of life, that of enjoyment, the political life, and that of contemplation, various men consider that the good or happiness is, viz. enjoyment, honour, and contemplation. And later he gives his own view, contending, with the help of an argument based on the idea that man has a function, that happiness is ψυχῆς ἐνέργειά τις κατ᾽ ἀρετὴν τελείαν.[1]

Here it has to be admitted that Aristotle is expressing himself in a misleading way. His question 'What is the greatest of goods?' can be treated as if it had been the question 'What is a man's ultimate end?' i.e. τὸ τέλος τὸ ἁπλῶς. For as Book I, 2, § 1 and Book I, 7 show, he considers that to find what is the greatest good, or the good, we must find a man's final end, i.e. that which he desires and aims at for its own sake, and in Book I, 5 he judges what men consider the good from what their lives show to be their ultimate aim. And his answer to this question, if taken as it stands, is undeniably absurd. For, so understood, it is to the effect that, though all men, when asked 'What is the ultimate end?', answer by using the same word, viz. εὐδαιμονία, yet, as they differ about what εὐδαιμονία is, i.e., really, about the thing for which they are using the word εὐδαιμονία to stand, some using it to designate pleasure, others wealth, and so on, they are in substance giving different answers, some meaning by the word εὐδαιμονία pleasure, others wealth, and so on. But of course this is not what Aristotle meant. He certainly did not think that anyone ever meant by εὐδαιμονία either τιμή or πλοῦτος; and he certainly did not himself mean by it ψυχῆς ἐνέργειά τις κατ᾽ ἀρετὴν τελείαν. What he undoubtedly meant and thought others meant by the word εὐδαιμονία is happiness. Plainly, too, what he thought men differed about was not the nature of happiness but the conditions of its realization, and when he says that εὐδαιμονία is ψυχῆς ἐνέργειά τις κατ᾽ ἀρετὴν τελείαν, what he really means is that the latter is what is required for the realization of happiness. Consideration of the *Ethics* by itself should be enough to convince us of this, but if it is not, we need only take into account his elucidation of the meaning of the

[1] *Ethics*, i. 13. 1.

C

question 'τί ἐστιν;' to be sure that when he asks 'τί ἐστι ἡ εὐδαιμονία;' his meaning is similar to that of the man who, when he asks 'What is colour?' or 'What is sound?' really means 'What are the conditions necessary for its realization?' We must therefore understand Aristotle in Chapter 4 to be in effect contending that while it is universally admitted that our ultimate aim is happiness, there is great divergence of view about the conditions, or, more precisely, the proximate conditions, of its realization.

But, this conclusion reached, we can plainly take one step farther and conclude that Aristotle himself is in agreement with the view that our ultimate end is happiness, and that, taking its truth for granted, his *Ethics* is concerned first to prove that it is by virtuous action that it will be realized, and then to work out in detail the character of virtuous action, so that we shall be better able to obtain our aim. In other words, we can conclude that his real answer to the question, 'What is τὸ τέλος τὸ ἁπλῶς, i.e. our ultimate aim?' is not, as we may at first think, ψυχῆς ἐνέργειά τις κατ' ἀρετὴν τελείαν but εὐδαιμονία, i.e. happiness. Putting this otherwise, we can say that the accurate statement of his own view is to be found in I. 12, where he gives as a reason why εὐδαιμονία is τίμιον, whereas ἀρετή is merely ἐπαινετόν, that it is for the sake of εὐδαιμονία that we all do everything.[1]

Now, if by thus going behind Aristotle's terminology we are driven to conclude that Aristotle really considered our ultimate end to be always our happiness, or alternatively some particular state of happiness on our part—for sometimes he seems to imply the one view and sometimes the other—we are also driven to conclude that, though he at times makes statements to the contrary, he also holds that where we are said to have as our ultimate end τιμή or ἐνέργειά τις κατ' ἀρετήν or anything else of a kind which we consider a condition of happiness, the thing in question is really according to him only our penultimate end, and the desire of it is only a derivative desire depending on our desire of happiness. And then it becomes obvious that when he implies, as he always does, that in desiring one of these things we desire it as an ἀγαθόν, what he means by ἀγαθόν is 'productive of a state, or rather a feeling, of happiness', i.e., as I think we may say in this context, a feeling of pleasure. Further, this being so, we have to allow that he fundamentally misrepresents his own problem. Assuming that we all always have either a single ultimate aim, or at least, alternatively,

---

[1] [ταύτης (i.e. εὐδαιμονίας) γὰρ χάριν τὰ λοιπὰ πάντα πάντες πράττομεν, *Ethics*, i. 12. 8.]

an aim of one sort, what he ostensibly maintains is that we are uncertain about its nature, and that therefore he has to discover its nature in order to help us to achieve it. But, as we must now conclude, what he is really maintaining is that though the nature of our ultimate aim, happiness, is known to us, for we all know the nature of that for which the word 'happiness' stands, we are doubtful about the proximate means to it, and that consequently he has to discover the proximate means. In other words, in maintaining ψυχῆς ἐνέργειά τις κατ᾽ ἀρετὴν τελείαν to be our ultimate end of the nature of which we are uncertain, he is putting what on his view is really the proximate means to our end in the place of what on his view is really our end. And if we ask 'How can he have come to misrepresent his own view so fundamentally?', then, if the contentions already advanced are true, we have at hand a satisfactory answer. We can reply that the misrepresentation is due to his making two mistakes to which we are all prone: first, that of thinking of the property of causing happiness as a quality of what causes it, and secondly, that of thinking that where we are aiming at something of a certain kind for its own sake, and so having it as our ultimate end, we are nevertheless aiming at it in respect of its having a certain character.

By way of conclusion it may be well to refer to an objection which will inevitably be raised, viz. that I have been, in effect, representing Aristotle as a psychological hedonist, and that to do this is absurd. I admit the charge, but do not consider the representation absurd. It seems not only possible, but common, to hold that there are a number of things other than pleasure which we desire for their own sake, and then when the question is raised, 'How is it that we desire these things?', to reply: 'Only because we think they will give us pleasure.' In my opinion, the reply is mistaken, and is made only because we are apt to think of the gratification necessarily consequent on the thought that something which we have desired is realized as that the thought of which excites the desire. But the mistake is a very insidious one, as, if I am right, is shown by the fact that Green, in spite of all the trouble he takes to point out that Mill falls into it, falls into it himself.

4

GREEN: POLITICAL OBLIGATION

I

GREEN's lectures on the Principles of Political Obligation are in the main an attempt to answer two related questions. The first of these is the question: *Why* is it the duty of a subject to obey his ruler or sovereign or government? This question of course takes for granted, as in ordinary circumstances we all do, that there is such a duty, i.e. that the mere fact of a sovereign's ordering us to do some action gives rise to a duty on our part to carry it out. And the question arises naturally out of this idea, for after all the mere receipt of an order backed up by a threat seems, if anything, to give rise to the duty of resisting rather than of obeying, and so we naturally ask, why is this otherwise in the special case where the order comes from a ruler?

The question, it should be noted, is similar to questions about acts of other kinds which we ordinarily think duties, such as, *why* ought we to speak truthfully or to consider the feelings of others? Hence an answer is really only part of a theory of Moral Obligation in general, viz. that part which concerns one special obligation, and unless we recognize this we are apt to go astray in looking for the answer.

Green puts this question in the form: What is the true ground or justification of obedience to law? At the same time his answer, as will appear later, has a peculiarity. This is that by its very nature it is at the same time a theory of Moral Obligation in general, i.e. an answer to the question, *why* ought we to do any of the actions which are duties? And indeed his lectures will be better understood if they are regarded as a theory of Moral Obligation generally rather than a theory of Political Obligation in particular, though they are both.

The second question is one the answer to which in Green's mind is bound up with the answer to the first. It is the question put by a *ruler*: What is the principle which should guide me in making laws, i.e. in ordering and enforcing various actions?

Green's treatment of these questions exerts a peculiar fascination. It gives the impression of propounding a profound truth, the ignoring of which has led his predecessors astray, and the discovery of which at last renders it possible to give the right answer.

At the same time the lectures are undeniably very obscure. And the impression of their obscurity is apt to grow rather than to diminish with further acquaintance. Indeed we more and more find ourselves asking not so much: Is the doctrine true? but: What *is* the doctrine?

Once the reader has realized the obscurity, what he would like to see offered in the first instance is a clear statement, kept clear of all commentary, of what the doctrine is. And he would prefer any comments to be reserved till afterwards.

Now I flatter myself that I could offer such an outline. But if I did, you would only call it a caricature. For it would differ so widely from Green's own statements that it would strike you as mere misrepresentation, and you would object that I have simply misunderstood him. To avoid this objection, it would be necessary simply to construct an outline by piecing together in as connected a way as is possible the statements to which Green seems to attach most importance. But you would find the result just as obscure as the lectures. It would, in fact, only present the obscurity in a tabloid form, and it would be no help towards discovering what the doctrine really is.

The chief reason of this lies in a fact which only becomes clear as the result of considering very closely what Green says. Underlying the lectures is a peculiar theory of Moral Obligation which is totally inconsistent with our ordinary moral ideas and therefore also with ordinary language, which is after all only the expression of our ordinary ideas. Unfortunately, however, Green does not realize this; and in consequence, when stating what he considers to be the truth, he retains ordinary language, thereby speaking as though our ordinary ideas were true, although it is really his object to make out that they are not. Thereby he conceals both from himself and from his readers the real nature of his view, and in fact fundamentally misrepresents it. And in consequence, to represent his doctrine accurately, radical restatement becomes necessary. Incidentally, it may be added, Green by expressing his view in ordinary language gives it a plausibility which it does not deserve, by making it seem consistent with our ordinary ideas although in fact it is not.

This being so, the only useful plan is to take the statements to which Green would seem to attach most importance, and ascertain what he is really implying in making them, and then to formulate his doctrine in accordance with these implications, regardless of whether or no the formulation agrees with his ordinary method of expressing himself.

And this is the procedure which I propose to adopt. It unfortunately, of course, involves a good deal of discussion of matters of interpretation. But this has to be regarded as inevitable.

At the same time, to do this with success some preparation is necessary. As any consideration of Green will show, he is on certain matters confused, and on these things we must first get ourselves clear.

1. It is important to bear in mind that to have a Legal Obligation and to have a Moral Obligation to do some act are facts of quite different sorts. The former consists in the fact that we have been ordered to do it and are subject to coercion if we do not, while the latter consists in our having the duty of doing the action.

2. Consider the meaning of the phrase 'a moral right'. As instances will show, we use 'having a moral right' in two senses according as that to which we are said to have a right is (a) our doing something, e.g. taking a holiday or killing someone in self-defence, or (b) another's doing something, e.g. our son's maintaining us in old age, or our government's protecting us from violence. In the former case we mean simply that our act would not be wrong, i.e. that we are not under a disobligation to do it. In the latter case, we are referring to the other's obligation to do the action, his obligation being from our point of view our right.

3. Consider a favourite phrase of Green's, viz.: 'a system of rights and obligations enforced by law'. Here the rights and obligations meant must be *moral* rights and obligations. For since our having a legal right or obligation is something which includes an enforcing, it cannot be enforced, since it is impossible to enforce an enforcing. Further, strictly speaking, what is implied to be enforced is not the rights and obligations but the acts to the doing of which there is a right or an obligation. In addition, when we speak of the ruler as enforcing a right of *mine*, we really mean his enforcing on another the doing of an act to his doing of which I have a right and he has an obligation, e.g. the ruler's enforcing on another the refraining from interfering with my body, to which refraining I have a right. Correspondingly, when we speak of the ruler as enforcing an obligation of mine, we mean his enforcing on me an act to the doing of which I have an obligation and someone

else has a right. Hence the phrase 'rights and obligations enforced by law' is really the equivalent of the obligations of others to a man and his obligations to them enforced by law, i.e. the system of mutual obligations enforced by law—so that the thing meant can be referred to in terms only of obligation.

4. Green always speaks of a right as being a *power* to do some action, i.e. really a power to do it in consequence of someone else's action. This cannot be true of a right in either the legal or the moral sense. At best such a power can only be something *to* which we have a right in either sense. And the only truth underlying Green's way of speaking is that where we have a legal right to do some action, i.e. where the government orders and enforces on others actions which will give us the power to do it, we shall to some extent have the power in consequence of the government's coercion. Where, however, we have a moral right to a power due to the nature of the action in question, we need not have the power.

We can now turn to Green. It is, of course, a prominent feature of the lectures that they are largely taken up with a criticism of previous theories of Political Obligation, and notably of the Social Contract theory, and in effect he regards this theory as enemy number one, and indeed as a theory to be demolished before it is possible to attain the true theory. And the ground of his objection to this theory lies in his denial of the existence of any such thing as a system of natural rights and obligations, as the phrase 'natural rights and obligations' is usually understood.

The first thing to do for any one who is trying to elucidate Green's theory is to ascertain what precisely he is maintaining in making this denial. For this denial is an essential part of the negative side of his doctrine, and the positive part has to be consistent with it. Whatever his positive doctrine is, it has to be one which is consistent with this denial.

The first question, therefore, to be answered is: What does Green mean when he denies the existence of natural rights and obligations, as the phrase is usually understood?

This denial first appears in § 9. He says:

There has been much objection to the admission of *natural* rights and obligations. At any rate the phrase is liable to misinterpretation. It may be taken to imply that rights and obligations can exist in a 'state of nature'—a state in which every individual is free to do as he likes; that legal rights and obligations derive their authority from a voluntary act by which individuals contracted themselves out of this state, and that the individual retains from the state of nature certain rights with which no legal obligations ought to conflict. Such a doctrine (he adds—and obviously with approval) is generally admitted to be untenable.

And he endorses the truth of this admission by implying that no such system ever did or could exist independently of force exercised by society over individuals. Then later, in § 20, he says: 'a law is not good [i.e. really is not one which the legislator ought to make] because it enforces "natural rights", but because it contributes to the realisation of a certain end'. And, as the context shows, he implies that the reason why a law cannot be good because it enforces natural rights is that there are no such things as natural rights.

Here, of course, he is referring to the social contract theory. And in § 22 he, in effect, represents this theory thus: Men originally existed in a state of nature, i.e. in a community *not* united by subjection to a government. In this state men had various rights against and obligations to one another. Then at some time with a view to the general interest men *agreed* to, and did, set up a government, i.e. a body which would order and enforce various actions which individuals were under an obligation to do, and also others the doing of which generally would be in the general interest. This done, if the question was raised 'Why is an individual bound to obey his government?', the answer in some instances would be 'Because there is an obligation to do the action, natural in the sense of being independent of the government's order', and in others, 'Because, though there is no natural obligation to do the action, yet there is a natural obligation to carry out the original promise or agreement to obey the government', so that in every case the duty to obey rests on a natural obligation.

The implication is that here by 'a system of natural rights and obligations' is meant a system of rights and obligations which existed before there was a government, and which therefore, being independent of any order, still exists after there has come to be a government.

Therefore what Green is denying is the existence of natural rights and obligations in this sense, i.e. in the sense of rights and obligations independent of a government's order.

This denial is, of course, very drastic, though until we consider closely what Green must be meaning by 'natural' we do not realize how drastic it is. He is here denying that you or I who are members of a state have any moral rights or obligations, apart from a law (i.e. a ruler's action of ordering and enforcing the acts in question).

And this denial is in two respects totally at variance with our ordinary convictions. (1) As regards our obligations to other members of the state to do certain actions, or their right to our doing them, *we* think that, while some depend on the ruler's order, e.g. our obligation to keep to the left of the road, or to give our shop assistant a half-holiday on Thursdays, others do not, e.g. our obligation to educate our children, or to refrain, except in self-defence, from killing another. In fact we should sharply divide our moral obligations to other members of our state into two kinds in this respect. (2) We do not regard our obligations to others as limited to obligations to other members of our state. We should regard it as absurd to maintain that an Englishman, e.g., can have no obligations to, say, a Frenchman or a German. And we regard Locke as right when he replies to the objection that there never has been a state of nature by urging that the rulers of two independent states, and again an Indian and a Swiss in the backwoods of America, are even now in relation to one another in a state of nature, and have certain obligations to one another arising out of that state, the obligation, e.g., to keep faith with one another, belonging to men *as men*, and independently of belonging to one and the same community.

And Green here, in denying the existence of natural obligations in the ordinary sense, is maintaining that in both respects we are mistaken.

In addition there is one special obligation to be considered which makes it look as though Green here is cutting the ground from under his own feet. His primary object plainly is to discover why we ought *to obey our government*, a task, of course, which implies that in fact we are so bound. But from the very nature of the case, if there be a duty to obey our sovereign, this particular duty cannot depend on the order of any *body* whatever. For, if it did, (1) it would depend on the order of a body other than our so-called sovereign, and that so-called sovereign would only be a *subordinate* body like, e.g., a County Council deriving its authority from the order of another body, and so not a sovereign body at all; and (2) the obligation to obey the other body would have in turn to depend on the order of a third body, and so on.

Hence it at least looks as if Green by denying the existence of natural obligations in the ordinary sense is rendering it impossible for himself to answer his own chief question. And to this objection it will in the end have to be admitted that there is no answer.

Here it should be noted that the social contract doctrine, how-ever weak it may be in other ways, is free from this objection, because, asked why we are bound to obey our ruler, it has a natural obligation to fall back on, viz. the natural obligation to keep a promise.

What Green would have replied to these objections is shown by § 9. He would have said that he had expressly only denied the existence of natural rights and obligations in the ordinary sense, and expressly asserted their existence in another and an important sense, and that this assertion meets the objections. This other sense he explains by saying: 'There is a system of rights and obliga-tions which *should be* maintained by law, whether it is so or not, and which may properly be called "natural", because necessary to the end which it is the vocation of human society to realise.' But this statement raises the question: 'What is this different sense of "natural"?'

The statement makes use of a phraseology frequently to be found in Green, viz. that in which he speaks of law, i.e. really the government, as maintaining and again as enforcing rights and obligations. Here, of course, 'rights and obligations' means moral rights and obligations, because a government cannot enforce its own enforcing, and what must be meant is that the govern-ment secures or enforces the doing by a subject *A* of those actions which he is under a moral obligation to do, and to the doing of which another subject *B* has a right. Now the use of this language, of course, implies the idea that the moral rights and obligations enforced exist independently of the enforcement, for otherwise there is nothing to enforce; and the language *is* appropriate for those who believe in natural rights and obligations in the sense to which he objects, i.e. rights and obligations independent of an order and enforcement. But for Green it is not, because according to him there are no independent rights and obligations to be en-forced. What he should from the point of view of his own doctrine have spoken of the law or the government as doing is *creating* rights and obligations, thereby making it clear that it is only by the government's action that there came to be moral rights and obli-gations. And his constantly speaking of the law as maintaining or enforcing rights and obligations is very unfortunate because it inevitably implies that, contrary to his own theory, there are moral rights and obligations which are independent of law. Hence, by using this language he misrepresents his own doctrine, giving both his readers and himself the false impression that some moral rights and obligations have an independence of law which he is really denying to them. And just for this reason his own statement of his view requires to be re-written, if it is to be made accurate.

If we bear this in mind we can answer the question: In what sense of 'natural' is he maintaining the existence of natural rights and obligations? His statement is: There is a system of rights and obligations which should be maintained by law whether it is or not, which may properly be called natural. Now if the word 'maintained' is kept, this must mean that there are rights and obligations which are natural in the very sense in which he objects to this, viz. existing independently of law. And this cannot possibly be right. If, however, we substitute as we should for 'maintained' 'created', Green is making the intrinsically untenable assertion that there is a system of rights and obligations which the law should create whether it does so or not, as though things which if they are to exist require to be created exist equally, whether or not they have been created. And once this becomes clear, it also becomes clear that what Green is really asserting the existence of in nature is the fact that the law should create certain rights and obligations whether it does or not. What, in fact, he is doing is denying the existence of natural rights and obligations in any sense whatever and representing the existing fact that the government should make certain laws, and thereby create certain rights and obligations, as the proper substitute for natural rights and obligations. In other words, he is saying: Where people assert that there are moral rights and obligations independent of law they are wrong, and the nearest fact corresponding to such supposed natural rights and obligations is the fact that a government *should and ought to* make certain laws and thereby create certain moral rights and obligations.

The main conclusion is, of course, that Green has completely failed to state a sense in which there really are natural rights and obligations, and substitutes for it the existence in nature of something quite different.

II

We have, however, not yet done with considering Green's treatment of the doctrine of natural rights and obligations. The view which has been attributed to Green has been based on statements taken from the first 20 paragraphs of Chapter A.

The later part of A, however, and subsequent chapters, and especially G, H, and I, appear to offer a different doctrine and one according to which it is possible for a ruler to *maintain* rights·and obligations. Thus in § 138 he speaks of the sovereign, and also of the State, as *presupposing* rights, and as an institution for their maintenance. And in § 148 he speaks of those rights which do not come into being with the State, and implies that they may exist where a State is not, it being the first, though not the only, office of the State to maintain these rights.

These statements, of course, directly contradict the view implied in the first part of Chapter A (that the member of a State has no rights and obligations independently of the sovereign's order, the sovereign creating his rights and obligations). And they agree with the Social Contract view to the extent of representing the sovereign's activity as mainly consisting in maintaining or enforcing already existing rights and obligations.

Green, however, when making such statements is usually careful to add that the rights (and he could always have added 'obligations') which the State maintains belong to a man only as a member of a society. Thus in § 134, e.g., he says: 'A state presupposes other forms of community, with the rights that arise out of them, and only exists as sustaining, securing, and completing them.' (N.B. 'completing' is difficult.) And he adds that in order to make a State there must have been families of which the members recognized rights in each other, and also tribes grown out of families, of which each similarly recognized rights in each other. Again in § 138 he insists that the rights which the State maintains belong to individuals only as members of a Society (cf. also § 148).

Indeed this insistence is the basis of his main criticism of the Social Contract theorists given in the later chapters.

By conflating §§ 113 (beginning of G) and 137–8 (beginning of H), we can state his criticism thus:

Their fundamental mistake (and also that of Spinoza) was that they misunderstood the very question: 'Why ought subjects to obey their ruler?' They took 'subjects' to refer to men who apart from being subjects were a mere aggregate as distinct from members of a society, and doing this committed them to giving a false answer. For it exposed them to a fatal dilemma. They had either to assert or to deny that this aggregate had rights and obligations apart from the ruler's action. If with the Social Contract theorists they did the former, they had, to answer the question, to represent individuals as having consented to being ruled. And this can only be done so long as the ruler rules in accordance with their several wishes (N.B. this is quite untrue) and as to some extent this is impossible, this answer is bound to fail. If, however, they did the latter, they were representing all rights and obligations as derived from the sovereign, and therefore were reduced to treating 'having an obligation' as meaning being *forced*, i.e. forced by the ruler—and this is untrue. To get a true answer we must think of 'subjects' as referring to men who are not an aggregate but members of a society.

Hence Green's correction of the Social Contract theorists seems to consist in substituting for their 'men in a state of nature' 'men in a society'. While seeming to agree with them that the sovereign *maintains* already existing rights and obligations, he represents these as possessed by the subjects not as men but as members of a society.

This doctrine, of course, requires the admission of 'natural' rights and obligations, as the phrase is used in §§ 1–20, i.e. in the sense of rights and obligations independent of a ruler's order. It therefore involves an abandonment of the view given in §§ 1–20 and is to that extent more plausible, because it leaves to the sovereign rights and obligations to enforce.

Unfortunately, however, there is reason to doubt whether the statements quoted, and therefore also this account of Green's view which is based on them, are accurate expressions of his view. The doubt arises as soon as we ask: When Green says 'The rights and obligations which the sovereign maintains imply membership of a society', what does he mean by 'a society'? This question is difficult and I propose to defer adequate consideration of it. But without this we can give an answer sufficient to decide whether these statements express his real view.

In § 116 Green makes a statement which, though surprising, is one by which he would evidently stand. Apropos of Rousseau's view that the social pact is the foundation not merely of civil government but of morality, Green says in support of Rousseau: 'It remains true that only through a recognition by certain men of a common interest, and through the expression of that recognition in certain regulations of their dealings with each other, could morality originate, or any meaning be found for such terms as "ought" and "right" and their equivalents.'

This and similar statements imply that Green thinks that there are no such things as rights and obligations apart from *regulations*, or as he calls them just afterwards (§ 117) rules, i.e. really that there can be no obligation to do an action unless there is a regulation enjoining the doing it. A regulation, however, implies the existence of a body which imposes and enforces the rule, which therefore is in fact at least the analogue of a ruler. And the underlying idea must be that where someone is under an obligation to do some action, and so also where another has a right to his doing it, the obligation and the right have been *created* by a regulating body's enjoining the action. Hence when Green maintains that the rights and obligations which the sovereign maintains are rights and obligations which the subjects have only as members of a society, he must at least mean by 'a society' a group of men who are subject to a regulating body which by its regulations has created the rights and obligations they have. Hence just as before, in the first chapter, Green implied that the rights and obligations of the members of a State are the creation of its sovereign, so now he is implying that the rights and obligations of the members of a society have been the creation of its regulating body.

But, this being so, Green would have had, if pressed, to withdraw as inaccurate his statement that the sovereign *maintains*, i.e., really, enforces, rights and obligations which the subjects have as members of a society. What he is thinking of is a supposed change in which men who were members of a society become members of a State. And he is exposed to a dilemma. He has either to maintain that the society survives the change and continues to exist along with the State, or else to maintain that it disappears and is in fact superseded by the State. If he does the former, he has to allow that the sovereign is only doing over again what the ruling body of the society is still doing, viz. creating the rights and obligations. On the other hand, if he does the latter, he is really maintaining that the sovereign is now re-creating, i.e. creating anew, those rights and obligations which the ruling body of the society created, until it was superseded and so disappeared. Consequently on neither alternative is Green justified in speaking of the sovereign as maintaining, as distinct from creating, rights and obligations. As a matter of fact, of the alternatives Green would obviously have accepted the second. For apart from its greater plausibility, he expressly says (§ 139): 'The state is a form which society takes in order to maintain them': and this implies not only that a State is a species of society, but that where a society which is not a State is followed by a State, it *becomes* that State. And this being so, instead of speaking of the State as maintaining the rights and obligations which its members have as members of a society, Green ought to have expressed his view by speaking of the State as re-creating the rights and obligations which its members formerly had as members of a society, and which were then the creation of the regulating body of that society.

The broad fact is, as should now be obvious, that in spite of the language in which Green expresses it, Green's second view is really only a more general form of his first, being the view that there are no *natural* rights and obligations, in the sense of rights and obligations independent of the action of a regulating body, whether that body be a government or not.

It is really the view that, there being societies or communities other than states, i.e. groups of individuals united by being under a regulating body other than a government, the rights and obligations of any individual whatever are created by the regulating body of a society to which he belongs, it merely happening that the rights and obligations of the members of a State are created by its government, as a particular case.

We therefore find that Green's second view is really just as paradoxical as the first, being the view that no one has any right or obligation independently of some order or quasi-order of a ruler or quasi-ruler of a society to which he belongs. It is, in fact, a complete denial of natural rights and obligations, not indeed in the first sense of rights and obligations independent of membership of a State, but in the second sense of rights and obligations independent of membership of a society whether a State or not, i.e. independent of some order or quasi-order.

Further, it should be noticed, in its application to the State the paradox of this latter view is disguised by his use of inappropriate language, and even by his speaking of rights and obligations, i.e. the rights and obligations which men have as members of a society, as *maintained* by the sovereign. This disguise is exactly parallel to that found in expressing his earlier view in the first chapter. But this time the disguise is more effective because it passes unnoticed until we ask: What does Green mean by 'a society'?

There is, too, something else to be noticed. Green's denial of natural rights and obligations even in the second sense exposes him to the criticism that he himself holds a view to which he expressly objects, viz. that all right in a State is derived from the sovereign. For this is precisely his own doctrine, in spite of his denial of this view in § 138. The nature of his view is only disguised by his use of inappropriate language. Consequently he is himself exposed to the charge which he makes against Hobbes of identifying 'I ought to do so and so' with 'I am forced to do so and so' (§ 137). And it is significant that even Green himself (§ 132) is driven to allow that there is a sense in which all rights are derived from the sovereign.

So far we have only succeeded in formulating the negative part of Green's political theory—viz. his denial that we can answer the question 'Why ought we to obey our government?' by maintaining the existence of any obligation independent of our government's order, this denial being as much really implied in what I have called his second view as in his first.

III

We now have to look for the positive part of Green's doctrine. Some clue is to be found in § 23. There he states a difference of principle dividing him from the Social Contract theorists. And he does this by expressing agreement in one respect with the Utilitarians. Of them he says—with approval—'They do not seek the ground of actual rights in a prior natural right, but in an end to which the maintenance of the right contributes.' This statement needs elucidation. It must mean: The Utilitarians consider that the reason why I, a subject, ought to do the various acts, to my doing of which others have a legal right, i.e. those acts which make up my duties, lies not in a prior natural right of others to my doing them, i.e. a natural obligation of mine to do them, but in the acts' contributing to the realization of an end. Further, by 'end' must be meant 'purpose', and since it is I that am bound, 'an end' here must be a loose phrase for 'my purpose'.

The difference of principle meant, therefore, is that while the Social Contract theorist represents as what renders obedience a duty its being the carrying out of some natural duty, he represents as the reason its contributing to the realization of the subject's purpose. And these reasons are, of course, of quite different sorts.

Further, Green must be tacitly attributing to the ruler in issuing and enforcing his orders the same purpose, and therefore also attributing to the various subjects a common purpose.

But what according to Green is this common purpose?

To this question we unfortunately get two different answers. The first is that implied by §§ 1–20—viz. the doing by the subjects of morally good actions, i.e. actions of which the motives are good. And in giving this answer Green takes the opportunity to urge that as the ruler can only exercise coercion, he can only achieve his purpose indirectly by producing conditions favourable to the doing of morally good actions. Then later we find substituted for morally good actions 'the public good' or 'public interest' (§ 108), or the general interest (§ 99), or the general well-being of the members of the society (§ 151), and this we may take to mean that state of affairs which would render all the subjects well off or happy. And this is unquestionably his *dominant* answer, the earlier answer afterwards simply dropping out.

Correspondingly as regards societies generally, of which states are implied to be a species, the common end attributed to the regulating body of a society and to its members must be the well-being of its members, and the ground of obligation is in both cases implied to be the conduciveness of the doing of the action to this purpose.

The view, of course, differs radically from the Social Contract theory. It is not merely that one asserts and the other denies the existence of *natural* rights and obligations. There is also a greater difference. We see this as soon as we consider what Green's doctrine implies as regards what is meant by the term 'ought'. The Social Contract theorist may be mistaken, but he does at least consider that by 'ought' what is meant is what we may call the 'ought' of moral obligation or duty. But Green really does not. This will be obvious to anyone who has considered the distinction which Kant draws between categorical and hypothetical imperatives. For unless we are prepared to maintain, as no one really will, that we consider it a duty to do whatever will contribute to the realization of our purpose, whatever that purpose may be, we shall have to allow that when we say of some man who has something β as his purpose, that he *ought* to do an act α because doing α will contribute to the realization of β, we only mean by 'he *ought* to do it' that α is an act he *must* do, if his purpose is to be realized. Consequently Green must be maintaining that what we call the 'ought' of duty is really resolved into 'ought' in this sense. Correspondingly, Green is at any rate not entitled to use the phrase 'a right' in the ordinary sense of the term. For suppose the act α enforced on X is one to his doing of which Y has a right, e.g. X's refraining from interfering with Y's body. Then if we ask: What in Green's view can be meant by 'Y has a right to X's doing α'? we have to answer: It can only mean that X's doing α is necessary for the realization of Y's end or purpose, viz. the happiness of the whole state—so that, oddly enough, for Green 'a right' comes to have the same meaning as an obligation.

Further, two characteristics of Green's answer need emphasis.

1. To make it successful even on its own lines, Green must succeed in showing that both the ruler and his subjects have the purpose he ascribes to them. (Since otherwise they will not be bound—in Green's sense—to do the actions he considers they are bound to do.)

Yet when we consider human nature we should at least hesitate to allow this.

2. There is a characteristic which when noticed looks very strange. There must be some actions such as refraining from playing a gramophone late at night in a town, which on balance would contribute to the happiness of the subjects as a whole, *even when not ordered*. Yet, according to Green, such actions are not duties, unless ordered. And not only do we think such actions duties, but Green on his own principles should have maintained that they are, because they contribute to the agent's purpose.

Similarly according to Green, in societies which are not states, such acts are not duties unless prescribed by a regulation: 'It remains true that only through a recognition by certain men of a common interest and through the expression of that recognition in certain *regulations*[1] of their dealings with each other, could morality originate, or any *meaning*[1] be found for such terms as "ought" and "right" and their equivalents.' And he adds, 'Morality (i.e. man's duty), in the first instance, is the observance of such regulations.'[2] Yet such acts would be contributing to the agent's purpose.

The fact is that even from his own point of view, Green's idea that for an act to be a duty it must have been ordered, either by a ruler or by the analogue of a ruler in anything we can call a society, is an arbitrary importation. This of course raises the question: What led Green to import it? And the only possible answer seems to be: His having somehow acquired a sort of fixed idea that there can be no such thing as a natural obligation.

[1] The italics are mine.   [2] § 117.

IV

The account of Green's theory, however, is still incomplete. (A rather complicated story cannot be told all at once.)

The account itself suggests this. For to attribute to rulers and subjects as their common purpose the realization of what he calls the public interest seems contrary to fact—or at least to involve exaggeration. And therefore we expect Green to consider it an essential part of his position to show that here he is right. And indeed, for a reason which will appear shortly, from Green's point of view it is specially important to do this.

Moreover, consideration of passages purporting to state the ground of political obligation suggests that a vital part has been omitted. For what they *emphasize* is not so much that the common purpose is the realization of the public interest as that this is, and presents itself to the subjects as, a common good; and so far this idea has not been referred to. As instances of this emphasis we may take the following statements. (Unfortunately they are vague.) 'No one can have a right' (and he could have added 'or an obligation') 'except as a member of a society . . . in which some common good is recognised by the members of the society as their own ideal good.'[1] In § 98 he says: 'An interest in common good is the ground of political society, in the sense that without it no body of people would recognise any authority as having a claim on their common obedience.' Again in § 117 he speaks of primitive morality as consisting in rules established for the common good. And in § 139 he speaks of the possession of a claim (i.e. really a right) as implying a 'consciousness of having an object', i.e., a purpose, 'in common with others, a well-being which is consciously his in being theirs and theirs in being his'.

These passages show that Green considers (1) that a subject *cannot* have the realization of the general interest as his purpose unless he conceives it as his own good, and (2) that he cannot really be bound to obey unless the general interest is his own good, in which case the subjects will have a common good.

To understand how Green came to have these ideas we have to go to the *Prolegomena*. There in § 91 he maintains that the motive of every deliberate action is desire for personal good in some form or other. And he adds in the next paragraph: 'By an instinctive action we mean one *not* determined by a conception . . . of any good

[1] § 25.

to be gained. . . . It is superfluous to add, good *to himself*; for anything conceived as good in such a way that the agent acts for the sake of it, must be conceived as *his own* good, though he may conceive it as his own good only on account of his interest in others, and in spite of any amount of suffering on his own part incidental to its attainment.' Again, in § 96 he represents Esau as selling his birthright because at the time he thinks of satisfaction of his hunger as his greatest good.

Here Green is advancing a view about all deliberate action. This he first represents as being that in such action what a man has as his purpose is always *some* good to himself, and afterwards as being that this is always his own good, i.e. his own greatest good— the latter account expressing his more considered view. Thinking this as he does, when he comes to consider Political Obligation he is inevitably driven to two conclusions. The first is that to vindicate his contention that in a state men have the realization of the public interest as their purpose, he must show that they conceive the public's interest as their own good. The second is that to prove that men ought to obey the ruler's orders—orders which he assumes to be devised in the public interest—he must show that the public interest really is their own good.

For the reader, therefore, the question at once arises: 'Can this be shown?' And this question should be considered before considering Green's attempt, because by doing so we shall better see the nature of the task which Green has set himself.

To answer this question, we have first to ascertain what Green means by (1) 'a good', and (2) 'your good', 'my good', &c.

In § 171 of the *Prolegomena* (where he is distinguishing himself from a Hedonist), he explains that in his view the common characteristic of the good is that it satisfies some desire, and he uses the phrase 'good, i.e., such as will satisfy desire'. This is really to say that he means by 'a good' a something which produces, i.e. directly produces, satisfaction of a desire, i.e. really gratification. And his use of the phrase bears out this statement. Also from this it follows that he must mean by 'my good' that which renders me completely satisfied, i.e. having the gratification consisting in the satisfaction of all my desires.

Once, however, we realize this, we become forced to deny that, except on one hypothesis to which we shall have to refer later, the realization of the public interest can be *conceived* by members of a state as, or *be*, their own good.

The reason lies in a consideration which, though apt to escape our notice, is conclusive.

A feeling of satisfaction or gratification can be excited only by a state or activity of ourselves. If, e.g., I desire a member of my family to get some post, and if I learn that he has got it, or even think that he has, or will, get it, I shall necessarily have a feeling of satisfaction or gratification. But what excites the gratification is the knowledge or belief that the thing I desire is or will be realized, and not the *realization* of the thing desired—so that, shortly speaking, the thing which I desired and the thing which gratifies me cannot be the same, and Green is mistaken in speaking of the realization of some object of desire as necessarily exciting satisfaction. And since by 'a good' Green means something which excites satisfaction, there cannot be such a thing as a good common to two different persons, unless the two so-called different persons are really one and the same, and so not different persons.

For even if X and I want the same thing, and so have a common object of desire, as where X and I both want X to get a certain post, we cannot have *a* common good, i.e. a common source of satisfaction connected with these desires, since the sources will be respectively *his* thought that he has the post and *my* thought that he has, and his thought cannot be mine and vice versa, unless he and I are really the same individual. And for the same reason my good, i.e. that state which renders me *completely* satisfied, cannot be identical with his, unless we are the same. For the same reason, too, what Green calls the public interest, by which here must be meant those states of all the individuals which render each completely satisfied, taken together, cannot be that of a single individual, unless he is identical with all the others, nor again can a single individual *conceive* the public interest as being identical with his own, unless he *conceives* the other as identical with himself.

Now though it is not very apparent on the surface, yet strangely enough the existence of this identity and of the thought of this identity is exactly what Green does maintain.

In spite of his conviction that in deliberate action men have always one and the same motive, viz. desire of what will excite satisfaction in themselves, there is nothing which he emphasizes more than our possession of disinterested interests, of which the most obvious are an interest in the welfare of others, commonly called benevolence, and an interest in the welfare of certain others, such as other members of our family, or of a society to which we belong, or of our country. These interests in other persons, he says (§ 199),[1] are not merely interests dependent on other persons for the means to their gratification, but interests in the good of those other persons, interests which cannot be satisfied without the consciousness that those other persons are satisfied. And he obviously considers that we not only have the desire of others' welfare which is involved in this interest, but often act upon it, .thus acting disinterestedly, i.e., as we should say, without regard to our own interest or happiness. Green has therefore to reconcile this latter conviction, which of course most of us share, with the former. For they at least seem violently inconsistent. For just so far as we are being moved by the disinterested desire of what would satisfy another, i.e. the desire of this for its own sake, the desire moving us, it would seem, cannot be the desire of what would satisfy ourselves; and even the thought of something which would give us satisfaction may be absent.

How then does Green seek to remove the appearance of inconsistency? It would, of course, be useless for him to contend that what is called the desire of what would satisfy another for its own sake is really only the desire of this as *a means* to what would satisfy ourselves. For to do this would be just to deny the disinterestedness. Nor does he. He is anxious to maintain the reality of the disinterestedness at all costs. Instead he adopts the only method open to him, viz. to maintain that where one man A has a disinterested interest in the welfare of another B, B and A are really identical.

Given this view it, of course, becomes justifiable for him to speak of a common good, i.e. a common source of satisfaction, since if B is A, what would excite satisfaction in B would excite satisfaction in A; and also to speak of B's good as identical with and also as thought of as identical with A's. But it is not justifiable otherwise. This should be emphasized, since to understand Green's doctrine that obligation implies the existence of a common good it has to be realized that it implies the idea that the persons to whom it is common are identical.

Here it is worth while for a moment to pass from elucidation to commentary.

The underlying thought is obvious. Green is taking his stand on the idea that in certain instances a man A disinterestedly, i.e. for its own sake, desires the welfare of (or as Green should rather say,

[1] Cf. *Prolegomena*, §§ 161, 200.

what would satisfy) another man B. And he is contending that A's possession of this desire shows that A is thinking of B as a being who is really identical with A, and not another being at all, since a man can only desire what would satisfy himself. He is further thinking that A in thinking this is right, i.e. that in this case B is identical with A. (The doctrine is one foreshadowed in *Republic* V (462), in which Plato says that the just state is one in which the largest number of citizens apply the terms 'mine' and 'not mine' to the same things in the same respects, and implies that this applies *inter alia* to pleasures and pains.)

The net result is that according to Green, where a group of, say, five persons are disinterestedly interested in one another, they are really not five persons but one, a state of A being related to a state of another, B, just as it is related to another state of A—these states being states of one self.

The first and most important comment is that when Green comes to consider the nature of disinterested action, instead of revising his previous account of the general nature of deliberate action, in such a way as to include disinterested action—as he should—he freely adapts his account of the latter to fit his general theory, and that by doing so he really abolishes its disinterestedness. Having laid down that in all deliberate action a man's motive is desire of what would satisfy himself, he nevertheless, when he comes to consider disinterested acts, at first thinks of them as moved by the desire of what would satisfy another. Then to square the two ideas he untruly represents the disinterested agent A, in desiring what would satisfy B, as really thinking of B as a being who is *not* another than himself, and if he were right here, A's desire would have lost any appearance of disinterestedness, since then, e.g., there would be no difference in kind between desiring, say, an honour for himself, and desiring an honour for B, i.e. disinterestedness would be resolved into interestedness.

The fact, of course, is that a disinterested desire is not a desire of a good to oneself at all.

In addition two minor facts should be noticed:

1. Green is undoubtedly implying that, whenever A has a disinterested interest in the satisfaction of B, B similarly has a disinterested interest in the satisfaction of A, as is normally the case with members of a family. For otherwise he cannot, as he does, represent the satisfactions of A and B together as

identical with the satisfaction of each. But this need not be so, and where it is not, B's satisfaction cannot be represented as identical with those of both together. And the curious conclusion emerges that if Green were forced, as he could be, into allowing that the disinterested interest need not be reciprocal, he would have to allow that where B did not reciprocate, B was identical with A without A's being identical with B.

2. Malevolence is just as much a fact as benevolence, i.e. what we can have a disinterested interest in is just as much the unhappiness (or dissatisfaction) of another as the happiness (or satisfaction) of another. And Green admits this in § 161. Hence he ought to have maintained that malevolence of A towards B equally with benevolence of A towards B implies the identity of B with A, and therefore also that in desiring B's unhappiness A is desiring his own.

v

We are now in a position to give a complete statement of Green's theory. His proof of the duty to obey the government is one which tacitly assumes that our being bound to do some action *is* the act's being one which we must do if our purpose is to be realized, i.e. its contributing to our purpose; and it may be stated thus: Our purpose is necessarily our own good. But we being disinterestedly interested in the good of other members of our State, the other members are necessarily identical with ourselves, and therefore the public interest, i.e. the various things which are the good of each subject taken together, is necessarily identical with our own good. But obedience to the ruler is contributory to the public interest, and therefore to our own good, and this being our purpose obedience is necessarily a duty. To this account, however, it ought to be added that he also maintains that only acts ordered are duties, a contention which is only consistent with the rest of the theory if it be also held that no act unless ordered will be for the public interest. This addition really has no connexion with the rest of the theory.

An analogous statement can, of course, be made for members of a society which is not a State.

The theory is, of course, a general theory of Moral Obligation which takes the form of a political theory in the case of members of a State.

It now becomes fairly easy to answer the question: What does Green mean by 'a society'? The question is one which we find ourselves constantly asking when reading the lectures, especially when trying to understand such statements as 'a man has rights only as a member of a society'.

He cannot be using the phrase in its ordinary sense of a voluntary association such as an essay society. For he speaks of a State as a society, and yet he certainly does not think it a voluntary association. Still he probably would have called a voluntary association a society. And 'a community'—a phrase he sometimes uses—would better express what he means. On the other hand, he cannot be using it so widely as to include any group of men related in some special way, e.g. as friends or as united by a promise. Unfortunately he never offers a definition though he uses phrases which are really though not ostensibly partial definitions, as when (§ 26) he speaks of 'a society [i.e. a group of men] in which some common good is recognized as their own good'. The proper clue lies in the reflection that he would have applied and only applied the term to groups of men who satisfy the conditions which he considers necessary for the existence of rights and obligations among them. For, this being so, he must really mean by a society a group satisfying these conditions. Now plainly these conditions are (1) that the members of the group have a common good, consisting in the respective goods of each taken together, and (2) that they are subject to regulation of their dealings with each other for this common good. Hence Green must really mean by 'a society' men, i.e. a group of men, having a common good and subject to regulations for this good.

A regulation or rule, however, implies an imponent. How then does Green think of this imponent? Certainly not as necessarily a definite body, such as a government or a committee. For in the case of a society which is not a state he is wont to speak of it as custom, or authoritative custom, or the law of opinion (§ 4). But if his idea of a society is to be plausible, this part has simply to be discarded, as putty used to fill up a gap. For we can only rightly speak, as Green always does, of a man's community as securing to him certain powers, if we think of it as doing so through an agent. To substitute something called custom or the law of opinion is useless, for the phrase can only be a veiled term for the thoughts held by individuals that certain acts are duties, and though these thoughts may help to secure the doing of the actions, it cannot be said that the community acts through them. Moreover—and this is decisive—according to Green there cannot be such thoughts apart from regulations, and therefore on his view they cannot be considered a substitute.

Hence, if Green's idea of a society is to escape absurdity, his society must include the analogue of a ruler in the shape of a regulating body.

If this be granted there is one thing which becomes obvious. His statement, 'Men have rights and obligations only as members of a society', is not one in which 'society' is being used in some ordinary sense, and which in consequence, if accepted, can be used as a *premiss* to justify his theory. It is simply a *statement* of the theory which he has to justify, being the statement that men only have rights and obligations where they have a common good and are subject to a regulating body.

Reverting to the consideration of Green's general theory, we should next consider what are the main comments it suggests. (And here it may, I think, be fairly asserted that it is one of those theories about which, when its nature is grasped, little need be said, the main difficulty being to discover it.)

If we survey the theory, the main contentions appear to be these:

1. The duty of doing an action *is* its contributing to the realization of our purpose (this contention being implied and *not stated*).
2. We always (except when moved by an impulse) act for our own good.
3. In view of our disinterested interests in others they are identical with us.
4. There is no duty without an order, or at least a quasi-order.

Of these, the fourth contention seems to stand apart from the rest—having, it would seem, no connexion with it. And of the rest, the second seems the one deserving the most attention, as the explanation of why Green puts forward the first and the third.

Consider the fourth first. Unfortunately it will not stand the test of instances. For we do think with Locke that one individual has certain obligations to and rights against another without their being members of the same state or community—and we do think again that we have certain obligations to certain animals, i.e. that they have certain rights against us. (Green denies that animals have rights, but the denial seems due to the exigencies of his theory.) Again, to take an instance specially unfortunate for Green, we think we ought to obey our ruler, and here the obligation *ex hypothesi* cannot depend on *orders* to obey.

In this connexion it is worth while to refer to the so-called eighteenth-century Rationalists, Cudworth and Samuel Clarke. They have been, to my mind, far too much neglected, for their main burden is just to insist against Hobbes, not only that there are such things as natural obligations, in the first sense, that of obligations independent of an order, but also that it is impossible for *all* obligations to be non-natural, since by its very nature the existence of a non-natural obligation implies the thought of a natural obligation. And, if I am right, they performed an outstanding service in doing this, but a service which would have been much more effective if subsequent writers had paid more attention to them.

Cudworth really comes first, for though his *Treatise* was not published till 1731, some sixteen years after Samuel Clarke's *Discourse on Natural Religion*, he died in 1688.

This is what Cudworth says:

Now the necessary Consequence of that which we have hitherto said is this, That it is so far from being true, that all Moral Good and Evil, Just and Unjust are meer Arbitrary and Factitious things, that are created wholly by Will; that (if we would speak properly) we must needs say that nothing is Morally Good or Evil, Just or Unjust by meer Will without Nature, because every thing is what it is by Nature, and not by Will. For though it will be objected here, that when God, or Civil Powers Command a Thing to be done, that was not before obligatory or unlawful, the thing Willed or Commanded doth forthwith become Obligatory, that which ought to be done by Creatures and Subjects respectively; in which the Nature of Moral Good or Evil is commonly Conceived to consist. And therefore if all Good and Evil, Just and Unjust be not the Creatures of meer Will (as many assert) yet at least Positive things must needs owe all their Morality, their Good and Evil to meer Will without Nature: Yet notwithstanding, if we well Consider it, we shall find that even in Positive Commands themselves, meer Will doth not make the thing commanded Just or Obligatory, or beget and create any Obligation to Obedience; but that it is Natural Justice or Equity, which gives to one the Right or Authority of Commanding, and begets in another Duty and Obligation to Obedience. Therefore it is observable, that Laws and Commands do not run thus, to Will that this or that thing shall become Just or Unjust, Obligatory or Unlawful; or that Men shall be obliged or bound to obey; but only to require that something be done or not done, or otherwise to menace Punishment to the Transgressors thereof. For it was never heard of, that any one founded all his Authority of Commanding others, and other Obligation or Duty to Obey his Commands, in a Law of his own making, that men should be Required, Obliged, or Bound to Obey him. Wherefore since the thing willed in all Laws is not that men should be Bound or Obliged to Obey; this thing cannot be the product of the meer Will of the Commander, but it must proceed from something else; namely, the Right or Authority of the Commander, which is founded in natural Justice and Equity, and an antecedent Obligation to Obedience in the Subjects; which things are not Made by Laws, but pre-supposed before all Laws to make them valid: And if it should be imagined, that any one should make a positive Law to require that others should be Obliged, or Bound to Obey him, every one would think such a Law ridiculous and absurd; for if they were Obliged before, then this Law would be in vain, and to no Purpose; and if they were not before Obliged, then they could not be Obliged by any Positive Law, because they were not previously Bound to Obey such a Person's Commands: So that Obligation to Obey all Positive Laws is Older than all Laws, and Previous or Antecedent to them.[1]

This is what Clarke says:

The true State therefore of this Case, is plainly this. Some things are in their own nature Good and Reasonable and Fit to be done, such as keeping Faith, and performing equitable Compacts, and the like; And these receive not their obligatory power, from any Law or Authority, but are only declared, confirmed and inforced by penalties, upon such as would not perhaps be governed by right Reason only. Other things are in their own nature absolutely Evil, such as breaking Faith, refusing to perform equitable Compacts, cruelly destroying those who have neither directly nor indirectly given any occasion for any such treatment, and the like; And these cannot by any Law or Authority whatsoever, be made fit and reasonable, or excusable to be practised. Lastly, other things are in their own Nature Indifferent; that is, (not absolutely and strictly so; as such trivial Actions, which have no way any tendency at all either to the publick welfare or damage; For concerning such things, it would be childish and trifling to suppose any Laws to be made at all; But they are) such things, whose tendency to the publick benefit or disadvantage, is either so small or so remote, or so obscure and involved, that the generality of People are not able of themselves to discern on which side they ought to act: And these things are made obligatory by the Authority of Laws; Though perhaps every

---

[1] Selby-Bigge, *British Moralists*, ii, pp. 249–50.

one cannot distinctly perceive the reason and fitness of their being injoined: Of which sort are many particular penal Laws, in several Countries and Nations.[1]

Then later, after pointing out that Hobbes was forced to suppose some particular things obligatory, originally, and in their own nature, he says:

If the Rules of Right and Wrong, Just and Unjust, have none of them any obligatory force in the State of Nature, antecedent to positive Compact, then, for the same Reason, neither will they be of any force after the Compact, so as to afford men any certain and real security; . . . For if there be no Obligation of Just and Right antecedent to the Compact, then Whence arises the Obligation of the Compact itself, on which he supposes all other Obligations to be founded? If, before any Compact was made, it was no Injustice for a man to take away the Life of his Neighbour, not for his own Preservation, but merely to satisfy an arbitrary humour or pleasure, and without any reason or provocation at all, how comes it to be an Injustice, after he has made a Compact, to break and neglect it?[2]

Further, here it is worth noting that on Green's own showing his theory is beginning to break down. For

1. In chapter i, §§ 148–51, he is forced to single out certain rights, viz. to liberty, life, and property (viz. those which we think of as natural rights), as forming a special class which do not come into being with the state and can be treated without reference to the form of the society which concedes them. And in § 154 he is reduced to admitting that the right to free life on the part of every man as man implies the conception of men as forming one society, and adds that if a claim is made on behalf of any and every human being, it must be a claim on human society as a whole. And as he obviously thinks there is such a right, he implies thereby that he considers mankind one large society, which it obviously is not, either in his or even in any other sense of a 'society'.

2. He attributes rights to individuals who plainly are not members of a society in his sense, viz. to (a) members of a family; (b) a group of slaves (§ 140); (c) a group of persons consisting of a slave and the family of his owner (§ 140); (d) certain citizens and certain slaves. And he even emphasizes the existence of the rights possessed by certain slaves by

---

[1] Ib., p. 9.   [2] Ib., p. 45.

insisting that though the state may refuse them rights it cannot extinguish them. (Here, of course, his moral convictions are, so to say, bursting through the theory.)

If all this be allowed, it becomes worth asking, Where does the root of Green's mistake lie? The answer is, it seems to me, obvious. It lies in his second contention, viz. that we always act for the sake of our own good. We are therefore brought to the consideration of this.

The contention is one which any one must in the end admit to be false. To convince ourselves of this we need only allow, as in the end we must, that some deliberate actions have at least shown some element of disinterestedness, whether this has taken the form of benevolence or malevolence, and others again some element of conscientiousness. And the contention seems only to arise from the idea, which, though plausible, is mistaken, that we can only be led to desire to do some action by coming to think of it as one which will be, or else cause, something which we shall like, i.e. give us either enjoyment or satisfaction.

I shall therefore take for granted that it is false. But once we realize that Green has this idea it becomes easy to see how most of the rest of his position follows. For if every one necessarily has his own good as his purpose, it becomes idle to maintain that there can be anything which it is his duty to do, and the only thing left for the term 'ought' to refer to is an act's being necessary for the realization of the agent's purpose, and then what we ought to do necessarily becomes those actions which are necessary for the realization of the thing which is our purpose, viz. our own good.

Green being driven to hold this, we have the paradoxical consequence that on fundamentals Green is in agreement with Hobbes, his chief enemy. For in maintaining that we always act for our own good, and therefore ought to do what is necessary for its realization, he is at bottom only repeating Hobbes's view, and his difference from Hobbes lies merely in a matter, though no doubt an important matter, of detail. He is in effect saying to Hobbes: 'I entirely agree with your general contention, but I differ completely as to what acts are necessary for the realization of our own good. You, ignoring our possession of disinterested interests, fail to see that, owing to this, it is just by contributing to the public good that we shall contribute to our own.'

And, of course, just because Green thinks this, we should all like to think that here he is right, for even though we do not think that the duty of obedience to the state arises from the fact that obedience contributes to our own good, we should all like to think that obedience is contributing to it.

There is, however, another comment which is important because it shows that Green's view will not work even on its own lines.

Green is really insisting that to maintain, as he does, that two subjects of a ruler, A and B, have a common purpose, he must show that B is identical with A, and thus that B's satisfaction is A's. Hence he is implying that when A considers how to get most satisfaction, he will consider it indifferent whether some satisfaction which an act would cause would arise in B or in himself.

Hence A's problem will be simply to ascertain what action would produce the greatest amount of satisfaction in A and B together, irrespectively of how the satisfaction will be distributed. And as Green considers the ruler's purpose identical with that of A and B, the ruler's problem in devising rules will be the same. Suppose then, e.g., the ruler found A and B each fetching his own newspaper before breakfast and realized that fetching two papers would be very little more trouble than fetching one. He would think he should issue an order as the result of which on any given occasion one of them fetched both papers, thereby diminishing the aggregate dissatisfaction. But he could only decide by tossing up who was to be ordered to do the fetching, i.e. whether it was to be A always, or B always, or A and B alternately, and so on—because any arrangement would be *equally* effective in diminishing dissatisfaction. Yet Green obviously thinks that the ruler would in fact order A and B to divide the fetching equally. And for this idea, for the reason just given, he has on his own theory *no* justification. To notice this is important. For (1) it shows that Green's theory is unable to take into account the idea of fairness, on which actual rules are based. And (2) it brings out the fact that the idea of fairness, which underlies actual rules, so far from implying that individuals have identical satisfactions, implies that individuals have satisfactions which are not only different but such that the conditions of their realization are incompatible. The fact is that, if a ruler's rules are to come out anything like what we ordinarily think of as rules, he must be implying that individuals' goods so far from being identical are inconsistent, i.e. that their interests so far from being the same are conflicting. And if Green, to meet this objection, were to allow that the rules should take account of fairness, he would in doing so both be allowing a natural obligation and going back on his view that the subjects have a common good.

VI

The drastic nature of the criticisms just made naturally provokes the question: Is there not after all some important truth to be found in Green's lectures?

To this question the answer seems to be Yes. The doctrine of Green's which seems closest to the facts is that epitomized in the title of Chapter A: 'Will, not force, is the basis of the state.' In this chapter he discards the question: 'Why *ought* a subject to obey his ruler?' for the very different question: 'Why *does* a subject obey?', i.e. what is the motive of his obedience? And here negatively his aim is to refute the view of Hobbes and certain others that the state rests simply on force or compulsion, i.e. that what gets a government obeyed is simply desire to escape its penalties. He is, of course, not denying that this desire is an essential factor, and with some individuals the only factor; he is only maintaining that if this were the only factor *no* government would in the long run get itself obeyed. And in consequence he thinks it fallacious to regard a state—as he thought Hobbes did—as an aggregation of individuals under a sovereign body able to compel their obedience (for the phrase see § 137)—by 'individuals' here being meant men who will be led to obey only by fear of penalties. Here Green seems perfectly right. Even with our experience of modern dictatorships—an experience, of course, denied to Green—it seems impossible to hold that over a long period *any* government could get itself obeyed if its subjects obeyed only so far as they thought the existence of penalties rendered obedience advantageous. General fear of the policeman will not *by itself* secure obedience.

What, however, is Green's positive contention, i.e. what does he consider the other factor necessary for obedience? The answer is: The desire of the public welfare, as being their own welfare, which the subjects have in consequence of recognizing that the other members of the public, being individuals in whom they are disinterestedly interested, are identical with themselves, the desire being accompanied by the conviction that obedience will be conducive to the public welfare.

This answer is, of course, less satisfactory. For it really just as much represents the additional factor as the outcome of selfishness. For the desire for what will give me satisfaction is the same in kind as the desire for what will cause me dissatisfaction. Yet after all Green is insisting on men's possession of disinterested desires, and if only he had dropped the representation of these as *interested* (by representing others as identical with ourselves), he would have been contending that the additional factor necessary to secure obedience is the subject's unselfish interest in the welfare of other members of the community; and then he would have been on very strong ground. For anyone would have to allow that this interest is a large factor in what gets the government obeyed—not because it is appreciable in those least likely to obey but because its existence in others makes practicable the task of enforcing laws on the reluctant minority. What, however, would have been *most* appropriate for Green to point out as the other factor is simply the thought itself that it is a duty to obey, combined of course with the desire to do what we ought. And he could have done this without entering into the question *why* individuals thought they ought to obey.

The Ground of Political Obligation

In conclusion I propose to make some general remarks about the question which Green is discussing, viz. why ought a subject to obey his ruler?

Two things may be noticed at the outset:

1. *We* are apt to assume that the question admits of a single answer, i.e. that whoever be the ruler, the answer will be the same.
2. Green assumes that the answer must take one or other of two mutually exclusive forms—basing the obligation either on a certain origin of the government, and indeed on some form of contract, or on the fact that obedience will help to bring certain things about.

These alternatives are of course poles apart. For on the latter alternative the mode of origin of a government is simply irrelevant—(since so long as obedience will achieve certain things, it does not matter how the government achieved its position, i.e. whether by violence or otherwise)—while on the former it is all-important.

Further, both Green's alternatives are to be found in actual political controversy. Thus on the one hand, before the Irish Free

State existed, the Southern Irish denied that they owed any allegiance to the British Crown and Parliament, on the ground that it was a mere coercive body, i.e. a body which had just imposed its power on them, and was acting without their consent and even against it. The extremists in India make similar statements about the Government of India. Similarly members of subordinate communities speak of their right to self-determination, i.e. really to be self-governed, i.e. governed by a government of their own appointment or creation.

On the other hand, it is often said by way of retort: 'That may be so; nevertheless the government in question is doing its work, i.e. the work of a government, with great efficiency; it is giving and enforcing on you subjects the laws which you need, and doing this much more effectively than would any government you could set up.'

And here what is chiefly noteworthy is the complete lack of common ground. Each simply ignores the contention of the other and substitutes his own. And in consequence they never get to grips—and completely fail to convince each other.

Now this makes one think. For it suggests that possibly the deadlock is due to the idea common to both that there can only be *one* ground of the duty of obedience, and that if we can satisfy ourselves that the idea is mistaken, we can get rid of the deadlock. In this connexion the doctrine of the *Crito* is suggestive. There Socrates is made to explain why he considers himself bound not to disobey the state by escaping from prison and so avoiding being put to death. And what is suggestive is that his answer gives *more than one* reason. He states three ideas, first that the state or the laws or the government is his father, second that it is his benefactor, to whom he owes his upbringing and education, and third that, as on growing up the laws had left him free to go elsewhere if he did not like them, he, by staying, had entered into a tacit agreement with the laws, i.e. the government, to do what the government commanded. φαμὲν τοῦτον ὡμολογηκέναι ἔργῳ ἡμῖν ἃ ἂν ἡμεῖς κελεύωμεν ποιήσειν ταῦτα.[1] And though he represents the three grounds of the obligation as concurrent, he says nothing which excludes the idea that any one by itself would be sufficient.

This leads us to ask whether there need be only one ground, the same in all cases, rather than different grounds in different cases, with the possibility of concurrent different grounds in any given

[1] *Crito*, 51 e.

case. If there need not, both contending views may contain an element of truth, each only making the mistake of putting forward as *the* ground what is *a* ground of political obligation. The question can be put in another form thus: We are apt to assume that the questions 'Ought an Englishman to obey the Crown and Parliament, an Italian to obey Mussolini, a German to obey Hitler?' are instances of the same question. But is this really so—because the thing called a state may in each case be different, and if there are kinds of state, the ground of the duty to obey may depend on the kind?

And our attitude, e.g. to the controversialists about India, suggests that on considering instances we may find the doubt justified. For we think there is something in what each party says— viz. in the one case, that in view of the greater efficiency of such a government, it ought to be obeyed in the interest of the other subjects, and in the other case, that if a government in some way appointed by the inhabitants of India had been in its place, the subjects would have been bound to obey by that fact alone, irrespectively of the effect of obedience—and that in any case such an appointment forms an additional ground for the duty to obey. How prevalent the latter idea is is shown by the attempts which most revolutionary governments make to get what at least looks like some form of election, however farcical it really is.

(N.B. What they really want is something which looks not like the legal right but the moral right to sovereignty. For the very phrase 'a legal right to sovereignty' involves contradiction, for, a law being the order of a sovereign, the act of creating a sovereign cannot be an act of law. And if we allow, as it seems we can, that there is some truth in this idea, we must allow that there is some truth in the social contract theory. For what we call appointing, or accepting, or consenting to a government, is some kind of agreeing.)

If, however, we allow, as it seems we must, that there are different grounds of political obligation, then we have to admit that strictly speaking the very question 'Why ought a subject to obey his ruler?' is fallacious, and is therefore bound to ensure a false answer—just because there are sorts of rulers, and the sort makes a difference, and that the question ought to be split up into the questions 'Why ought the subjects of certain specified *sorts* of government to obey them?' If so, the question is like the question: 'Why ought we to read books?'; for here obviously there is no proper question, so long as we are considering books generally, as distinct from books of a particular sort.

In addition, even if we ignore this, we have to allow that in another way the question requires modification and that unless we modify it, we only get into confusion.

As it stands, the question Why ought a subject to obey his ruler? is parallel to similar questions about other moral rules, e.g. Why ought a man to speak the truth? or Why ought a man to educate his family? Now consideration of instances of what seem conflicting duties is enough to show that no kind of action whatever can, strictly speaking, be a duty, if only for the reason that if it were, there might be occasions on which we were bound to do two actions, although we could only do one or other of them. This reflection forces us to allow that what we at first think of as a duty must really be something else, for which, in my opinion, the least unsatisfactory phrase is 'a claim', and that the proper question with regard to some moral rule is of the form: 'Why is there a claim on us to do such and such an action?' For this reason the proper form of the question: 'Why ought a subject to obey his ruler?' must at least be: 'Why is there a *claim* on the subject to obey his ruler?' And unless we put the question in this form, we shall only find ourselves in a state of confusion when considering whether we ought to obey in instances where obedience involves the failure to satisfy certain other claims—the question then really being: 'Does the claim to obey outweigh the other claims?'

5

MORAL OBLIGATION

1. *The Main Questions about Moral Obligation*

THE object of this inquiry is first to consider, with the help of the treatment they have received, the chief questions which have been raised about moral obligation, and then to examine certain questions which arise as the result of this consideration. To many it will come as a surprise that there are questions to be raised about moral obligation. For although a normal person, once he has reached a certain age, plainly has the idea of moral obligation, since he thinks of himself as morally bound to do certain actions and as morally bound not to do certain others, and although he will have asked himself on various occasions whether he ought or ought not to do certain actions, he is not thereby necessarily led to ask any general question about moral obligation, such as: What character must an act have for us to be morally bound to do it? Yet the existence of such questions is shown by the existence of what are called books on moral philosophy, in whose subject duty undeniably occupies an important if not the central place.

To ascertain the chief questions raised it would seem necessary only to refer to the chief writers. Yet the attempt to do this is apt to be bewildering. For it will be found difficult to find a single set of questions which each writer in his own way is trying to answer. And in some cases, as in that of Butler or, to take a modern instance, that of Bradley, it is even difficult to be sure about the questions which they are trying to answer. Even if we find a formula such as the question: What is the basis of moral obligation?, it may be vague and in need of clearing up.

Nevertheless, consideration seems to show that four chief questions have been raised, though not necessarily by the same thinkers.

First, there is the question which Plato raises in the Republic: 'Will a man be better off for doing his duty?'—a question which he puts in the form: 'Is just action profitable?'

Second, there is the question, the answer to which Plato considered to turn on the answer to the first question: viz. 'Should or ought a man to do his duty (or, as Plato put it, do what is just)?'

In putting this question it is of course implied that 'should' or 'ought' is being used in some sense other than that in which to say that I ought to do so and so is only another way of saying that I am morally bound to do so and so. And the sense implied must be one in which we use it in connexion with any action which we do not think of as a duty, as when we ask: 'Should I take the first turn to the left?'

Third, there is the question which almost inevitably arises as soon as we recognize that the various acts which we think duties fall into groups of different sorts, such as speaking the truth, obeying the government, keeping a promise. For, this once noticed, it is almost bound to occur to us that acts of different sorts cannot all be duties unless they possess some common character, the possession of which renders them duties. And if this does occur we are led to ask: What is the character which an act must have for us to be bound to do it, and the possession of which by our action is the reason why we ought to do it? The question is sometimes put in the form: What is the criterion of a duty? And by 'a theory of moral obligation' seems to be meant an answer to this question.

Fourth, there is the question: What is moral obligation? i.e. what is it for someone to be morally bound to do some action?, along with which goes the corresponding question: What is it to be morally bound *not* to do some action?, where plainly 'morally bound not to do some action' does not mean 'not morally bound to do some action' but stands for something positive.

These questions are, of course, not necessarily independent. Thus it would at least seem impossible to answer the question whether we shall be better off for doing our duty without first ascertaining the character common to the acts which form our duties. And for this reason it will not be easy to settle which question should be considered first. Moreover, though they are few they may none the less be difficult to answer, possibly partly because to get an answer to them we may have first to find the answer to other and difficult questions, such as, e.g., 'What is doing something?'; and when we have found an answer, we may find ourselves still faced by other and difficult questions.

Of these questions, the last will be considered first, because although it is not the first which anyone is likely to raise, the answer to it bears on the answers to the others. Then the first and the second will be considered together, as being the questions which most men raise first. And then the ground will be cleared for consideration of the third, which will be found to need much more discussion.

II. *The Question 'What is Moral Obligation?'*

As has already been implied, we, in our ordinary unreflective state of mind, regard statements of the form, 'X ought to do so and so', 'X has the duty of doing so and so', and 'X is morally bound to do so and so', as equivalent in meaning. And Hume is only expressing the necessity of answering the question 'What is moral obligation?' in the phraseology of 'ought' when he says:

I cannot forbear adding to these reasonings an observation, which may, perhaps, be found of some importance. In every system of morality, which I have hitherto met with, I have always remark'd, that the author proceeds for some time in the ordinary way of reasoning, and establishes the being of a God, or makes observations concerning human affairs; when of a sudden I am surpriz'd to find, that instead of the usual copulations of propositions, *is*, and *is not*, I meet with no proposition that is not connected with an *ought*, or an *ought not*. This change is imperceptible; but is, however, of the last consequence. For as this *ought*, or *ought not*, expresses some new relation or affirmation, 'tis necessary that it shou'd be observ'd and explain'd; and at the same time that a reason shou'd be given, for what seems altogether inconceivable, how this new relation can be a deduction from others, which are entirely different from it. But as authors do not commonly use this precaution, I shall presume to recommend it to the readers; and am persuaded, that this small attention wou'd subvert all the vulgar systems of morality, and let us see, that the distinction of vice and virtue is not founded merely on the relations of objects, nor is perceiv'd by reason.[1]

For the context shows that he is here thinking of the terms 'ought' and 'ought not' as terms used in connexion with actions, and from other passages it is clear that he would accept the statement, 'X is under a moral obligation to educate Y' as equivalent in meaning to 'X ought to educate Y'. Indeed, as Hume is putting the question, it is in effect the question 'What distinguishes a statement of the form, "X *ought* to do so and so", from a statement of the form, "X *is* doing so and so"?' And it will refer to something which we should have in mind if we said to someone, as we might: 'I am not considering the question whether X is doing (or was doing, or is going to do) a certain action, but the quite different question whether X is (or was, or will be) morally bound to do it.' We substitute 'is

[1] Hume, D., *A Treatise of Human Nature* (ed. Selby-Bigge), pp. 469–70.

morally bound' for 'ought' only because 'ought' does not admit of
difference of tense. And the question is in the first instance best
considered in Hume's formulation of it, because the form 'X ought
to do so and so' is the more usual, and the other, if used in preference, seems intended as an elucidation of it. To make sure, however, of not misunderstanding the question when thus formulated,
it is necessary to apprehend clearly that the sense in which 'ought'
is being used here is quite different from that to which Kant refers
when he speaks of hypothetical imperatives. Kant designates all
statements of the form 'I ought to do so and so' imperatives,
choosing this term because he considers that they express commands. And he divides them into two kinds which he calls respectively hypothetical and categorical according as the idea on
which the statement is based is (a) the idea that the doing of the
act is necessary for the realization of something which I am or
possibly might be willing, i.e. which is or might be my purpose in
action, or (b) the idea that the act is one which I ought to do of
itself, i.e. independently of its being necessary for the realization
of some actual or possible purpose of mine. Instances of the former
would be 'I ought to get up early', when asserted on the ground
that my purpose in acting is the maintenance of my health and
that my early rising is necessary for this; and, again, 'I ought to
make friends', when asserted on the ground that my happiness is
my purpose and that its attainment requires the making of friends.
Further, he subdivides what he calls hypothetical imperatives
into two kinds which he calls respectively counsels of prudence
and rules of skill according as the purpose implied is or is not our
happiness.

Kant, here, in drawing his main distinction, viz. that between
categorical and hypothetical imperatives, does not say that the
term 'ought' has a different meaning in each of the two kinds of
statement. Indeed, what he says suggests the contrary, for he uses
the same term 'imperative' for both, and represents the difference
as consisting solely in the difference of the grounds on which they
are asserted—grounds which can only be ascertained from the
context; so that when told, e.g., that we ought never to drive a hard
bargain, we cannot tell whether the imperative is 'categorical' or
'hypothetical' unless we know whether the speaker is or is not
attributing to us some purpose, such as increase of our business.
Yet plainly Kant thinks that there is a difference of meaning, for
he goes on to speak of categorical imperatives as *moral* impera-

tives, or imperatives of *morality*. And, in fact, there is a difference and indeed a total difference of meaning. This difference becomes obvious if we consider instances. Thus, to borrow from Kant an instance of a hypothetical imperative, we say to a would-be poisoner: 'You ought to give a second dose'; the thought which we wish to convey is that if he does not, his purpose, viz. the death of his would-be victim, will not be realized. Indeed, this is what we really mean by our statement. At first, no doubt, the statement, 'If you do not give a second dose, your purpose will not be realized', seems to state our reason for our assertion, 'You ought to give a second dose', rather than what we mean by it. But this cannot be so, for if it were, we should in making the assertion be implying the idea that whenever a man has a certain purpose, no matter what the purpose be, he ought to do whatever is necessary for its realization, and no one has such an idea. Hence, to put the matter generally, whenever we use the term 'ought' thus, what we really mean by the categorical statement 'I ought to do so and so' has to be expressed by the hypothetical statement: 'If I do not do so and so, my purpose will not be realized.'

It may be noticed that this is the real justification for Kant's designating as hypothetical the imperatives which he distinguishes from imperatives of morality. On the other hand, if we say to a man 'You ought to tell the truth' and mean by it what Kant evidently understood it to mean in calling it a categorical imperative, we do so, as Kant saw, without any reference to some purpose we may think he has, and if we are asked what we mean, we should, ordinarily at least, only answer by using what we considered a verbal equivalent such as 'should' or 'duty' or 'morally bound'. Indeed, as we cannot fail to allow on reflection, the difference in meaning is complete. And for this reason the distinction which Kant is formulating is really not, as he represents it as being, one between two statements containing the word 'ought' made on different grounds, but one between two statements in which 'ought' has a completely different meaning. Consequently the two kinds of statement should be referred to not by Kant's phrases 'categorical' and 'hypothetical imperatives' but rather by phrases indicating the difference in meaning borne by 'ought' in each. And for this purpose the least unsatisfactory phrases seem to be moral and non-moral imperatives. But if this be done, 'moral' must be understood not in its ordinary sense of morally good, but as simply the equivalent of 'duty' or 'morally bound'.

Hume's question then, stated unambiguously, is: 'What distinguishes our assertion, e.g., that X *ought* to be educating his son Y—where "ought" is being used in the moral sense—from our assertion, e.g., that X *is* educating his son Y'?

To this question one answer can be ruled out at once. This is the answer implied by Hume when he speaks of 'ought' and 'ought not' as expressing some new relation, i.e. some relation different from that implied by 'is' and 'is not'. For to speak thus is to imply that what distinguishes the former assertion from the latter is that instead of asserting that a certain subject of attributes, viz. X, stands in the relation to a certain attribute, viz. that of educating Y, of being something which *does* possess it, it asserts that the subject stands to the attribute in the relation of being something which *ought* to possess it, the problem being to ascertain what this relationship is. And there can neither be nor be thought to be any such relationship. For as we recognize when we reflect, the only relations in which a given subject of attributes can possibly stand to a given attribute are those of possessing and not possessing it, no third alternative being possible. And consequently, when we assert that X ought to be educating Y, we cannot possibly be asserting that X stands to the act of educating Y in a relation indicated by the word 'ought' which is neither that of possessing it nor that of not possessing it. As Kant pointed out when considering the term 'sollen', the very question: 'What ought to be the properties of a mile?', as distinct from: 'What are the properties of a mile?', is absurd.

This being so, what seems to distinguish the second assertion from the first is that in it we are attributing to the same subject of attributes X, i.e. asserting him to possess, an attribute of a different kind, viz. that of being under an obligation to educate Y, as distinct from that of educating Y, so that Hume's question becomes: 'What is the *being under an obligation to do some action*?', as distinct from doing some action. And if this be right, the nature of the thought which we express by a statement of the form 'X ought to do so and so' is more clearly expressed by substituting a statement of the form 'X is under an obligation to do so and so'.

It might, however, be maintained that if we consider the nature of the thought which the assertion that X ought to be educating Y expresses, we find that (1) although in making the assertion we are attributing an attribute to a subject of attributes, yet in this case the subject of attributes to which we are attributing an attribute is not X, as it is when we assert that X is educating Y, but the action, viz. educating Y; and that (2) we use the term 'ought' to indicate the nature of the attribute which we are attributing to the action. But if this contention be advanced, the question will have to be answered: 'If so, what is the attribute indicated by the term "ought"?', and the only possible answer will be: 'That of being something which ought to exist.' Consequently the view will be that in asserting, e.g., that X ought to be educating Y, what we are really asserting is that X's educating Y is something which ought to exist. And if it be objected that the phrase 'ought to exist' is artificial, it can be replied that at any rate we are prepared to apply it to things which we think to be good.

Nevertheless, this way of interpreting what we mean by 'X ought to educate Y' is open to a fatal objection. For we can no more either think or assert of something which we think does not exist that it ought to exist than we can think or assert anything else about it. Of what we think does not exist we can think and assert nothing at all. Yet unquestionably, in asserting that X ought to be educating Y, we need not be thinking of X's educating Y as existing, since we think the truth of our assertion independent of whether X is educating Y. Consequently we cannot be asserting that X's educating Y is something which ought to exist. Consequently anyone who begins by offering this interpretation can be forced into modifying it to the extent of allowing that 'X ought to be educating Y' is really hypothetical in meaning, and that if the thought which it is used to express is expressed accurately, it must be expressed in the form: '$If X$ is, or will be, educating Y, his educating Y is, or will be, something which ought to exist.' And if this interpretation be right, there will be no such thing as the attribute of being under a moral obligation to do some action, but only that of being something which ought to exist, this being attributable only to acts which we think were, are being, or will be done, and the very phrase 'being under an obligation to do so and so' will be misleading, as standing for something which can have no existence.

There seems, therefore, to be no way of avoiding the admission that an assertion of the form: 'X ought to do so and so', when 'ought' is being used in a moral sense, has to be interpreted in one or other of two ways. We have either to maintain that it means 'X is under a moral obligation to do so and so', being under a moral obligation to do some action being implied to be a special kind of attribute of a man; or else to maintain that it means: If X does so and so, his doing so and so ought to exist.

We at once find the second interpretation very difficult to accept, partly because the phrase 'ought to exist' strikes us as artificial, but still more because we find it hard to convince ourselves that such a statement is not in meaning as well as in grammatical form categorical. And it does not seem possible to find any thinker who has explicitly offered this interpretation. Nevertheless, as will appear later, there are many who when they raise the question, '*Why* is a man bound to do a certain action?' give answers which imply this interpretation. And it should be noticed that this interpretation cannot be ruled out on the general ground that any assertion which is grammatically categorical cannot be hypothetical in meaning, for we have to allow that at any rate a non-moral imperative though categorical in form is hypothetical in meaning.

Nevertheless, when we consider the matter thoroughly we find ourselves forced to admit that when we assert, e.g., that X *ought* to be educating Y, we *are* attributing a certain attribute to X, and therefore are implying the existence of such an attribute as the being under an obligation to do some action.

This being so we must allow that Hume's question really reduces to the question: 'What is the kind of attribute to which we refer when we say, e.g., that X is under a moral obligation to educate his son Y?'

If we consider this question in connexion with instances, we soon become forced to admit that the kind of attribute is *sui generis*, i.e. unique, and therefore incapable of having its nature expressed in terms of the nature of anything else. To bring the necessity of making this admission home to ourselves, we need only consider various definitions which have been offered and which fail either because they treat 'ought' in the moral sense as if it were the same as 'ought' in the non-moral sense, or because they imply that the statement 'I ought to do so and so' is really hypothetical in meaning. Hobbes, e.g., is implying such a definition when he implies that to be morally bound to do some action is to be coerced, i.e. constrained to do it, by the fear of the sovereign's penalties; and so is Paley when he maintains that it is to be urged by a violent motive resulting from the command of another. So, also, is Hutcheson when he says that by a man's being obliged we mean that every spectator or he himself upon reflection must (i.e.

really does) approve his action. So again is Joseph[1] when he says that being obliged is being moved by the thought, being moved by which makes the act which a man does right. For we have only to consider these alleged definitions to become certain that what we refer to as our being morally bound to do some action is none of the things which it is being asserted to be. Thus it is plain that even though when we think ourselves bound to do some action we do feel ourselves constrained to do it, we do not mean by our being bound our feeling constrained, but something else; and again, that even if, when we do the action, we do approve it, we do not mean that we approve it. Recognition of the failure of these supposed definitions is no proof of the unique and therefore indefinable character of the thing meant by 'our being morally bound to do some action', but it does help us to recognize its unique character by forcing us to recognize its difference from other things with which it has been confused. Further, it should be noted that the summary attempt to elucidate the nature of moral obligation by the analogy of law, an attempt illustrated by Kant's phrase 'categorical *imperative*' and by the reference to a principle of duty as a moral *law*, is only mischievous, because it represents our being morally bound to do some action as if it were our being commanded to do it.

III. *The Relation between Moral Obligation and the Agent's Happiness*

The next question to be considered is: Does a man's performance of his duty necessarily render him happier? It will, however, be found in the course of considering it that a stage is reached at which it will be appropriate to consider the second of the questions enumerated, viz. Ought a man to do his duty?

The treatment of this question has differed, and necessarily differed, radically according as those who have considered it have or have not distinguished 'ought' in the moral from 'ought' in the non-moral sense. And I propose first to consider its treatment by the latter. For these the attempt to give an affirmative answer has to take one or other of two forms. It must *either* contend that it is a condition of our being bound to do some action that doing it would make for our happiness, *or* else contend that though this is not so, yet the performance of our duty by its own nature must

---

[1] *Some Problems of Ethics*, p. 54.

bring us happiness. As an instance of the former class I propose to consider Butler, and as instances of the latter, Plato and Aristotle.

Butler at least seems to be declaring himself a member of the former class when he says, in a well-known passage:

Let it be allowed, though virtue or moral rectitude does indeed consist in affection to and pursuit of what is right and good, as such; yet, that when we sit down in a cool hour, we can neither justify to ourselves this or any other pursuit, till we are convinced that it will be for our happiness, or at least not contrary to it.

Common reason and humanity will have some influence upon mankind, whatever becomes of speculations; but, so far as the interests of virtue depend upon the theory of it being secured from open scorn, so far its very being in the world depends upon its appearing to have no contrariety to private interest and self-love.[1]

This interpretation is sometimes disputed on the ground that here he is only arguing *ad hominem*, contending that even if conduciveness to our happiness were a condition of our having an obligation to do some action, as some think it is but as he does not, we should really be bound to do the acts which we ordinarily think we are bound to do, viz. virtuous actions, since they will be for our happiness. But that he himself considers conduciveness to happiness to be the condition of a duty seems conclusively shown by two earlier passages. In leading up to the statement quoted, he says:

And to all these things may be added, that religion, from whence arises our strongest obligation to benevolence, is so far from disowning the principle of self-love, that it often addresses itself to that very principle, and always to the mind in that state when reason presides; and there can no access be had to the understanding, but by convincing men, that the course of life we would persuade them to is not contrary to their interest. It may be allowed, without any prejudice to the cause of virtue and religion, that our ideas of happiness and misery are of all our ideas the nearest and most important to us; that they will, nay, if you please, that they ought to prevail over those of order, and beauty, and harmony, and proportion, if there should ever be, as it is impossible there ever should be, any inconsistence between them: though these last too, as expressing the fitness of actions, are real as truth itself.[2]

Again, in his Preface to the *Sermons*, he asserts that interest, one's own happiness, is a manifest obligation, and (considering as he does that vicious action constitutes what we ought not to do)

---

[1] Selby-Bigge, *British Moralists*, i, p. 240.
[2] Ibid., pp. 239–40.

meets the objection that in a case where a vicious action is for our interest there would be an obligation to do the vicious act, only by saying that it is always uncertain whether some vicious action *is* for our interest, thereby implying that if it is, as it may be, for our interest, there is an obligation to do what is vicious. There seems to be no doubt then but that Butler considered that no act can possibly be really a duty unless it will be for our happiness.

If we now go on to consider whether he is right it takes only little consideration to satisfy ourselves that he is not. To do this we need only imagine ourselves unwilling to do some action, e.g. to get up early in the morning, and then thinking of some substantial gain which it would bring us which we consider would more than outweigh the loss of comfort. For we then find that though the thought might make us less unwilling to do it, it would do nothing to make us think that it was a *duty* on our part to do it. And by doing this we can come to recognize that conduciveness to our advantage is simply irrelevant to the question whether it is a duty to do some action. In fact, this seems so obvious when we consider the matter that we then find it difficult to see how Butler and others who follow him can have come to think what they have. Light, however, on this question seems to be thrown by a passage in Butler's *Dissertation of the Nature of Virtue*. He says:

It deserves to be considered, whether men are more at liberty, in point of morals, to make themselves miserable without reason, than to make other people so; or dissolutely to neglect their own greater good, for the sake of a present lesser gratification, than they are to neglect the good of others, whom nature has committed to their care. It should seem, that a due concern about our own interest or happiness, and a reasonable endeavour to secure and promote it, which is, I think, very much the meaning of the word prudence in our language; it should seem that this is virtue, and the contrary behaviour faulty and blameable; since, in the calmest way of reflection, we approve of the first, and condemn the other conduct, both in ourselves and others.[1]

This suggests as the explanation that our admitted approval of some act of prudence, i.e. an act in doing which a man with a view to his own welfare overcomes a disinclination to do it, is regarded as either identical with or, if not, as at least carrying with it, the thought that it is a duty on his part to do it.

We have now to consider the other form of the attempt to connect happiness with the performance of a duty, viz. that of trying

---

[1] Selby-Bigge, *British Moralists*, i, pp. 249–50.

to show that the latter by its very nature carries happiness with it. Of this form Plato's is undoubtedly the best to consider, partly because he puts with unrivalled force the difficulties to be overcome, and partly because he realizes better than others a condition essential to success.

In attributing this attempt to Plato two assumptions have been made. The first is that in the *Republic* what Plato means by just and unjust actions is the various actions which we ought, in the moral sense, to do and not to do respectively. And the second is that his object in dealing with just and unjust actions is to show that it is by doing what is just, i.e. what we ought, rather than what is unjust, i.e. what we ought not, that we shall become happy. But both assumptions can be justified. There is no obvious word in Plato for 'ought' in the moral sense, duty or obligation; and in the *Republic* χρῆ or δεῖ, as in χρῆ δίκαιον εἶναι, except in one passage, are shown by their context to mean 'must do' if the happiness which a man is seeking is to be attained. And we are driven to think, especially when we take into account the wide sense in which Plato is obviously using δίκαιον, that when he says of an action that it is δίκαιον (just), that is his way of saying that we ought to do it. Again, as regards the second assumption, Plato usually puts the conclusion he wants to draw in the form 'just action is profitable' (λυσιτελεῖ), and, in the wide sense in which he is using 'profitable', we may fairly say that he means that it makes for one's happiness.

To follow his argument, however, we have to elucidate what he means by two terms by the help of which he expresses it, viz. ἀγαθόν and κακόν, which would ordinarily be translated 'a good' and 'an evil'. And to do this with success we need first to notice that in English there are two usages of the word 'good' and that in these there is a complete difference of meaning. The term 'good' is used both as an adjective, as in the statement 'courage is good', and also as a part of a substantival phrase, as in the statement 'having friends is a great good' or 'the goods of life are numerous'.

---

[1] Cf. the distinction between the adjectives ἀγαθός and ἀγαθόν, and the substantival phrases ἀγαθόν τι and ἀγαθά. It may be noted that 'bad', the contrary of 'good', is only used adjectivally, and that the corresponding substantival phrase is 'an evil', as in the statement 'The loss of reputation is an evil'. It may also be noted that when someone considers the question 'What is the origin of evil?' he does not always stop to ask himself whether the question to which he is addressing himself is the question 'What is the origin of what is bad?' or the very different question 'What is the origin of evils?'

When we use the term 'good' as an adjective, as when we make the statement 'Courage is good' or 'That man is good in respect of his courage', we can be said—provided that we use the terms 'character' and 'quality' in a very wide sense—to be attributing to what we state to be good a certain character or quality which it possesses in itself, i.e. independently of its relatedness to other things. The character or quality meant seems coextensive, though of course not identical, with that of being something the thought of which excites approval. It is not, however, a quality of the ordinary kind of which it is true to say that one quality exists side by side with others. We can say, e.g., of a certain plate that it is round and hard; and if, having said that it is round, we go on to say that it is hard, we are thinking of its hardness as something separate from its roundness. Similarly we can say of a certain man that he is generous and courageous; and if, having said that he is generous, we go on to say that he is courageous, we are thinking of his courage as something separate from his generosity. But if we then go on to say that a man is in these respects good, we are not thinking of his goodness as something separate from his courage and his generosity; on the contrary we think that, in being generous, although he is not being courageous, he is being good, and similarly that in being courageous, although he is not being generous, he is being good. The quality, however, to which we refer by the term 'good' plainly cannot be defined. Although we mean to attribute a certain character to, e.g., a courageous disposition when we state that it is good, just as we do when we state that some body is red, that a line is continuous, or that the soul is not extended, we can no more state the nature of this character in other terms than we can in the case of 'red', 'continuous', or 'extended'.

As regards the application of the term 'good', it may be observed that we apply it most naturally either (1) to certain capacities or dispositions, or to the actualizations of certain dispositions, of human or sentient beings—the word 'disposition' being used here in a wide sense—or (2) to human or sentient beings in respect of these dispositions or of their actualizations. Indeed, it even looks as though we apply the term exclusively thus. For if we are asked 'Is pleasure good?'—though at first we may be inclined to answer 'Yes', yet if we reflect, we are likely to answer: 'It all depends on the disposition of which it is an actualization; the pleasure, for instance, excited by the thought of the ill fortune of someone we hate being bad, and the pleasure excited by the thought of a friend's good fortune or, indeed, the pain excited by the thought of his ill fortune, being good.'

When, however, we use the word 'good' as part of a substantival phrase, as in speaking of having friends as a good, we are *not* stating that that to which we apply the phrase 'a good' has a certain quality in itself. In using the phrase thus we are no more doing this than we are when we state that something, e.g. the possession of power or pleasure, is an object of desire. We mean by 'a good', 'a good *to someone*'. Thus when we speak of the having of friends as a good, we mean that it is a good to the man who has the friends. And where this addition is not stated it is always implied.[1] In the same way by 'an evil' we mean an evil to someone. What, however, precisely we mean by 'a good to someone' and by 'an evil to some-one' is not easy to elucidate. As the first step it seems necessary to recognize that in ordinary speech we apply these phrases with a certain looseness. We should, for instance, as a matter of ordinary language say that to most men a son's having done something dis-graceful was a great evil. Yet if we were asked whether X's son's having done something disgraceful would have been an evil to X if X had not learned of the action, we should have to say 'No'; and then, if pressed, we should have to say that what, as a matter of accuracy, we should have stated to be evil to X was the *thought* that his son had done the disgraceful action. Similarly we might with-out artificiality say of a certain man who, having one ticket for the theatre, is considering whether to use it himself or to send a friend that, though his seeing the play himself would be a good to him, his friend's seeing the play would be a greater good to him; yet, if pressed, we should have to allow that what we vaguely had had in mind, and ought to have spoken of, as a greater good to him was *the thought* that his friend was seeing the play. As a result of recog-nizing the need for this correction we should probably at first go on to say that what we really mean by 'a good to us' is something which gives us, i.e. excites in us, satisfaction, i.e. a feeling of satis-faction, and similarly what we really mean by 'an evil to us' is something which gives us dissatisfaction. But these statements would be inaccurate. For a feeling of satisfaction implies the prior existence of a desire, viz. a desire of that the thought of the realiza-tion of which excites the satisfaction; and we should also apply the phrase 'a good to us' to what we call enjoyments, such as that of

---

[1] ἀγαθόν has a similar implication.

seeing a beautiful landscape, which do not imply a preceding desire. This being so, we seem forced to allow that we mean by 'a good to us' something which *pleases*, i.e. excites pleasure in us, pleasure being something which admits of two forms, viz. satisfaction (or gratification) and enjoyment; and similarly that by 'an evil to us' we mean something which excites pain, pain admitting of two forms, viz. dissatisfaction and something for which we have no word but 'pain'.

It has, however, to be added that if this account is to stand, 'to excite pleasure' or 'to excite pain' must be understood as meaning to excite it whether *directly or indirectly*. For we do not restrict the phrase 'a good to us' (to consider that only) to things such as seeing a beautiful landscape, of which we should say that they are *in themselves* a good, i.e. which create pleasure directly, but apply it also to things such as our being healthy or rich, of which we should say that they are a good though not in themselves, meaning that though they do not directly excite pleasure yet they indirectly excite pleasure by causing other things which directly excite pleasure.

If then, as seems clear, we mean by 'a good to us' something which directly or indirectly excites pleasure in us, the difference in meaning between it and the term 'good' must be radical, in spite of the occurrence of the word 'good' in both. Indeed, in the end we have to allow that statements of the forms 'X is good' and 'X is a good to us' are *totally* different in meaning, so that the meaning of neither is capable of being stated in terms of, or even derivable from, the meaning of the other.[1] The difference, however, is one which we have no difficulty in admitting in particular cases. Thus we readily allow that although a certain act of revenge was bad, it was a good to the agent, though, no doubt, we should add that so far as he felt compunction, it was also an evil to him. Again we readily allow that to a given man, A, the thought that he is courageous himself, or, again, the thought that his friend, B, is courageous, is a good, although this could not be so unless A thought courage a good quality, whether in himself or in another. And examples like these last are important in two ways. First, they

---

[1] 'To be valuable' and 'to be of value', except where they mean being capable of being exchanged for money, appear to mean 'to be valuable or of value to someone', and to be identical in meaning with 'to be a good to someone'. Hence it seems impossible to allow that there can be such things as judgements of value except in the sense of estimates of the extent to which various things will excite pleasure in individuals; and it seems merely the result of confusion to describe a judgement that such and such an act or character is good as a judgement of value.

illustrate a use of the term 'good' as part of a substantival phrase which *presupposes* its use as an adjective. Second, consideration of them shows us that where that which is a good to us is a thought, that thought has what may be called a personal reference which is absent in the thought that something is good. Where, e.g., to one man, *A*, the thought that another man, *B*, is good (say in respect of being courageous) is a good, this is only because he is thinking of *B* as in some special relation to himself, as being, e.g., a friend, or a fellow countryman or a man of whom he is fond, and if he were to abstract from any such relationship the thought of *B* as good would cease to excite satisfaction, whereas, of course, in thinking of *B* as good in respect of his courage, he is abstracting from any such relationship. And just for this reason *A*'s thought of his own goodness and his thought of his friend *B*'s goodness are goods to himself of different kinds; for the one implies the desire to be himself good and the other the desire for his friend to be good— and these desires are different, for the former is the desire for himself as being himself, and not as just being someone, to be good, and similarly the latter is the desire for his friend to be good, as being his friend and not just as being someone.

Kant, it may be observed, emphasizes the difference in meaning between 'good' and 'a good to us'. He speaks of the ambiguity of the terms *bonum* and *malum* and says that German has fortunately two expressions which prevent the difference from being over-looked. 'For *bonum*', he says, 'it has *das Gute* (good) and *das Wohl* (well), for *malum*, *das Böse* (bad) and *das Übel* (ill, evil).' He adds later that '*das Wohl oder Übel*' (well or ill) implies only a reference to our condition of pleasure or pain; and concludes that we make two quite different judgements when we consider the goodness or badness of an action and when we consider its relation to our *Wohl oder Weh* (good or evil).

It is also to be observed that connected with the phrase 'a good to ourselves' we have the phrases 'our good' and 'our own good', and that by this we mean either our happiness or else the totality of the things which render us happy. And for this reason we have to distinguish sharply between the meanings of 'my good' and 'your good' on the one hand and those of 'my goodness' and 'your goodness', i.e. the goodness of me and that of you, on the other. Consequently, when Professor Moore[1] criticizes the doctrine that a man ought to aim at his own good as self-contradictory, the

[1] *Principia Ethica*, §§ 58–62.

basis of his argument, viz. the contention that the goodness of anything good is independent of what or whom it is the goodness of,
must be admitted to be irrelevant. For what the doctrine criticized
represents as what a man ought to aim at is not his own goodness,
i.e. the goodness of himself as opposed to the goodness of another,
but his own happiness as opposed to the happiness of another; and
Professor Moore seems here to be treating the phrase 'a man's
good' as if it meant 'a man's own goodness'.

We are now in a position to consider Plato's treatment of justice,
i.e. of the acts which form our duties, in the *Republic*. In Plato,
corresponding to 'good' and 'a good to us', there is the use of
ἀγαθός (good) as an adjective and of its neuter ἀγαθόν as a substantival phrase. By the adjective ἀγαθός he, of course, means good,
as when he speaks of a man or a city as good, and maintains that
there is a better and a worse element in the soul. And by the substantival phrase ἀγαθόν he must be admitted to mean not something good but what we mean by 'a good to us', i.e. something
which excites pleasure in us whether directly or indirectly. The
admission is inevitable for various reasons; but two considerations
may be mentioned as decisive. The first is that in Plato ἀγαθόν
means ἀγαθόν τινι, a good to *someone*, as in the statement put into
the mouth of Thrasymachus that just action is ἀλλότριον ἀγαθὸν τῷ
ὄντι, τοῦ κρείττονός τε καὶ ἄρχοντος συμφέρον, οἰκεία δὲ τοῦ πειθομένου
τε καὶ ὑπηρετοῦντος βλάβη,[1] i.e. is a good to another, being advantageous to the stronger and the ruler but being loss to the agent.

The second consideration concerns what is ostensibly a division
of ἀγαθά (goods) but is really a division of objects of desire, at the
beginning of the second Book. There he divides the things which
we desire into three classes:

1. things which we desire for themselves and not for the sake of
   their consequences, such as rejoicing and harmless pleasures,
2. things which we desire both for themselves and for the sake of
   their consequences, such as intelligent activity, seeing, and
   being healthy,
3. things which we desire only for the sake of their consequences,
   such as gymnastic training, receiving medical treatment, and
   practising medicine.

These he represents respectively as (1) goods in themselves,
(2) goods both in themselves and on account of their consequences,

---

[1] *Rep.* 343 c.

and (3) goods on account of their consequences. And since in referring to these as ἀγαθά, i.e. as goods, he cannot possibly be meaning
that they are objects of desire, and so just stating in other words
that we desire them, the only meaning which it is possible to attach
to ἀγαθά is that of 'goods to us', i.e. things which directly or indirectly excite pleasure in us, these being divided into three kinds
according as they excite pleasure directly, indirectly, or in both
ways. No doubt this interpretation requires us to allow that Plato
is involved in holding that we only desire anything so far as we
think it will excite pleasure directly or indirectly. But this cannot
be helped.

It is now possible to state Plato's treatment of justice. His first
task is to state as strongly as possible the case against thinking that
it is just rather than unjust action which is profitable. He represents the Sophists as presenting the case in two forms, in both of
which just action is held—with, of course, some plausibility—to
consist in carrying out the laws of the state, i.e. obeying the orders
of the government. In its *more* superficial form, put into the mouth
of Thrasymachus, the government is held to consist of a ruler who
has successfully devised the laws in his own interest, so that it is
the ruler who gains by just action, and the agent suffers whatever
evil is incurred by conferring the benefit in question on the ruler.
And Socrates is made to refute this view by an argument which
even on its own lines, although showing that 'the ruler does not
gain', does nothing to disprove what *prima facie* is the truth, viz.
that by obeying the law, e.g. by refraining from stealing, it is not
the agent but another subject who gains. In its *less* superficial
form, put into the mouth of Glaucon, the case put forward is more
complicated. According to Glaucon, men originally pursued their
own interest regardless of that of others. But they found that they
lost more by others acting regardless of any interest other than
their own, than they gained by acting thus themselves. In consequence they mutually agreed to abstain from gaining at the
expense of others, and to set up a government to order and enforce
this abstinence. And a government having been thus set up,
justice consists in refraining from gaining at the expense of others
in a state thus set up, and so a state where this abstinence is
ordered and enforced. Hence for most men it is not a good, but
only a lesser evil than unjust action—being a lesser evil because
the loss incurred by doing what is just is a lesser evil than suffering
the penalty for doing what is unjust; but for those men—and there

are such—who are either strong enough or skilful enough to avoid the penalties, just action is an evil, and unjust action a good.

In addition, Glaucon is made to strengthen the case in the following way. He is made to say that if Socrates is to show that the man who does what is just is necessarily happier than he who does what is unjust, he must succeed in taking into account both the case of the completely successful unjust man, who by his skill manages to obtain the advantages of a reputation for complete justice as well as those of his injustice, and also that of the completely just man, who in spite of his justice has the reputation for the greatest injustice, and so not only fails to gain the advantages of his justice but also suffers the penalties which attach to injustice. And though the reason for this which Glaucon is made to offer is irrelevant, viz. that otherwise the just man may be considered to be doing what is just for the sake of its rewards, he should have been made to offer a good reason, viz. that such a case is possible.

Finally, Glaucon is made to state what, in view of the case to be met, is the only possible method of meeting it, if it can be met. According to him, since all the rewards normally open to a just man are equally open to an unjust man, and since a just man may suffer all the penalties which normally go to unjust action, just action can only be shown to bring happiness by ignoring rewards altogether, and by showing that just action is *in itself* a good so great as to outweigh any possible combination of resulting evils.

Plato certainly did not underrate his task. Indeed, in reading his statement of it, we wonder how he ever came to think that he could execute it.

To carry it out he naturally thinks that he has first to get the right answer to the question 'What is justice?', i.e. 'What is the character common to the acts which are just or those which it is our duty to do?' And ostensibly he proceeds thus: He first considers what he represents as only an analogy to the just action in individual men, viz. the just action of members of an ideal community, and finds it to consist in each of what he finds to be the three parts of the community (the rulers, their subordinates, and the artisans) contributing that service to the community for which the special nature of each is best suited. Then, turning to the individual man, he finds that he also has three parts, viz. the intellectual, the spirited, and the concupiscent, and that his just action, and so justice proper, consists in each part doing in the interest of the individual that for which its special nature is best suited. And finally he urges that once we have realized this it becomes ludicrous even to ask whether a man gains by just action.

Yet this can only ostensibly be his procedure. For, in spite of what he says, he must be implying that his 'justice in the state' is identical with and not only analogous to his 'justice in the individual', and he must be going too far when he asserts that justice must really concern the internal and not the external performance of a man's proper work.[1] For the just actions, the profitableness of which his speakers are considering, are certain acts of a man to others, and unless he holds that the activity within the soul, which he maintains that just action consists in, shows itself outwardly in these acts, his argument is broken-backed. For otherwise there is nothing to connect the activity of which he is maintaining the profitableness with that whose profitableness the various speakers are considering. Moreover, Plato himself maintains this connexion when he makes Thrasymachus say that the just soul, i.e. the man whose parts work properly, will keep the ordinarily recognized commandments. And plainly Plato's own answer to the question which Thrasymachus answered by saying that justice is promoting the interest of the ruler is: 'Doing that in the service of the community for which our nature is best suited.'

What then is Plato's argument to show that the just man, i.e. the man who carries out his duty by serving the state, necessarily gains thereby? To answer this question we have to bear in mind that Plato's three parts of the soul are really certain capacities of desiring. This must be so, even though Plato introduces the rational part as reasoning, and afterwards speaks of it as exercising forethought on behalf of the whole soul. For his test for a difference of parts of the soul is the existence of a mental conflict, and the only things which can conflict are desires. Hence Plato must mean by the rational part of the soul the capacity for a desire of a special kind entitled to be called rational. In addition, the objects of this desiring part must be held to include the doing of what is just, i.e. serving the community. For he represents the just individual as one in whom the rational part is dominant, and so requires the doing of what is just, although the other parts prompt him to act otherwise. Plato must, therefore, be attributing to the just man a desire to do his duty of serving the State, and maintaining it to be stronger in him than any other desire.

[1] *Republic,* iv. 443 b.

This being so, we can, of course, understand how Plato came to maintain that just action is in itself a good. For where we desire something, the thought that it is being or has been realized necessarily excites satisfaction, and if we desire to serve the State, either as serving the State, or as a duty, then serving the State, or (to speak accurately) the thought involved in doing it that we are serving the State, will necessarily itself excite satisfaction and so be a good to us, and we can distinguish its being thus in itself a good from the action's causing something which will be a good to us. But even so, strictly speaking what will be a good will not be serving the State, as Plato implies, but the thought that we are serving the State. And we can now see what he means when he says in effect that when we understand the nature of the just soul it is ludicrous even to ask whether the just man gains by his justice; viz. that just action will in itself excite in him a satisfaction so great as to outweigh any possible evils in the way of consequences. In fairness to Plato, however, two things should be noted. First, he seeks in Book IX to supplement the argument of Books I–IV by trying to show in detail that the pleasures obtained from satisfying the rational part of the soul are more permanent and less bound up with pain than those of the other parts. Second, at the end of the fourth Book he makes it clear that he does not go so far as to contend that any given man will *at once* gain in happiness by doing what is just, but is only contending that he will gain in the long run, first by a course of just action developing the just disposition (i.e. really the desire to do what is just), and then, though not before, by attaining a satisfaction, by doing what is just, which will outweigh all possible evils.

This being Plato's argument, what comments does it suggest? It has at least one outstanding merit. It does proceed on the only plan which has any hope of success, that of trying to make out that doing our duty is in itself a good so great as to outweigh any combination of resulting evils. For whatever be the kinds of action held to be our duty, since *ex hypothesi* they cannot be that of making ourselves happy (for if they were, there would be nothing to be proved), they must consist of acts causing things of another sort or sorts, and an act consisting of causing something of one kind cannot possibly be shown necessarily to cause something of another kind. Hence no consideration of the results of the acts held to be our duty can succeed in showing that we shall necessarily be the happier for doing them. And in this respect Plato's argument is only a special form of the endeavour to show that obedience to conscience is itself a reward sufficient even to outweigh any resulting evils.

Nevertheless, there is no denying that it is open to two fatal objections. The first is that even if for one whose desire to serve the state, or, alternatively, to do his duty, is at the maximum possible for any human being, the satisfaction excited by the thought that the object of this desire is realized would outweigh all possible resulting evils, yet any given individual may be incapable of having this desire developed to that extent, and so may not even in the long run become happier by doing what is just. Indeed, it is more plausible to say that the actions conducive to a given man's happiness will depend on his nature and that, e.g., if he is initially ambitious and little anxious to serve the state, he will gain most happiness by first developing and then gratifying his ambition rather than his desire to serve the state. And though Plato in Books VIII and IX does much to mitigate the force of this objection, what he says can only be a mitigation; and even Plato himself insists that those who, after contemplating the good, return to the cave to take their share of ruling and in doing so do what is just are making a sacrifice of happiness. And the second objection is that even for the man whose desire to do what is just is at the maximum possible for anyone, there must come a point at which, if the evils resulting from doing what is just continue to be piled up, they will outweigh the good to the man of knowing that he is doing what is just.

Here it may be noted that these objections are independent of Plato's view of what a man's duty consists in, viz. serving the state, so that if any other be substituted they still hold; and for that reason, in considering the success of Plato's argument, there is no need to consider whether he is right in thinking that what justice consists in is serving the state. The plain truth is, of course, that apart from theological reasons for thinking that the results of doing what we ought and doing what we ought not are specially adjusted by rewards and penalties, no general answer either way is possible to the question: 'Will doing our duty be for our happiness?' The only possible answer must be: 'It all depends; in some instances it may be and in others it may not.'

Aristotle, it may be noted, appears to follow Plato in offering a proof that it is by doing our duty that we shall become happy, but in his case the argument is curiously crude. In contrast to Plato he appears to hold that our duty consists in exercising the various virtues, and his argument appears to be this.[1] A man, to be a special craftsman such as a flute-player or a shoemaker, has a function, i.e. is an instrument, and indeed is a human instrument. Now in the case of an instrument of a given sort, e.g. a flute, there is a difference between its performing its function, i.e. exercising the activity the capacity for which renders it an instrument of the sort it is, and performing its function well, i.e. exercising that activity well. And in the case of a human instrument, its happiness arises from its performing its function well. Therefore, to find what will render a man happy, we must find what the function of a man is and then find what performing that function will consist in. But to find the function of a man, as of any instrument, we have to find the capacity for activity special to a man. This consists in the capacity for rational activity; and to exercise this function well is to exercise good rational activity, i.e. to exercise the various virtues. And, therefore, it is by the exercise of the various virtues, the exercise of which is our duty, that we shall be happy.

The argument, however, is really only verbal. For (1) a man is not an instrument, nor does Aristotle refer to any special skill possessed by a man, which would justify his implying that man is an instrument. (2) There is no distinction other than one of degree between an instrument's performing an activity and its performing that action well. Unless the activity included in its nature something of what is meant by 'well', it would not be the activity of the instrument. We could not, e.g., distinguish a knife's cutting from its tearing a piece of paper, or playing the flute from making a noise on the flute, unless we meant by 'cutting' something only different in degree from cutting well, and by 'playing the flute' making in some degree beautiful sounds, i.e. playing the flute well. (3) Consequently Aristotle cannot reach his conclusion that it is *virtuous* activity that is required for a man to perform his function well from consideration of what the function of a man is; and in fact he only speaks of virtuous activity because, independently of an idea of man's having a function, he thinks of it as the best activity of which a man is capable. All we are left with, therefore, is a bare *assertion* on Aristotle's part that it is by doing the best actions of which we are capable that we shall become happy.

[1] *Eth. Nic.* i. 7. 9–15.

iv. *Do We Always Seek Our Own Happiness?*

In considering Plato's treatment of the connexion between duty and happiness, an underlying idea with which he approached the question has, for clearness' sake, been ignored. The idea lies in the background, and it may even escape notice. Yet it is undeniably there, and its presence explains the intensity of Plato's desire to prove that justice leads to happiness. Moreover, as the idea has not only been not infrequently shared by others, but may also affect either the questions asked about obligation or the answers given, its truth ought to be considered. The idea is one which concerns not how men ought to act but how they do act, and at first at least it strikes us as having little plausibility. It is that whenever we act deliberately, and not on an impulse, and so have a purpose, our final purpose, i.e. that the desire of which for its own sake leads us to do what we are doing and so forms our motive, is always the realization of our own good, i.e. of what will make us happy, or, more accurately, of our own happiness. The idea is one which Plato had formulated in the *Gorgias*,[1] where after contending that men do all that they do for the sake of the good (τὸ ἀγαθόν), i.e. as the context shows, of what is a good to themselves, he says of anyone who kills or exiles a man or despoils him of his wealth that he does it because he thinks it will be better for himself. In the *Republic* the idea first emerges in a rather disguised form at the beginning of Book II. There Glaucon is made to contend that men in fact only do what is just, i.e. their duty, ὡς ἀναγκαῖον, i.e. as an evil which has to be endured only to avoid a greater evil, and to urge in support that no one, like Gyges, able to do what is unjust with impunity would in fact do what is just. And that Plato himself here accepts this contention is shown by his representing Socrates, the mouthpiece of the truth, as having to show not that Glaucon's contention is mistaken, but that men in acting thus are mistaken in thinking just action the incurring the lesser of two evils. Later, however, in Book VI[2] the idea is explicitly stated, though in a way which may be misunderstood. There, in introducing the subject of the Idea of good, Socrates says that, while we are willing to put up with things which *seem* just and beautiful, it does not suffice us to obtain things which seem a good (τὰ δοκοῦντα ἀγαθά), but we seek things which are really a good (τὰ ὄντα ἀγαθά). And he goes on to speak of the good (τὸ ἀγαθόν) as that which

---

[1] 468 *b*.   [2] 505 *d–e*.

every soul pursues and for the sake of which it does everything that it does, divining its existence, but perplexed about it and unable adequately to grasp its nature, and so misses such benefit as it might have got from other things. This statement, especially when taken in connexion with the earlier books, must be taken to mean that in all action what we are striving to bring into existence is—not what is good but—what is really good for us, or for our own good.

If we allow, as we must, that this interpretation is right, then we can, of course, understand the intensity of Plato's desire to prove to us that we shall gain by doing our duty. For plainly he was passionately anxious for men to do what is just, and if he considered that men always seek their own good, he must have thought that men could only be persuaded to do what is just by being persuaded that it was the course of action by which they would gain. Also, we can then understand his contention that the ultimate question under consideration, for the sake of which he is considering whether justice is profitable, is: 'Should or ought we to do what is just, i.e. our duty?' For this question will have the intelligible meaning of: 'Ought we to do our duty', in the non-moral sense of 'ought', i.e. is doing it necessary for the realization of our purpose in all action? And in view of what has been said, we may take it that this is the ultimate question to which Plato is addressing himself. We are, therefore, brought to the conclusion that the ultimate question which Plato is considering is: 'Should or ought we, in the non-moral sense, do our duty?' and that it is forced on him by his idea that men always pursue their own good. Further, *if* we share this idea, then for the reasons already given we shall have to conclude that the true answer is:

No general answer is possible; on some occasions it may be that we ought to do our duty, and on others it may not, but as we never know all the consequences to ourselves of an action, we never *know* whether we ought, in the non-moral sense, to do any particular action, whether a duty or not, though sometimes we may be able to have a fairly good opinion about it.

The idea that we always seek, i.e. act for the sake of, our own good is one which has not infrequently been held. Aristotle shared this idea with Plato, and it was in effect held by Hobbes, Bentham, Mill, and T. H. Green. And we ought to consider whether it is true, if only because our conclusion may affect the question: Should or ought we to do our duty? For if we think our purpose in acting is not always the realization of our own good, the question will have disappeared as one admitting of a general answer, since the answer on any particular occasion will depend on what our purpose happens to be. And if, further, we think that sometimes our purpose is the doing of our duty, the question will have disappeared as a general question, since if our purpose on a given occasion is the doing of our duty, we cannot even ask 'Should we do our duty?' since it will mean: Is the doing our duty necessary for the realization of what it is *ex hypothesi* itself? Doing our duty cannot be necessary for the realization of our purpose, unless our purpose is something other than doing our duty.

There is, however, a much more important reason for considering whether the idea is true. This is that if we accept the idea, we shall be involved in very awkward consequences. For we shall then be forced to allow (1) that there is really no such thing as a conscientious action or a benevolent or a malevolent action, and also (2) that there is really no difference of motive between the acts of a so-called good man and those of a so-called bad man.

The idea is, of course, limited to deliberate actions, i.e. to actions in doing which we should be said to have a purpose. No one would maintain that a man who acts on an impulse is seeking his own good, or indeed *seeking* anything. Yet even though the idea is thus limited, it by no means seems even plausible to anyone to whom it is presented for the first time. And it appears to be one of those to which men are only driven by a course of reflection, the process in this case being started by raising the general question: What is required, for a man to be led to act? In dealing with this question we take for granted, and (it seems) truly, that for us to do some action deliberately, there must be something which we think of as non-existent and the existence of which we desire, the desire of this being what we call our motive, i.e. what leads us to do the act if we do it. In other words, we take for granted that in all action we must have a purpose, since we mean, by our purpose in doing an action, that the desire of which leads us to do the action, i.e. that the desire of which is our motive. And the idea in question appears to arise by our taking three steps. First, having asked what our purpose is, we think of it as always something, other than an action, which we think an action likely to cause, directly or indirectly, such as the disappearance of a headache which we think taking some drug will effect. Mill expresses this idea when he says that all action is for the sake of an end. And Plato in the *Gorgias*[1] expressly states this idea. In trying to show that orators and tyrants have the least power in states, he lays down generally that what a man wishes for in doing some action is not the action but the result for the sake of which he does it, the man who takes a drug, e.g., wishing not for this but for health, and the man who takes a voyage wishing not for the sailing and the incurring of dangers but for the resulting wealth. Here, however, Plato is plainly going too far in asserting that a man does not want to do the action: what he meant and should have said is rather that though he desires to do the action this desire depends on the desire of a certain result, this latter desire being more properly said to be what is moving him, as being what gives rise to the desire to do the action. Further, it is worth observing that it is because we are apt to think of our purpose in action as being always something, other than our action, which we think our action will cause, that we have come to use as we often do two metaphorical expressions for our purpose. First, we are apt to refer to our purpose as our aim, or as what we are aiming at. And the justification of the metaphor is that if, e.g., our health is our purpose, it is that by reference to which we have devised what we are doing, e.g. taking some drug, as being what we think most likely to cause it, just as a target is that by reference to the position of which a shooter arranges his weapon before shooting. And, second, we are apt to refer to our purpose as our end, as being that which will be realized only at the end of the action. It should, however, be borne in mind that the terms 'aim' and 'end' thus used are only metaphorical expressions for our purpose, and that they are appropriate only if our purpose is something, other than our action, to which we think it will lead.

Having thus come to think that our purpose is always some expected result X, we are led to take the second of the three steps referred to. This is to insist that the action requires the desire of something for its own sake. For we recognize that it is impossible to desire everything for the sake of something else; since otherwise, as Aristotle said, all desire would be empty and vain; and that in particular in desiring X we must either be desiring X for its own sake or else desiring it for the sake of something else which we are desiring for its own sake. In this way we are led not only to distinguish the desire of a thing for its own sake and the desire of a thing for the sake of something else, as respectively independent and dependent desires, but also to distinguish our ultimate purpose in doing some action from some non-ultimate purpose, and to insist

that in all action we must have some ultimate purpose, i.e. something the desire of which for its own sake is what is independently
moving us, our other desire being dependent on this. Finally we
are led to take the third step referred to. We ask: What is that in
our various actions desire of which for its own sake moves us to do
them and so forms our ultimate purpose? And our first answer is
likely to be: 'This is of different sorts in different instances; we
desire things of very varied kinds for their own sake.' And Aristotle
in effect gave this answer.

v. *Teleological Theories of Obligation*

There remains for consideration the third of the main questions
which were said to have been raised about moral obligation, viz.
the question: 'What is the character which an act must possess for
it to be one which we are morally bound to do?' or, as it is sometimes expressed, 'What is the criterion of duty?' To put the question
is to imply the idea that we can only be morally bound to do the
various acts which from time to time we are morally bound to do,
in virtue of some common character, their possession of this
character being what renders us bound to do them; this being
what we call the *basis* of our obligation to do them. And the idea
is at least very plausible, for unless it be true, it would seem that,
to use Joseph's phrase, 'our obligations will be an unconnected
heap',[1] and there will be no connexion between the nature of an
act which we are bound to do and our obligation to do it. And
given that we have the idea—and the idea is certainly shared by
most thinkers—we think of the question as one to which we are still
without the answer, since if we survey the acts of these various
kinds into which we ordinarily think duties fall, such as telling the
truth, sparing the feelings of others, and so on, it is not even
obvious that they have a common character. And even for practical purposes we seem to need the answer, since, unless we can
find it, it would seem that we never can be sure that any of the acts
which we ordinarily think duties are duties.

In considering the question, it seems best to begin by considering
the various answers it has received—these answers being what is
usually meant by theories of obligation. And the great divergences
between these theories suggest that the endeavour to find the right
answer is a long and laborious process. Of these I propose to consider first the theories which have been called by Paulsen and

[1] *Some Problems in Ethics*, 67.

Muirhead teleological, my reason being that once we have grasped their real nature, they are the easiest to make up our minds about once for all. Early in his *Methods of Ethics*, Sidgwick says:

It is not necessary, in the methodical investigation of right conduct, considered relatively to the end either of private or of general happiness, to assume that the end itself is determined or prescribed by reason: we only require to assume, in reasoning to cogent practical conclusions, that it is adopted as ultimate and paramount. For if a man accepts any end as ultimate and paramount, he accepts implicitly as his 'method of ethics' whatever process of reasoning enables him to determine the actions most conducive to this end.[1]

Unfortunately, although Sidgwick constantly makes use of the term 'end', he does little to explain what he means by it. But his use of the term seems to show that he uses it as a synonym for purpose, and this interpretation is borne out by his statement[2] that all he means by 'end' is 'an object of rational aim—whether attained in successive parts or not—which is not sought as a means to the attainment of any ulterior object, but for itself'. And if, as we seem to have to allow, this interpretation is right, by 'accepting X as an ultimate end' he must mean 'having X as our ultimate purpose'. This being so, Sidgwick is here laying down that to discover what he ought to do a man has only to discover what his end is and then discover what actions will most contribute to it. He is, therefore, implying the idea that, at any rate where we have something X as our purpose, the character which an act must have, to be what we ought to do, is that of contributing more than any other in our power to the realization of X. Now Sidgwick in making the statement quoted is not implying that we always have one and the same purpose or even that we always have a purpose. But some who have taken the same view about the connexion between our purpose, where we have one, and our duty, have held that we always have a purpose and that that purpose is always the same, and consequently according to them the task of discovering what we ought to do consists in ascertaining first what that purpose or end of ours is and then what the acts are on various occasions which would do most to effect its realization, the character required for an act to be what we ought to do being that of contributing most to its realization. And such a theory appears to be what Muirhead means by a 'teleological theory of duty'. For in

[1] Sidgwick, H., *Methods of Ethics*, p. 8; cf. p. 77 n.
[2] Ibid., p. 134.

E

Rule and End in Morals, although his language is vague, he refers to the theory which he thus designates as one which takes its start from the idea of benefits to oneself and others to be obtained, ends to be gained by the conduct in question, and deduces that of duty (i.e. deduces the duty of doing the action) from it.[1]

Further, Professor Muirhead makes a sweeping division of all theories of duty into two species, of which teleological theories form one, and of which the other consists of those in which the idea of an end is replaced by that of rules according to which men should direct their conduct; and he calls the latter deontological to mark their difference from the former. And among exponents of a teleological theory he includes both Plato and Aristotle, and of English thinkers Bentham and Mill, and, in recent times, Green and Bosanquet, and he seems to regard Kant as the most prominent exponent of the opposite theory.[2]

Now of teleological theories of duty there are really only two forms. For if we try to make out that we always have a single final end in action, there are only two things which it is at all plausible for us to represent as this end. These are (1) the realization of a life of enjoyment on our part, and (2) the realization of our own good, i.e. really the realization of the totality of things which will give us a life of satisfaction. On the one hand, we may, as Mill was, be struck by the idea that what we want for its own sake is always something we shall enjoy, and thence conclude that as we think of our life as going to continue, our purpose is always the realization of the things which will give us most enjoyment in life generally. On the other hand, we may be struck by the idea, as Plato, Aristotle, and Green undoubtedly were, that what we want for its own sake is always something which will give us satisfaction, and thence conclude that as we think of our life as going to continue, our purpose is always the realization of the totality of those things which will render us satisfied in life generally, those being what we call our own good. There is no third idea which has any plausibility whatever.

Further, between these two ideas there is no distinction of importance, as becomes obvious when we realize that each requires a certain correction. For the enjoyment of something which we enjoy, e.g. the enjoyment of seeing a beautiful landscape, is related to the thing we enjoy, not as a quality but as an effect,

---

[1] J. H. Muirhead, *Rule and End in Morals*, p. 3.
[2] Ibid., pp. 6–8.

being something excited by the thing we enjoy, so that if it be said that we desire some enjoyment for its own sake, the correct statement must be that we desire the experience, e.g. the seeing some beautiful landscape, for the sake of the feeling of enjoyment which we think it will cause, this feeling being really what we are desiring for its own sake. And for an exactly similar reason, when it is said that we desire for its own sake something which will gratify us, e.g. the thought that some friend is prosperous, the correct statement must be that what we are desiring for its own sake is the feeling of gratification, and that we are desiring the thought only for the sake of the feeling of gratification which we think it will cause. Hence, given the necessary correction, the one view will be that our final aim is our being constantly in the state of feeling enjoyment, and the other will be that it is our being constantly in the state of feeling gratified. And since it must be allowed that enjoyment and gratification are species of pleasure, the views only differ in that the one implies the idea that enjoyment is the only form of pleasure, and the other the idea that gratification is the only form of pleasure. Further, as there seems to be no denying that by being happy we mean being pleased, whether the being pleased takes the form of enjoying ourselves or of being gratified or, for that matter, of both at once, as obviously may happen, both views seem only different forms of the view that our final end or purpose is always our happiness.

It does not, however, take much consideration to discover that a teleological theory, whichever form it takes, is open to a fatal objection of principle. This is not that it represents as what renders some act a duty something which we know does not do so. This is undoubtedly an objection, and a fatal one. For we have only to ask ourselves whether some act's being that which would do most to make us happy would render it what we are bound to do, to *know* that it would not. The fatal objection of principle is that it resolves the moral 'ought' into the non-moral 'ought', representing our being morally bound to do some action as if it were the same thing as the action's being one which we must do if our purpose is to become realized. And in consequence, strictly speaking the theory is not a theory of *obligation*, or *duty*, at all, but, if anything, is a theory that what are called our obligations or duties are really something else.

An attempt to meet this criticism may be made in the way indicated by Muirhead, who himself accepts the teleological theory.

Attributing the theory to Plato, he represents Plato as, while agreeing with the extreme Sophists that all men are moved by desire of profit to themselves, meeting them by so deepening the meaning of profit as to make it scarcely recognizable under that name. And he represents Plato's argument thùs: 'Man sought his profit or advantage in all that he did. But there was all the difference in the world between the things in which he sought his profit: whether, for instance, he sought it in what satisfied the desires of the body which he appeared to be or those of the soul which he really was; in material possessions which are at best mere means, or in the possession of qualities which are good in themselves wholly independent of anything they bring.' And Muirhead then meets the objection that nevertheless Plato and the Sophists are agreed in principle by saying: 'If the meaning they respectively attach to profitableness does not constitute a difference of principle, what would? As well say that there is no difference of principle involved in a famous question as to the exchange value of the world as against one's soul.'[1] Here the argument is, of course, that Plato in differing from the Sophists as to what the actions are which are necessary for a man's attainment of his purpose, viz. happiness, and so are profitable to him, was altering the meaning of the term 'profit', and that, consequently, when he maintained that a man ought to satisfy his better desires, he was using the term 'ought' in a different sense from that in which the Sophists maintained that a man ought to satisfy his worst desires.

But unfortunately the argument fails. For (1) though, of course, there can be different views as to what is profitable, there are not two 'senses' of 'profitable', and even to differ from another as to what is profitable is to imply that there is only one sense. And (2) as Muirhead interprets Plato, Plato is differing from the Sophists about what a man ought to do, and, if so, he must be using 'ought' in the same sense as that in which the Sophists were using it, viz. the non-moral sense. Otherwise there need not be any quarrel between them. And the alleged difference of opinion, so far from implying that what they meant is different, implies that it is the same. Moreover, even Professor Muirhead's own language implies a tacit admission that a teleological theory is treating the moral 'ought' as having a non-moral sense. For he describes any opposed theory as *deontological*, and this amounts to saying that any opposed theory is one which represents duty as really duty and not

---

[1] The references are to *Rule and End in Morals*, pp. 24–5.

as something else, and therefore implies that a teleological theory does represent duty as something else. It should, however, be added as a matter of caution that it must not be assumed that this division of theories into teleological and deontological is correct, since if a thinker does not resolve the 'ought' of duty into the 'ought' of 'necessary for one's purpose', he may nevertheless be resolving it into another 'ought', and so not be a deontologist; and, as will be seen later,[1] this has been done.

It has to be admitted then that any teleological theory of duty can be rejected, even without considering its details, on the ground that it represents the moral 'ought' as if it were the non-moral 'ought', and so is not a theory of moral obligation at all.

It may be objected that, this being so, there cannot really have been any adherents of a teleological theory, since the difference of meaning of 'ought' in the two senses is so obvious that no one can have failed to be aware of it. To this, however, the reply can be made that there have been instances, and prominent instances, of this failure. The failure can, of course, take place in either of two ways. Someone may ask himself whether when we say that we are morally bound to do some action we mean the same thing as we do when, thinking of some action as necessary for some purpose, we say we ought to do it, and he may answer that we do. Or again, he may simply fail to notice the difference in meaning, i.e. fail to distinguish the things meant.

Now unquestionably Bentham did the former.

Nature [he says[2]] has placed mankind under the governance of two sovereign masters, *pain* and *pleasure*. It is for them alone to point out what we ought to do, as well as to determine what we shall do. On the one hand the standard of right and wrong, on the other the chain of causes and effects, are fastened to their throne. . . . The *principle of utility* recognises the subjection. . . . By the principle of utility is meant that principle which approves or disapproves of every action what-soever, according to the tendency which it appears to have to augment or diminish the happiness of the party whose interest is in question: or, what is the same thing in other words, to promote or to oppose that happiness. . . . Of an action that is conformable to the principle of utility, one may always say either that it is one that ought to be done, or at least that it is not one that ought not to be done. . . . *When thus interpreted, the words ought, and right and wrong, and others of that stamp, have a meaning: when otherwise, they have none.*[3]

[1] See Chapter 6.   [2] Selby-Bigge, *British Moralists*, i, pp. 339–42.
[3] The italics are mine.

This passage is, of course, sufficient to show that Bentham explicitly maintained that the so-called moral 'ought' is the non-moral 'ought', and the explicitness of his contention renders further comment superfluous. And the mistake is so obvious that it is not often made. But a failure to distinguish the two senses is common, and of this failure Mill and T. H. Green may be taken as instances illustrating the two forms which the teleological theory may take.

Mill so often uses the terms 'moral obligation', 'right' and 'wrong', and 'conscience' that at first we are very unwilling to allow that he is really failing to distinguish the moral from the non-moral 'ought'. And we are thrown off our guard by his initial statement of his doctrine, viz. that actions are right in proportion as they tend to promote happiness, wrong as they tend to promote unhappiness.[1] But we get a rude awakening when we find him saying on the next page that the basis of this doctrine is the theory that pleasure is the only thing which is desirable as an end, and then find later that he means by 'desirable as an end' desired for its own sake. And we have to conclude that his view is quite different when we take his statement of the basis of his doctrine along with (1) his statement:[2] 'All action is for the sake of some end, and rules of action, it seems natural to suppose, must take their whole character and colour from the end to which they are subservient', and (2) his idea that the proof of his view consists in showing that pleasure is the only thing which we want for its own sake.[3] It then becomes clear that his view is simply that what we ought to do is whatever would be most conducive to our pleasure or happiness, just because our pleasure or happiness is always our purpose. And the only comment needed is that this implies that 'ought' in the moral sense really only means necessary for the realization of our purpose, and so is not a theory of obligation at all.

Green, in the *Prolegomena to Ethics*, introduces his theory of obligation by giving an account of the motive of all deliberate action which is rather like Aristotle's. He contrasts what he calls moral actions in the sense of actions which may be good or bad, i.e. actions which would be called deliberate actions, with instinctive actions. And he maintains that what distinguishes a moral, i.e. a deliberate, action from an instinctive action is that what determines it is not an impulse but what he calls a motive, consisting of a desire for personal good in some form or other; meaning

[1] Mill, *Utilitarianism*, p. 8.   [2] Ibid., p. 2.
[3] See ibid., chapter iv.

by an instinctive action one not determined by a conception, on the part of the agent, of any good to be gained or evil to be avoided by the agent. It is superfluous, he continues, to add good *to himself*, for anything conceived as good in such a way that the agent acts for the sake of it must be conceived as *his own* good (i.e. as a good to himself), though he may conceive it as his own good only on account of his interest in others, and in spite of any amount of incidental suffering on his own part.[1] A little later, however,[2] when he takes into account the fact that an agent thinks of himself as having a future and as having various desires to be satisfied, he substantially modifies this account and represents the desire which forms the motive of every moral action, virtuous or vicious, as the desire of some possible state or achievement of his own as being for the time his greatest good—Esau's motive, e.g., in selling his birthright, being the desire of the satisfaction of his hunger, as that which for the time he conceives as his greatest good. And, as the sequel shows, this is his more considered doctrine.

Here Green is plainly intending to state what he considers to be our *final* purpose when acting deliberately; and, as he explains later[3] that he means by 'good' such as will satisfy desire, and as his usual use of the phrase 'a good' is in conformity with this explanation, his general statement must be an inaccurate statement of the view which he is expressing. For something which excites satisfaction, e.g. the thought of some friend's success, is related to the satisfaction as cause to effect, and therefore to desire something as a good, i.e. as something which excites satisfaction, is to desire it not for itself but for the sake of the satisfaction which it will excite. And, therefore, to express his view accurately he should have said that our motive is always the desire of a life of satisfaction, and that in desiring what we consider our greatest good, we are desiring this only as a means to our final end, viz. the continued realization of a state of satisfaction. It, therefore, may be noticed incidentally that although he regards Mill, a psychological hedonist, as his chief opponent, the line dividing himself from Mill is very thin; Mill considers the only form of happiness to be enjoyment, while Green considers it to be satisfaction.

Now the contention that in *all* deliberate action our motive is desire of a continued state of satisfaction has, of course, an awkward implication. For we ordinarily regard a good act as distin-

[1] *Prolegomena to Ethics*, §§ 91–2.   [2] Ibid., §§ 95–9; cf. § 128.
[3] Ibid., § 171.

guished from a bad one by its motive, and yet if in all actions our
motive is the same, this idea must be false, and it will only be
possible to hold that what really distinguishes the acts which we
ordinarily regard as good and as bad is a difference of opinion as
to how a continued state of satisfaction is to be attained. The contention therefore implies the view that our ordinary idea of what
distinguishes good from bad acts is mistaken. But the contention
does not *by itself* involve a teleological theory of obligation. Acceptance of it, no doubt, involves us in holding that what we ought to
do in the non-moral sense is whatever would cause us most satisfaction. But such acceptance does not preclude us from thinking,
as I have contended Plato thought,[1] that there are such things as
moral obligations, distinct from obligations in the non-moral sense,
although if we do, we shall have to allow that we shall carry out
our moral obligations only so far as, and because, we think that
doing so will be what would give us most satisfaction. So far, then,
Green has said nothing which commits him to a teleological theory
of duty.

But in Book III he does. For after reiterating that his account of
moral actions, which he now calls acts of will, is formal, i.e. is an
account of all acts of will whether good or bad, he lays down that
the distinction between the good will and the bad will must be at
the root of any system of ethics. And to do this is to imply that he
has the idea that he, like others, has to find the character of an act,
required to render the doing of it a duty, in its goodness. And as,
according to Green, the motive of all deliberate acts whether good
or bad is the same, viz. the desire of continued satisfaction, what
Green must be considering as that whose goodness renders an
action a duty is its contributing most to the continued satisfaction
which is the agent's purpose—since there is no other alternative
open to him. He must therefore be thinking of the moral 'ought' as
if it were the same thing as the non-moral 'ought', i.e. representing
our duty of doing some action as being its contributing most to the
realization of our purpose. Consequently it is not surprising to find
that later[2] he expresses this view almost in so many words. Apparently speaking of a man's desire to satisfy himself as the impulse
which becomes the source, according to the direction it takes, both
of vice and of virtue, he speaks of this impulse thus:

It is the source of vicious self-seeking and self-assertion, so far as the

---

[1] pp. 103–11.   [2] *Prolegomena*, § 171.

spirit which is in man seeks to satisfy itself or to realise its capabilities in modes in which, according to the law which its divine origin imposes on it and which is equally the law of the universe and of human society, its self-satisfaction or self-realisation is not to be found. . . . So it is again with the man who seeks to assert himself, to realise himself, to show what he has in him to be, in achievements which may make the world wonder, but which in their social effects are such that the human spirit, according to the law of its being, which is a law of development in society, is not advanced but hindered by them in the realisation of its capabilities. He is living for ends of which the divine principle that forms his self alone renders him capable, but these ends, because in their attainment one is exalted by the depression of others, are not in the direction in which that principle can really fulfil the promise and potency which it contains.[1]

It seems clear, then, that Green must be holding that what renders an act good and so what we ought to do is its contributing most to our purpose, viz. our continued satisfaction, and must therefore equally with Mill be resolving the moral into the non-moral 'ought'.

Yet it may be objected to this interpretation (1) that Green constantly insists that we have and are influenced by disinterested desires for the welfare of others, and so cannot be holding that at bottom all our actions are selfish; and (2) that in him the idea of duty is plainly so vivid that he, least of all men, can have resolved the 'moral' into the 'non-moral' 'ought'. These objections need consideration, especially as no reference so far has been made to an idea which is prominent in his exposition of this theory of obligation, viz. the idea that the existence of obligations among a group of men implies that of what he calls 'a common good'.

In his lectures on Political Obligation, where, though he is primarily occupied with a question about a particular obligation, viz. 'Why is a subject bound to obey his ruler?', he has also to state a general theory of obligation, Green insists that there are no such things as natural obligations in the sense of obligations independent of what he calls a society. And as a close examination of his use of the phrase 'a society' will show, he really means by 'a society' not a society in any ordinary sense but a group of persons which satisfies what he considers the two conditions necessary for the existence of a system of obligations. These are (1) that each of the members has as his own good, and so as his purpose in action, the totality consisting of the various goods of each member, this

[1] Ibid., § 176.

totality being referred to by Green as the public good,[1] or as the 'general interest' or 'general well-being' of the members;[2] and (2) that there are rules devised by a regulating body, the observance of which is required for the realization of this public good. And it is implied that a man's obligations consist in obeying the rules of a group to which he belongs, and that the reason why he ought to obey these rules is that obedience is necessary for the attainment of his purpose, viz. his own good, it, however, happening that his purpose is identical with that of the other members of the group, since the good of each is the same, viz. the respective goods of all the members of the group.

In consequence Green is able to make it appear as though in his view (1) a man in carrying out his duties is actuated by public spirit and not by self-interest, and (2) the acts which are a man's duties at least correspond to the acts we ordinarily think duties, since it is at least plausible to say that the latter are for the public interest; and this correspondence at any rate helps to disguise Green's resolution of the moral into the non-moral 'ought'.

The question, however, at once arises: Can Green justify his contention that what he calls the public good, i.e. the totality consisting of the good of each member, is the good of each member, so that they have a *common* good, two members, A and B, e.g., having as their own good one and the same thing? For prima facie, at least, the existence of such a thing as what Green calls 'a common good' is impossible. By 'a good to a man A' he means a something which excites, i.e. directly excites, satisfaction in A, and by 'A's good' the totality of the things which excite satisfaction in A. And the only thing which can excite satisfaction in A is a state or activity of his own, such as the thought that another man B is satisfied. Consequently nothing can be a good to A and also to another man B, unless in reality B is not a person other than but actually identical with A, so that what we should call B's thought, e.g. that B is satisfied, is really A's thought. No doubt in certain instances the satisfaction which each has implies a common *object of desire*. Thus the satisfaction which each gets from thinking that B is satisfied implies a *desire* by each for the satisfaction of B. But it is not the satisfaction of B which gives them satisfaction but their thought that B is satisfied, as is obvious from the fact that even where B is satisfied A and B could get no satisfaction unless they either knew or believed that B was satisfied. Consequently it cannot be maintained that A and B can have a good in common or, again, their good in common, unless it be maintained that A and B are really the same individual.[1]

Strangely enough, although it is not obvious on the surface, this is just what Green does maintain. Though he insists that we always seek our own satisfaction, there is nothing which he emphasizes more than our possession of *disinterested* interests, of which the most obvious are benevolence, i.e. a disinterested interest in the welfare of others, and interests in the welfare of other members of our family or of our country.[2] 'These', he says,[3] 'are not merely interests dependent on other persons for the means to their gratification, but interests in the good of those other persons, interests which cannot be satisfied without the consciousness that those other persons are satisfied.' And by way of emphasizing their disinterestedness he ridicules[3] the idea that the man who looks forward to the well-being of his family after he is dead is desiring the satisfaction of seeing it well off. Further, he evidently considers that often we act on the desires involved in such interests, and so have the satisfaction of certain others as our end. Consequently he has to reconcile this conviction with his idea of the nature of all deliberate action, with which it at least seems utterly inconsistent. To do this, it would, of course, be useless for him to contend that when the desire moving us seems to be the desire of something which would excite satisfaction in another for its own sake, it is really the desire of this as a means to something which would excite satisfaction in ourselves. For to do this would be to deny the disinterestedness of the desire. Nor does he do so. Anxious to maintain the disinterestedness at all costs, he tries to effect the reconciliation by what is really the only method open to him, viz. that of contending that where one man A has a disinterested interest in another, B, B is identical with A.

The first hint of this view is given in paragraph 200 of the *Prolegomena*. There, apropos of the interest in other persons, or, as he also calls it, a distinctively social interest, he speaks of the feeling of pleasure or pain which arises in response to manifested pleasure or pain on the part of another sentient being, and he says that this feeling does not contain the germ of such an interest unless the subject of it is conscious of the agent occasioning the feeling as an

---

[1] It may be noted that for the same reason there cannot be such a thing as a *goodness* common to two people unless they are one and the same.

[2] *Prolegomena*, § 167.   [3] Ibid., § 199.

'alter ego'. And later on (paragraphs 229–32), the view is stated, though we may fail to notice this from reluctance to think that he intends his statements to be taken literally.

He speaks (paragraph 229) of a man who reflects on the transitoriness of the pleasures by the imagination of which his desires are from hour to hour excited, and asks himself what can satisfy the self which abides throughout and survives those desires. And he says of such a man that his mind becomes possessed by the thought of the well-being of a family, with which he identifies himself, and of which the continuity is as his own (i.e. with whose members he thinks of himself as identical and whose continuity therefore he thinks of as his own continuity). He also speaks of him as looking forward to the well-being of his family, even though he may expect to be laid in the grave before it is realized, and as in doing so thinking of himself as still living in this welfare when dead, thus immortalizing himself (i.e. thinking of himself as immortal). Again later (paragraph 231) he says: 'At a stage of intellectual development when any theories of immortality would be unmeaning to them, men have already, in the thought of a society of which the life is their own life but which survives them, a medium in which they carry themselves forward beyond the limits of animal existence.' Lastly, in paragraph 232, he speaks of a man's thought of himself as permanent as inseparable from an identification of himself with others in whose continued life he contemplates himself as living, and he draws the general conclusion that the distinction commonly supposed to exist between considerate benevolence and reasonable self-love, as co-ordinate principles on which moral approbation is founded, is a fiction of philosophers.[1]

The underlying thought is obvious. Assuming it to be undeniable that in certain instances a man A has a disinterested desire for something which will satisfy another, B, he is contending that the disinterestedness of the desire implies that B is really identical with A and so not another at all. Again, assuming it to be undeniable that A in having this desire is thinking of B's satisfaction as being his own satisfaction in being B's, he is contending that this thought implies that A is thinking of B as being himself. The doctrine indeed is that foreshadowed by Plato where he says of the just citystate that it is one in which the largest number apply the terms 'mine' and 'non-mine' to the same things in the same respects, and

---

[1] Cf. § 233 end, where he speaks of the *identity* as distinct from the *co-ordination* of these principles.

implies that the application applies *inter alia* to pleasures and pains.[1]

The net result is that, according to Green, where the members of a group of two or more persons are disinterestedly interested in one another's welfare they are really only one person, and not more than one at all—a state of B, e.g., being related to a state of A in exactly the same way that some other state of A is related to that state of A, the states being all states of one and only one self. Consequently Green, in thinking as he does of the duties of the members of the group as consisting in carrying out rules devised for the greatest satisfaction possible of the group, is thinking of the carrying out of their duties as a sort of enlarged prudence, i.e. a prudence enlarged by taking into account the fact that the self to be made happy is the so-called plurality of selves taken together. And thereby Green seems able to represent a man who does his duty as at once acting *both* disinterestedly *and interestedly*, thus seeming to be able to have it both ways.[2]

Comment on Green's view that a duty implies the existence of a common good is, of course, almost superfluous once it is realized that a common good requires the identity of the persons to whom the good is common. For whatever be the paradox which the exigencies of a theory may tempt us to maintain, there is in the end no denying that two individuals, however disinterestedly interested in the welfare of each other, are two persons and not one, and indeed that for an interest in another to be *disinterested* that other has to be *another*, since otherwise it would not be *disinterested*. Three minor comments, however, may perhaps be usefully made. (1) Green, instead of trying to make his theory fit the facts, is trying to make the facts fit his theory. Starting with the idea that a man can only desire his own satisfaction, when he comes to consider disinterested desires, instead of abandoning his idea, as he should have done, he represents them as really interested. (2) By doing this, he resolves benevolence into self-love and so abolishes it, thereby rendering himself open to a criticism which he passes on the Hedonists. (3) Even on its own lines Green's doctrine is exposed to two very awkward objections. For (*a*) plainly in fact a man A may have a disinterested interest in B without B's having a disinterested interest in A, and in such a case Green would have to allow that A was identical with B, without B's being identical with A. And (*b*) plainly malevolence, i.e. a disinterested

---

[1] *Republic*, p. 462.   [2] Cf. *Prolegomena*, § 203.

interest in the unhappiness of another, is, as he himself admits,[1] as much a fact as is benevolence. He would, therefore, have to allow that malevolence equally with benevolence implies the identity of the persons concerned, and therefore also that where A desires the unhappiness of B, he is in doing so desiring his own unhappiness.

VI. *Quasi-teleological Theories of Obligation*

Teleological theories of obligation are based on two general ideas, first, that in all deliberate action we have a single final aim or purpose, and second, that an act is rendered what we ought to do by being that which conduces most to the realization of this aim, so that to discover what we ought to do we have first to discover what this aim is, and then to discover the act which would most conduce to its realization. And, as has been contended, these theories break down because we have no single final aim and because, if we had, these theories would resolve the moral into the non-moral 'ought'. Nevertheless, it may be contended that they are on the right track in making use of the idea that in action we have an aim or purpose, and that given a certain, though no doubt a radical, alteration in the first general idea, a tenable theory can be found. This consists in substituting for the idea that there is a single something at which we *are aiming*, the idea that there is a single something at which we *ought* to aim, and thereby representing an act as rendered what we ought to do by being the most conducive to whatever it be that we ought to aim at—as distinct from our actually aiming at it.

Theories which involve this idea may, for lack of a better term, be called quasi-teleological, and Sidgwick goes so far as to maintain that they form one of the two main kinds into which all theories of obligation fall, their underlying ideas being held by all except those who consider that there are kinds of action which in their nature are duties, and whose views he calls intuitional.[2] And in view of their at least seeming to have an affinity with teleological theories they seem to be those which next need consideration.

Such theories will, of course, differ from one another by the particular view taken of what we ought to aim at. And according to Sidgwick[3] there are four which deserve serious consideration,

[1] *Prolegomena*, § 161.
[2] *Methods of Ethics*[7], pp. 1–3. Inconsistently with this, however, p. 8 and p. 77 (note) he admits teleological theories of a third kind.
[3] Ibid., p. 9.

viz. those which represent what we ought to aim at as respectively (1) our own happiness, (2) the general happiness, (3) our own perfection, and (4) the perfection of human beings generally. And strangely enough, he maintains, inconsistently, that *two* of these theories are true, viz. the first and the second, as though there could be two things which are what we ought to aim at.

The two general ideas underlying such views are of course very attractive. For when we reflect we are apt to think (1) that there must be some one thing at which we ought to aim in acting, however difficult its discovery seems to be. And if we think this, we are also apt to think (2) that the character of what we ought to do must be determined by the character of what we ought to aim at, what we ought to do having to be what would be most conducive to what we ought to aim at, so that the initial task has to be that of discovering what we ought to aim at.

Nevertheless, when we consider the first of these underlying ideas we find it exposed to an objection so formidable that it is advisable to consider it before considering any particular theory or what Sidgwick has to say in favour of the first and the second.

The objection can be stated thus: In ordinary speech a statement containing the term 'ought' in the moral sense is always of the form: 'I ought to do so and so', i.e. I ought to effect a certain change, or else, if this elucidation of 'doing something' be not accepted, to make an effort to effect a certain change, and so, on either alternative, to perform a certain activity. But by 'aiming at something X', or 'having something X as our aim', we mean having X as our purpose, and by 'having X as our purpose' we mean having the desire of X as our motive, i.e. being moved to act by the desire of X, so that the statement 'I ought to aim at X' will mean: 'I ought to be moved to act by the desire of X.' The question therefore arises: Can a statement of this form be true if the term 'ought' be used in the moral sense? And the answer seems to have to be 'No', on the ground that a moral obligation is by its very nature a moral obligation to perform some activity, and that therefore there cannot be such a thing as a moral obligation to be moved by a certain desire, since whatever our being so moved may be, it is not an activity. To this reason can be added another, viz. that we can only be bound to do what it is in our power to do, and while it is in our power to perform certain activities, it is not in our power to desire something, still less to desire it enough to enable

us to overcome some aversion, and still less again to be moved to
act solely by the desire.

No doubt we think that we can often do something to excite or
to strengthen a desire of which we already have the capacity. Thus
we may think that by making ourselves dwell more upon the
advantages of some piece of hard work we can bring ourselves to
desire it more, and that we can stimulate, or strengthen, the desire
to relieve A's suffering by imagining his suffering, or by imagining
it more fully. But to think that we ought to stimulate or to
strengthen a certain desire is one thing, and to think that we ought
to act from that desire is another. To think the former is really to
think that we ought to *do* a certain action, viz. that act which will
stimulate or strengthen the desire; and though that act may render
it more likely that we shall act from that desire, it is different from
acting from that desire.

These reasons receive confirmation in two ways. For, first, if we
ask of some particular desire, e.g. the desire to help our friend A,
'Is it a *duty* on our part to be moved by it to act?' we answer 'No',
although we may wish to be moved by it on account of its goodness, and may think it a duty to do some act to which the desire
prompts us. And, second, if we consider any instance of what we do
in fact think a duty we find that it always consists simply in doing
a certain action, e.g. paying a certain debt, and not in doing it
from a certain motive, e.g. paying the debt from desire to help the
creditor, and that, therefore, we do not in fact think of the duty as
including the having a certain motive. In addition we find that
when we consider whether some past act is one which the agent
ought to have done, we think the question independent of the
question of what his motive was in doing it; we think, e.g., that
the question whether X ought to have paid the bill he paid is
independent of whether he paid it, e.g., to retain his neighbour's goodwill or to spite a third party, although of course we
think the latter question bears on the *goodness* or *badness* of his
action.

Underlying this objection is the idea that an act has a character
of its own which is independent of that of its motive, so that it is
possible to do the same act from different motives. And anyone
trying to meet the objection can do so only in one or other of two
ways. For he must either accept this underlying idea or else attempt
to reject it. If he accepts it, his attempt has to take the form of contending that in spite of the difference between doing some action

and being moved to do it by a desire, the term 'ought' in the moral sense is applicable to some things of the latter kind as well as to some things of the former kind; and this view is, in fact, taken by Sidgwick when he speaks of acts as capable of two kinds of rightness, which he calls objective and subjective rightness, the former being the rightness of the act and the latter the rightness of the motive. Such an attempt, however, must be admitted to fail, on the ground that it is really self-evident that an obligation is necessarily an obligation to perform a certain action, and not to have a certain motive. He may, however, attempt to reject the idea on the ground that an act has no character which is independent of that of its motive, and if he succeeds in establishing the dependence of the character of the act on that of its motive, he will then have an effective way of meeting the objection. For he can then argue thus: It is admitted by everyone, including the objector, that an obligation is necessarily an obligation to do some action, i.e. some particular action. But the character of a particular action being dependent on, and so inseparable from, that of its motive, to assert that there is an obligation to do some particular action is really to assert that there is an obligation to do an action having a certain motive, and so is to assert that there is an obligation to have that motive. And, therefore, the ground is cut from under the objector's feet, since the very thing which he contends there is an obligation to do is, as is obvious when its nature is apprehended, an action having a certain motive—and, therefore, it must be true that there is something at which a man ought to aim.

Now Joseph in *Some Problems of Ethics*[1] takes this course. He allows that an obligation is always an obligation to do some *action*. But he distinguishes two senses of 'action', viz. (1) that in which we speak of an automatic action, e.g. locking a desk from force of habit, as an action (he calls this an act of behaviour), and (2) that in which we speak of a deliberate action as an action; and he maintains that 'ought' and 'ought not' are applicable only to actions in the second sense. He then insists that actions in this sense include a motive. 'I submit then', he says, 'that there is no action in which we must not include a motive: at least none that concerns Ethics.'[2] And he states the reason thus: 'No act exists except in the doing of it, and in the doing of it there is a motive; and you cannot separate the doing of it from the motive without

---

[1] Joseph, H. W. B., *Some Problems in Ethics*, chaps. iv and v.
[2] Ibid., p. 43.

substituting for action in the moral sense action in the physical, mere movements of bodies.' And a little later[1] he adds:

What is left, if you take away the motive, is conscious behaviour like that of animals. . . . Whether there be not, in some animals, the germ of action proper, I do not discuss: but if there be, the instances of it are not behaviour and something besides, an undeveloped motive: the behaviour is no longer itself just the same. And so an act proper is not analysable into behaviour and motive; it is indivisible. You cannot conceive that the motive might be taken away, and the behaviour left really the same.

Further, in accordance with this he denies that it is possible for the same act to be done from different motives, contending that, e.g., eating a plateful of oysters is different when done (a) by someone who is fond of oysters and eats them for the sake of their flavour, (b) by someone who loathes them but eats them to avoid hurting his host's feelings, and (c) by someone who loathes or is indifferent to them but eats them to prevent his neighbour's getting a second helping.[2] To the objection that it is not in our power to act from some particular desire, he replies as follows: When I do have a certain desire, it may be my duty to act on it. Thus if I am prompted by affection to do some act of kindness but hesitate from desire to amuse myself, I ought to do the act of kindness, and ought to do it because it would be prompted by affection. On the other hand, when I do not have a certain desire it may be my duty to do the act to which the desire would have prompted me from another motive, viz. the idea that I ought to do the act as one which would realize a certain goodness,[3] this being different from the idea of duty in general, and in that case the act will be a duty because it would have this motive.[4] And as regards this second contention, Joseph is alive to the objection that an act cannot be rendered a duty by being one which if a man were to do it he would do because he thought it a duty. But he considers that he escapes it because the motive which he is attributing to himself in the instance taken is not the idea of duty in general (i.e., really, the idea that he ought to do the act as being one of a system of duties), but the idea that he ought to do the act as being one which would realize a certain goodness. Here, however, it must be allowed that he is mistaken; for he *is* representing as the reason why he ought to do the act the

[1] *Some Problems of Ethics*, pp. 45-6.   [2] Ibid., p. 45.
[3] This seems the only way of understanding an obscure passage, ibid., pp. 46-7.
[4] Ibid., pp. 47-8.

fact that it would have as its motive the thought that he ought to do it, and to represent the agent as having as his special reason for this thought that the act would have a certain goodness makes no difference whatever.

We have now to consider this view. It should first be noticed that Joseph cannot here be stating his doctrine accurately. When he uses the phrase 'separating an action from its motive' he is undoubtedly thinking of an act of abstraction, and means by it abstracting an act from its motive, i.e. considering an action in abstraction from, i.e. without taking into account, its motive. Hence when he says 'you cannot separate the doing of an action from its motive without substituting for action in the moral sense mere movements of bodies' (i.e. acts of behaviour), he cannot be intending to say exactly what he does. For if he were he would be implying that the abstracting is possible, and that when we perform it, i.e. consider an act in the moral sense in abstraction from its motive, we find that it is an act of behaviour. And that it is an act of behaviour is just what he is denying. What he must really be meaning, i.e. intending to say, is that to abstract an act in the moral sense from its motive, i.e. to consider it in abstraction from its motive, is *impossible*; and he must be implying as the reason for this that an action in the moral sense has no *character* of its own, i.e. one which is independent of that of its motive. And what he says about substituting for an act in the moral sense an act of behaviour must be regarded as offering a *reductio ad absurdum* to show the impossibility of the abstraction, the argument really being that if you try to perform the abstraction, you will find yourself trying to think of a moral action as an act of behaviour, which you know it is not.

Certain parallels will make the doctrine clearer. If we try to think of some universal, e.g. greenness, in abstraction from some instance, i.e. some particular colour, we find that we cannot, the reason being that a universal has no nature which is independent of its relation to instances of it. And the difficulties which we find in admitting the reality of universals arise from our trying to think of them as things having a nature which is independent of their relation to instances of them. Again, while we can consider the movement of a piece of lead in abstraction from its being the movement of *a piece of lead*, as we do when we consider it as the movement of a body, we cannot consider it in abstraction from its being the movement of *a body*, just because a movement has no nature, apart from its being the movement of a body. For a similar reason, though we can consider the pitch of a particular sound in abstraction from its being the pitch of *that sound*, we cannot consider it in abstraction from its being the pitch of *a sound*, and if we try we shall find ourselves ceasing to think of anything at all. In the same way Joseph is really contending that no moral action can be considered apart from its motive because it has *no* nature independently of its motive; and this view is implied when he maintains that to do the same action from different motives is impossible.

It has, however, to be admitted that when the nature of Joseph's view is thus made clear it is on the face of it untenable. For if an action in the moral sense has no character independently of that of its motive, there is no action for a motive to be the motive of, and therefore no motive either. Indeed, on this view what is called doing a certain action from a certain motive cannot even be illustrated. And even Joseph in giving illustrations of motives is forced to use language which implies, contrary to his theory, that the acts of which they are the motives have a nature which is independent of their motives, referring to the act, e.g., as one of eating a plateful of oysters, where *ex hypothesi* the act to which he is referring is not an act of mere behaviour. And no escape from this procedure is possible, because otherwise he cannot state what the motive of which he is thinking is the motive of. It should, moreover, be added that Joseph in trying to show that acts are done from different motives does not choose his instances quite fairly. For the acts of his three oyster-eaters are, on his own description of them, acts which will have different effects and so are really different actions irrespective of their motive. And if, as it seems clear that he could and should have done, he had taken as instances acts of which the effects would have been the same, it would not have been possible for him to deny that the acts were the same in spite of the differences of motive.

Yet this criticism may provoke a retort. 'The preceding argument', it may be said, 'is undeniably hard to refute. But there must be a mistake somewhere. For at any rate when we are considering actions already done we distinguish them as good or bad or neither according to their motive, thereby implying the idea that acts differ on account of a difference of motive, and that even where these effects are the same, but the motives are different, the acts are different.'

To speak thus, however, is to imply the idea that an action is something which includes a motive, and though, no doubt, we often think of an act thus, the idea cannot be right. An act, no doubt, must have a motive. But one thing may be necessary to another without being part of it. We cannot, e.g., think without mental imagining; but though mental imagining is necessary to a process of argument, it is not part of it. Again, we cannot hit something unless there is something to hit, or know something unless there is something to be known, yet the thing to be hit is not *part* of the hitting it and the thing to be known is not a *part* or a *constituent*, to adopt a phrase sometimes used, of the knowing it. And similarly a motive, though necessary to an action, is not a part of it. By the term 'action' we mean an activity of a certain kind, though of what kind we may find it difficult to say. But the being moved by some desire to perform an activity of a certain kind is not an *activity*. And should anyone be inclined to persist in maintaining that an action includes a motive, he should ask: 'If so, what is that part of an action which is not a motive?' The answer will have to be 'an action', since that is that to which a motive moves us; and then an action will be represented as being part of itself, which is, of course, impossible. And this being so it must be allowed that when we speak of actions as good or bad in respect of their motives, we should, to be accurate, restrict the application of the terms 'good' and 'bad' to their motives, and refuse to apply them to the actions. In conclusion it may be noted that if Joseph were right the question which we frequently put to ourselves: 'Ought we to do so and so?' must be an improper question. For in asking this we mean by 'doing so and so' such things as going to bed, or knocking someone down, or, if not, at least making an effort which we think likely to have a certain effect, and according to Joseph, such a question is as improper as the question: 'Is a noise greedy?'

The general conclusion reached is, of course, that there cannot be anything at which we ought to aim in action, the ground for this conclusion being that to aim at something is to have the desire of it as our motive and there cannot be an obligation to have a certain motive. And, incidentally, the conclusion has been reached that where there is an obligation to do some action it is independent of what our motive would be if we were to do it, so that if we were to do the action we should carry out the obligation, whatever our motive in doing so was.

This conclusion is, of course, the conclusion that the first of the two ideas underlying quasi-teleological theories of obligation is mistaken. But when we consider the second, viz. the idea that what we ought to do is whatever would most conduce to what we ought to aim at, we find that it also must be mistaken. For it can only be true if there be something at which we ought to aim, and there is not. But even if we thought that there were something at which we ought to aim, we could not vindicate the second idea. No doubt there is plausibility in Sidgwick's assertion that it can hardly be denied that the recognition of an end as ultimately reasonable (i.e. as something which we ought to have as our ultimate aim) involves the recognition of an obligation to do such acts as most conduce to the end.[1] But this is not really so. For even if we were bound to have something X as our final end, we should not *in consequence* be bound to do what would most conduce to X, nor would it be self-evident that we ought to do what would most conduce to X as being what we ought to aim at, and so irrespectively of whether we are aiming at it.

Quasi-teleological theories then can be rejected on general grounds, and so irrespectively of the special character which distinguishes one from another. Therefore, strictly speaking, there is no need to consider them. Nevertheless, Sidgwick is so emphatic in maintaining the truth of two of them, viz. that we ought to aim at, respectively, our own happiness and the general happiness, that it seems worth while to consider what he has to say on their behalf.

He prepares the ground for his vindication of these theories by urging that they are widely accepted either by men in ordinary life or by theorists. As regards acceptance of the idea that we ought to aim at our own happiness he argues as follows: The teacher of an art who advances an imperative of skill assumes that a man wants that to which the imperative relates, e.g. a physician in telling a man that he ought to take hard exercise assumes that he wants health. And it is sometimes maintained that someone who advances a prudential imperative, e.g. that you ought to make friends,[2] assumes that the man to whom it is addressed wants that to which the imperative relates, viz. his own happiness, and that if he does not, the imperative is untrue. But this contention is false. For

We do not all look with simple indifference on a man who declines to take the right means to attain his own happiness, on no other ground than that he does not care about happiness. Most men would regard

---

[1] *Methods of Ethics*, p. 35.   [2] The instance is mine.

such a refusal as irrational, with a certain disapprobation; they would thus implicitly assent to Butler's statement that 'interest, one's own happiness, is a manifest obligation,' though the phrase might strike them as unusual. In other words, they would think that he *ought* to care for his own happiness. The word 'ought' thus used is no longer relative: happiness now appears as an ultimate end prescribed by reason.[1]

Here it need only be noted (1) that the argument is curiously weak, since while the conclusion drawn is that most men think that a man ought to be moved by the desire of his own happiness, he only urges in support of it that most men *disapprove* a man's *refusal* to do what his happiness requires on the ground that he does not want happiness—which is quite different, and (2) that the conclusion is palpably false since no man thinks it a *duty* to be moved by the desire of his happiness.

As regards acceptance of the idea that we ought to aim at the general happiness, he contends (1) that the moral rules prescribed to one another are really—though in part unconsciously—prescribed as means to the general happiness, and (2) that Utilitarians even more widely think that such rules are only valid so far as they conduce to the general happiness. And about these contentions it need only be remarked that neither does anything towards showing that any men think that they ought to *aim at* the general happiness.

Having thus prepared the ground, Sidgwick offers his vindication of the two theories in an obscure passage of Chapter XIII in Book III of his *Methods of Ethics*, in which he is looking about for principles of obligation which are really self-evident.

The principle just discussed, which seems to be more or less clearly implied in the common notion of 'fairness' or 'equity', is obtained by considering the similarity of the individuals that make up a Logical Whole or Genus. There are others, no less important, which emerge in the consideration of the similar parts of a Mathematical or Quantitative Whole. Such a Whole is presented in the common notion of the Good —or, as is sometimes said, 'good on the whole'—of any individual human being. The proposition 'that one ought to aim at one's own good' is sometimes given as the maxim of Rational Self-love or Prudence: but as so stated it does not clearly avoid tautology; since we may define 'good' as 'what one ought to aim at'. If, however, we say 'one's good on the whole', the addition suggests a principle which, when explicitly stated, is, at any rate, not tautological. I have already referred to this principle[2] as that 'of impartial concern for all parts of our

---

[1] *Methods of Ethics*, p. 7.   [2] Cf. ibid., note to p. 124.

conscious life': we might express it concisely by saying 'that Hereafter *as such* is to be regarded neither less nor more than Now'. It is not, of course, meant that the good of the present may not reasonably be preferred to that of the future on account of its greater certainty: or again, that a week ten years hence may not be more important to us than a week now, through an increase in our means or capacities of happiness. All that the principle affirms is that the mere difference of priority and posteriority in time is not a reasonable ground for having more regard to the consciousness of one moment than to that of another. The form in which it practically presents itself to most men is 'that a smaller present good is not to be preferred to a greater future good' (allowing for difference of certainty): since Prudence is generally exercised in restraining a present desire (the object or satisfaction of which we commonly regard as *pro tanto* 'a good'), on account of the remoter consequences of gratifying it. The commonest view of the principle would no doubt be that the present *pleasure* or *happiness* is reasonably to be foregone with the view of obtaining greater pleasure or happiness hereafter: but the principle need not be restricted to a hedonistic application; it is equally applicable to any other interpretation of 'one's own good', in which good is conceived as a mathematical whole, of which the integrant parts are realized in different parts or moments of a lifetime. And therefore it is perhaps better to distinguish it here from the principle 'that Pleasure is the sole Ultimate Good', which does not seem to have any logical connexion with it.

So far we have only been considering the 'Good on the Whole' of a single individual: but just as this notion is constructed by comparison and integration of the different 'goods' that succeed one another in the series of our conscious states, so we have formed the notion of Universal Good by comparison and integration of the goods of all individual human—or sentient—existences. And here again, just as in the former case, by considering the relation of the integrant parts to the whole and to each other, I obtain the self-evident principle that the good of any one individual is of no more importance, from the point of view (if I may say so) of the Universe, than the good of any other; unless, that is, there are special grounds for believing that more good is likely to be realised in the one case than in the other. And it is evident to me that as a rational being I am bound to aim at good generally,—so far as it is attainable by my efforts,—not merely at a particular part of it.

From these two rational intuitions we may deduce, as a necessary inference, the maxim of Benevolence in an abstract form: viz. that each one is morally bound to regard the good of any other individual as much as his own, except in so far as he judges it to be less, when impartially viewed, or less certainly knowable or attainable by him.[1]

---

[1] *Methods of Ethics*, pp. 380–2.

The passage is evidently intended to convince us of the self-evidence of two principles which he calls the principles of Prudence and Rational Benevolence. Unfortunately it is obscure owing to its use of vague phrases such as 'impartial concern for', 'reasonably to be preferred to', and 'of importance to'; but there seem to be three main clues to its interpretation, viz. (1) the designation of the principles as those of *Prudence* and *Rational Benevolence*, which implies that the principles concern a man's motive, (2) his idea that the self-evidence of each is connected with the necessary relation which must hold between a certain whole and its parts, and (3) his idea that the procedure by which the second principle becomes self-evident to us is similar to that by which the first becomes self-evident. Further, by 'a good' Sidgwick here appears to mean something directly exciting satisfaction, and by 'our good on the whole' what would more accurately be called our whole good, viz. the totality of the states and activities which, if they occurred during the various parts of our life, would excite satisfaction during those parts; and though our good and our happiness can be dissociated, his use of the terms 'Prudence' and 'Benevolence' to designate his principles seems to show that he is implying that satisfaction is identical with happiness.

On this basis the argument of the first part seems to be as follows: In the first instance we think of various states or activities of ourselves as things which if they occurred during various parts of our life would be goods to us, and so desire them. And when we reflect we come to form the idea of these as forming one whole, which we may call our whole good; and then we come to desire this totality. But besides desiring this totality we on some occasions specially desire one of these particular goods, possibly because we think it will come soon; and then the desire of our whole good and the desire of some particular good prompt us to do different actions. And when this happens it is self-evident that we ought to aim at, i.e. be moved to act by the desire of, our whole good, rather than aim at, i.e. be moved to act by our desire of, the particular good.

On this part of the argument the only comment needed is that it is self-evident that there is no such duty.

The second part of the argument looks as if it were meant to be a demonstration that we ought to be benevolent, and the consideration of it is plainly more important. It appears to start thus: In the preceding process of thought we started with the idea of particular goods to ourselves, and thence formed the idea of a whole which they make up, viz. our whole good. This done we can now start afresh and, having formed ideas of the whole good of other persons similar to that of our own, we can then form the idea of a second whole which these make up, viz. the totality of the whole good of everyone. To this whole or totality Sidgwick then without any justification whatever gives the name 'universal good', by which he means the totality of things which are good. And then he continues:

Here again, just as in the former case, by considering the relation of the integrant parts to the whole and to each other, I obtain the self-evident principle that the good of any one individual is of no more importance, from the point of view (if I may say so) of the Universe, than the good of any other.[1]

Now being of importance, as he here implies, is being of importance to someone, and he appears to mean by it 'being something for which someone has concern', i.e. being wanted by someone. He is therefore implying (1) that the Universe is a *person*, a *benevolent* person, and indeed *simply* a benevolent person, i.e. a person who desires only and equally the good of all the inhabitants of the Universe, and also, since the argument is to apply to us, (2) that we are benevolent and simply benevolent persons, i.e. beings who desire only and indeed equally the good of all the inhabitants of the Universe. Consequently, if he had proceeded on the lines of his first argument, what he would have concluded to be self-evident is that we, being simply benevolent beings, ought to aim at, i.e. be moved to act by the desire of, the totality of the whole goods of all others, rather than by that of the whole good of any single person, whether ourselves or another. And had he proceeded thus his failure would have been obvious. For plainly (1) we are not purely benevolent beings, (2) the desire of *our own* whole good cannot be included, along with the desire of the whole goods of others, in benevolence, since the desire of our own good cannot be disinterested, and (3) even if we had been purely benevolent beings, there would not have been a *duty* to be moved by the desire of the good of all others.

But his actual procedure is an even worse failure. For at this point there is a complete break in his argument. He substitutes for the totality of the whole goods of all individuals something quite

[1] *Methods of Ethics*, p. 382.

different, viz. what he calls universal good, i.e. the totality of all
the things which are good—and then asserts it to be self-evident
that he as a rational being is bound to aim at good generally, i.e.
the totality of things that are good, and not at a particular part
of this totality, thereby treating being someone's whole good,
i.e. being what renders someone satisfied throughout life, as if it
were the same thing as being good. And of the various confusions
to be found in the *Methods of Ethics* perhaps the most fundamental
and the most prevailing is the treatment of 'being a good to someone' and 'being good' as identical.[1]

The inconsistency of his two conclusions, that we ought to aim
at our own happiness and also at the general happiness, which has
already been pointed out,[2] comes home to Sidgwick himself later.[3]
For on p. 420 he has to allow that an egoist, by which he means a
man who thinks that he ought to aim at his own happiness, cannot
be argued into thinking that he ought to aim at the general happiness, since to such a man his own happiness is the only thing of
importance, i.e. the only thing which he wants. Driven to this
admission, he tries to mitigate its force by maintaining that an
egoist *can* be thus persuaded if he can be made to allow, as he need
not, that his own happiness cannot be a more important part of
good than that of any other person. But the attempt is futile. For
it treats being of importance to someone, i.e. being wanted by
someone, as if it were the same thing as being good. And if this
mistake is removed Sidgwick is only saying that if he can convert
a man who wants only his own happiness into a purely benevolent
being, such a man will have to admit that the happiness of all others
is what he ought to aim at, because he has ceased to want his own.

---

[1] Some case can be made out for holding that Sidgwick does not mean by 'aiming
at X' 'having X as our purpose', but doing what is most conducive to X. Thus on p. 412
he treats the statement, 'Each ought to seek the happiness of all', as identical with the
statement, 'That act is right which will produce the greatest amount of happiness.'
And if this interpretation is adopted it can be urged that his fundamental idea is that
where something would be good this fact involves that we ought to do what would
most conduce to it, the notion of 'end' or 'purpose' having nothing to do with obligation. To this interpretation there are various objections into which it seems unnecessary
to enter. If it be right, then Sidgwick's theory of obligation will be subject to the criticism advanced on pp. 152–3, 158–63. What seems most likely is that he failed to distinguish the two doctrines which it is possible to attribute to him, and that there are
streaks of both to be found in him, that which I have attributed to him preponderating.

[2] p. 129.

[3] See *Methods of Ethics*, p. 420, and the concluding chapter.

VII. *Goodness and Obligation*

Teleological and quasi-teleological theories of obligation having been examined, there remains to be considered a group of three theories which between them include most of those which have been advanced. Indeed, it is plausible to represent them as forming an exhaustive division of theories of obligation. For it is plausible to argue thus: 'It is an idea common to everyone that no act can be a duty unless there is something good connected with the action, so that if the act be done, something good will come to exist which otherwise will not. It is therefore only possible to differ about what the good thing is. The only things, however, connected with an action which it is possible to represent as good are (*a*) some effect and (*b*) the action itself. Hence what has to be represented as the thing the goodness of which is necessary, for an act to be a duty, must be either (1) some effect, or (2) the action itself, or (3) either some effect or the action.' And in fact each of these views has been taken, and so there are three and only three possible views. These are that the character which an act must have, to be a duty, is respectively (1) that of *causing* something good, (2) that of *being* good, and (3) either that of *causing* something good or that of *being* good.

The three theories just referred to are those to be now considered. They have certainly been held. The first, for instance, has been held by those called Ethical Hedonists who *inter alia* maintain that only the results of actions can be good. Again, the second is to be found in Kant, who considers that only actions are good, and in those who, like Bentham, Hutcheson, Butler, and Price, are greatly impressed with the goodness of certain actions. And, as will appear shortly, the third is to be found in certain modern writers, of whom Rashdall and Professor Moore are notable examples.

It should be noted, however, that each of these theories is apt to be modified if it occurs to a supporter that the doing of one action is incompatible with doing various others. For then the question 'What is required to render an act a duty?' is apt to be transformed into the question 'What is required to render an act, out of all those any one of which I can do, the act which I ought to do?'; and given this alteration the answers become respectively: the act's being (1) that which would cause *most good*, (2) that which itself is the *best*, and (3) that by doing which *most good* would come to exist, whether in the act or as a result.

The three theories, although they at least seem to have a common idea, nevertheless are very different. For while, according to the first, to discover whether there is an obligation to do some action we must consider only the goodness which its results would have and ignore any goodness which it would have itself, according to the second we must do the opposite, and according to the third we must consider both. And these differences will be more obvious if we allow, as we must, that with one exception, which will be considered later,[1] those who speak of the goodness of certain actions themselves really mean by it the goodness of their motives; for, plainly, to consider the goodness of a result is one thing and to consider the goodness of the motive is another. The third, too, seems to have an element of queerness about it which distinguishes it from the other two in a special way. For the question being: 'What is the character which an act must have for us to be bound to do it?' its answer is: '*Either* that of causing something good *or* that of being good', and thereby it implies, as the others do not, that there is no such single character, and that two quite different characters are somehow equivalent. The difference between the theories seems to become more marked if we ask whether they all share what Joseph calls the idea that good is the fundamental notion of Ethics.[2] By this, it appears, he means the idea not that while goodness is *sui generis* obligation is not, but that while obligation equally with goodness is fundamental in this sense, it is dependent on goodness in the sense that an obligation to do some action depends on the goodness of something connected with the action, so that unless something connected with an action was good, there could be no such thing as an obligation. For while the third view plainly does imply this idea, the other two seem not to do so. For what the first view appears to represent an obligation as dependent on is not the goodness of *anything* good connected with the action but the goodness of some *result*, since it seems to be implied that for there to be an obligation a result of the act has to be good, whether or not the act is itself good. Indeed, it looks as though the first view could be expressed by saying that the fundamental notion of Ethics is not that of goodness but that of the goodness of certain *results* of action. Similarly, what the second view appears to represent an obligation as dependent on is the goodness of certain actions, and it appears capable of being expressed by saying

[1] See p. 150.
[2] *Some Problems in Ethics*, p. 75.

that the fundamental notion of Ethics is that of the goodness of certain *actions*.

Nevertheless, it will have to be considered later whether the three views are really as different as they seem, and whether the third is as queer as it looks.

The truth respectively of these three theories is to be found insisted on in recent writings.

Thus Rashdall is insisting on the truth of the first view when he says:

All Kant's difficulties arose from the attempt to give a meaning to, and to find a context for, the idea of 'right' without appealing to the idea of 'good'. In our view the idea of 'good' or 'value' is logically the primary conception. . . . That action is right which tends to bring about the good. There is no attempt here to get rid of the ultimate unanalysable 'ought'. The good is that which 'ought to be'.[1] . . . Our moral judgements are ultimately judgements of Value. The fundamental idea in Morality is the idea of Value, in which the idea of 'ought' is implicitly contained. . . . The idea of 'good' and the idea of 'right' are, as it seems to me, correlative terms. It is implied in the idea of 'good' that it ought to be promoted: the idea of 'right' is meaningless apart from a 'good' which right actions tend to promote.[2]

Again, Professor Moore is insisting on the truth of the first view when he says that it is demonstrably certain that the assertion 'I am morally bound to perform this action' is identical with the assertion 'This action will produce the greatest possible amount of good in the Universe'.[3]

Again, Laird, in his *Study in Moral Theory*, asserts the truth of the second view very emphatically.[4] He speaks of an inescapable question set by the fact of action, viz. 'Is any given action what it ought to be?' and he refers to moral theories, i.e. to attempts to answer the question, as concerned with reasons which justify or else condemn actions. And he goes on to say:

It is plain that the only consideration relevant to the justification or condemnation of an action is its value or lack of value, its goodness or badness. . . . Accordingly, we are bound to maintain that the only

---

[1] Rashdall, H., *Theory of Good and Evil*, i, p. 135.

[2] Ibid., pp. 137–8.

[3] *Principia Ethica*, § 89. For the justification of this interpretation see pp. 145–6, below.

[4] In his later *Enquiry into Moral Notions*, p. 10, he says that he wants to renounce his past *in toto* and to make no attempt to defend any opinion formerly held. I only refer to the doctrine of his earlier *Study* as a typical view.

reason which can justify or condemn is a reason based upon worth or its opposite.[1]

Later he adds:

When we say, for short, that duty is the adoption of the best, . . . we are asserting a necessary and a fundamental connection between value and obligation, excellence and authority, worth and duty. In the language of philosophers this connection is a *synthetic* connection, a union of things significantly different. . . . We are saying, indeed, that the character of excellence implies a command, that excellent things, just because of their excellence, ought to be sought and achieved.[2]

Again, Joseph expresses his adherence to the third view by saying that he believes good to be the fundamental notion of Ethics,[3] and he expresses this belief in an earlier passage, thus:

A right act, some say, is not to be defined as one causally related to what is good; and it may have no value in itself; nevertheless, I ought to do it. In spite of the arguments by which this position has been defended, it seems to me absurd. Why ought I to do that, the doing which has no value (though my being moved to do it by the consciousness that I ought, has), and which being done causes nothing to be which has value? Is not duty in such a case irrational?[4]

When, however, we come to consider the various statements made by the four writers just referred to, we find to our surprise that not one of them is content with only one view and that each, while beginning with one of the three, ends with another.

Professor Moore says: 'All moral laws, I wish to shew, are merely statements that certain kinds of action will have good effects. . . . What I wish first to point out is that "right" does and can mean nothing but "cause of a good result", and is thus identical with "useful".'[5] He adds that it is demonstrably certain that the assertion, 'I am morally bound to perform this action', is identical with the assertion, 'This action will produce the greatest possible amount of good in the universe'. And a little later he says: 'Our "duty", therefore, can only be defined as that action, which will cause more good to exist in the Universe than any possible alternative.'

Here the context shows that Professor Moore is using 'right' as the equivalent of 'ought' or 'duty'. Hence, in the sentence just quoted he is in effect asserting that the statement, 'I ought to do

---

[1] *Study in Moral Theory*, pp. 17–18.   [2] Ibid., pp. 21–2.
[3] *Some Problems in Ethics*, p. 75.   [4] Ibid., p. 26.
[5] *Principia Ethica*, § 89.

an act of a certain kind', e.g. help my neighbour, *means*: 'An act of a certain kind will cause something good', and consequently he is here offering a *definition* of the terms 'ought' and 'duty', viz. causing something good. And this interpretation is confirmed by his repeatedly contending that in Ethics, i.e. in the inquiry into what we ought to do, the goodness of something is the one thing which is simple and therefore incapable of definition.

Yet, if anything is certain, it is that by 'I ought to do so and so' we do not *mean* 'doing so and so will cause something good'. Hence, if we are to attribute to Professor Moore a view which has at least some plausibility, we must interpret him as if he had said: We always *base* the assertion, 'I ought to do an act of a certain kind' on the assertion, 'Such an act will cause something good', thereby implying that what renders such an action a duty is that it will cause something good. For this interpretation there is the additional justification that in his later *Ethics* he in effect makes this modification himself by saying:

It is indeed quite plain, I think, that the meaning of the two words[1] is *not* the same: for if it were then it would be a mere tautology to say that it is always a duty to do what will have the best possible consequences. Our theory does not, therefore, do away with the distinction between the *meaning* of the words 'duty' and 'expediency'; it only maintains that both will always apply to the same actions.[2]

The interpretation is also borne out by his refutation of Egoistic Hedonism, which can be shortly stated thus: Either the agent's happiness is good or it is not. If it is not, there can be no reason why the agent ought to aim at (i.e. cause) it. If it is, another's happiness is also good, and there is equally a reason why the agent ought to aim at (i.e. cause) that.

Further, Professor Moore, in stating his theory, constantly distinguishes between 'right' and 'absolutely right', thus implying a distinction between a duty and an absolute duty, and he confines the term 'absolutely right' to the act which will cause most good in the universe. This being so, the doctrine stated in the sentences quoted must be this: 'Any act in our power is rendered a duty by being one which will cause something good. But since at any moment there is a variety of acts which will cause something good, only one of which we can do, one of these acts is rendered our

---

[1] Sc. 'right' and 'expedient', i.e. useful, or causing something good.
[2] *Ethics*, p. 173.

absolute duty by being that which will cause more good than will any of the others.'

The doctrine so interpreted, however, is open to the charge of inconsistency. For the term 'absolute' applied to 'duty' can only add emphasis. There cannot be two kinds of duty, the one absolute and the other not. Either we are bound to do some action or we are not; we cannot be bound to do something but not absolutely. Consequently one act cannot be rendered a duty by causing something good, while another is rendered an absolute duty by causing the most good. And it seems only fair to represent Professor Moore as originally adopting the first of the three views in its modified form, viz. that causing something good renders an act a duty, and then on consideration substituting the modified form, viz. that causing most good renders an act a duty, as his more considered view.

This, however, is not the whole story. For Professor Moore frequently implies not only that an act may cause something good but also that it may itself have intrinsic value, i.e. *be* good. And when he has goodness of this kind in mind, he maintains[1] that in considering what action is our absolute duty we must take into account the goodness of various actions as well as that of their effects. Moreover, in one passage he states almost in so many words the third of the three views under consideration, in its modified form. 'In short', he says, 'to assert that a certain line of conduct is, at a given time, absolutely right or obligatory, is obviously to assert that more good or less evil will exist in the world, if it be adopted, than if anything else be done instead.'[2] It is, then, plain that there are to be found in Professor Moore two inconsistent views, viz. the first and the third of those under consideration, each in its modified form, and also that of these the third (which of course implies the third of the three underlying ideas[3]) is his more considered view, and that by which he would stand if forced to choose.

In Rashdall also we find the same transition from the first to the third view. For while we find such statements as 'That action is right which tends to bring about the good'[4] and 'The right action is always that which (so far as the agent has the means of knowing) will produce the greatest amount of good upon the whole',[5] we find that when he has in mind the goodness which certain actions

---

[1] See e.g. *Principia Ethica*, §§ 17 and 89.   [2] Ibid., § 17.
[3] See p. 143, above.
[4] *Theory of Good and Evil*, i, p. 135.   [5] Ibid., p. 184.

themselves have, he insists as emphatically as does Professor Moore that the goodness of various acts, as well as that of their effects, has to be taken into account in estimating their rightness.[1]

In Laird also we find a transition, but a different transition, viz. that from the second view to the third. For although in the passage quoted[2] he speaks of the only consideration which can justify an action as being its goodness, he also speaks of things which because of their excellence ought to be *sought and achieved*,[3] and when he considers the application of moral rules, he holds that goodness of results should be taken into account.

Joseph, however, differs markedly from the others by first proclaiming himself an adherent of the *third* of the three views, and then afterwards substituting for it the second in a modified form. Early in *Some Problems in Ethics* he says: 'Let me state here by way of anticipation what I propose to argue for. An act may be right because productive of good results. . . . An act may also be right not because productive of good results; but if so, it must have intrinsic goodness, which goodness must involve the agent's motive.'[4] In a later chapter, however, entitled 'An ambiguity in the word *right*', he puts forward a quite different doctrine. He allows that we often mean by calling an act right that we ought to do it, but he asserts that we also use the term to mean some character in the act, because of which we ought to do it.[5] And he maintains that this character must be a sort of goodness, although it is difficult to state what it is. And as, of course, to *cause* something good is not to *be* good, he is here abandoning his original contention that an act can be a duty because productive of good results, and limiting the reason to the goodness of the act itself. Afterwards he devotes himself to the problem of ascertaining what this goodness is which is common to all right acts, although he is ultimately forced to allow that he can find no account of it which is wholly satisfying.[6] He is, however, driven to deny that it can be the goodness of the motive, on the ground that at least in one instance we think we ought to do one act rather than another although the motive of each would be the same and so equally good, viz. the thought that we ought

---

[1] *Theory of Good and Evil*, i, p. 97.   [2] See p. 144 above.

[3] See p. 145 above. The italics are mine.

[4] *Some Problems in Ethics*, p. 28; cf. the statement quoted on p. 145 above.

[5] Ibid., p. 59. The statement is hard to understand unless it means that we also mean by calling an act right that it has a certain character—the character being in fact that character which we think renders an act a duty, although its so rendering it is not part of the meaning of 'right'.   [6] Ibid., p. 83.

to do the action.[1] The instance is that of our thinking that we ought to give to another the means for a much-needed holiday rather than to use it for a much-needed holiday for ourselves. Here, he holds, the superior goodness which we are thinking of as involved in the former action cannot be that of the other's having a needed holiday, since this cannot be better than our having such a holiday; but neither can it be that of the motive, since *ex hypothesi* we are asking what we ought to do, so that, whichever we do, we shall be moved by the thought of the rightness of (i.e. a certain goodness in) the action, and therefore the motive in each case will be the same.[2] And he becomes driven to find it in the goodness which the act would have if it were the manifestation of a rule of action such that if all the members of a community acted on it, their actions in acting on it would as a system be good.[3]

Unfortunately, however, this conclusion is undeniably exposed to two fatal objections. For, first, on Joseph's own showing, the goodness which he attributes to giving another a needed holiday is one the act usually would *not* have, since the goodness is one which the act would only have as one of a system of similar acts done by all, and at least in most cases, if not in all, not all the others would act similarly. Secondly, there cannot be any such goodness. For avowedly the goodness which he is attributing to the act is one which it has only as a part of a system of such acts, and to attribute a character to the parts of a system only as parts of that system is really to attribute the character to the system and to deny it to the parts. Thus, to assert that the parts of a picture are beautiful only as parts of the picture is really to attribute beauty to the whole picture and to deny it to its parts. And, for the same reason, to maintain that the goodness of which he is thinking belongs to the act *only* as part of a system of acts is in effect to deny that the act has any goodness of its own.

At this point it may be noted that a survey as a whole of the

[1] Ibid., pp. 96–7. Here, it may be noted, Joseph *is* admitting, contrary to his general account of 'moral' actions, that a moral action has a character which is independent of the character of its motive (see p. 133, above).

[2] Ibid., p. 96.

[3] This seems to be the only interpretation possible of an obscure passage which runs thus: 'We must look beyond the particular action not to its effects but to the rule of action of which it is a manifestation. This, however, is not enough. We must look to the whole form of life in some community, to which all the actions manifesting this rule would belong, and ask whether it, or some other form of life is better, which would be lived by the community instead, if this rule were not helping to determine it.' Ibid., p. 98.

writers under consideration suggests two comments. The first is that there is a tendency in them all to treat causing something good as if it were a special way of being good—a treatment encouraged by the misleading phrase 'instrumentally good'—for without such a tendency they could not have failed to notice their transition from one view to another. The second is that, if we except Joseph, who is driven into what must be allowed to be an untenable view of the goodness of an action required to render it a duty, there is a tendency to begin with one or other of the first two views and to end with the third, and this tendency raises the question whether after all the first two views are not arbitrarily restricted versions of the third.[1]

At this point, also, it may fairly be objected that so far no instance of the expression of the second view has been given, since though Joseph's more considered doctrine finds the goodness required, for an act to be a duty, in the goodness of the action, the goodness is one which the act cannot have. The truth, however, appears to be that, with the exception of Joseph, those who place the goodness necessary, for an act to be a duty, within the action itself are thinking of the goodness of its motive, and are thinking of the act as something which includes its motive. And this being so, to give instances is easy. Kant, e.g., is expressing the second view when he says:

Since every practical law represents a possible action as good and *on this account*,[2] for a subject who is practically determinable by reason, necessary,[3] all imperatives are formulae determining an action which is necessary according to the principle of a will good in some respects. . . . If now the action . . . is conceived as good *in itself* and *consequently*[2] as being necessarily the principle of a will which of itself conforms to reason, then it is *categorical*.[4]

The second theory, again, is to be found in Hutcheson when he insists on our disinterested approval of certain acts—an approval which he sometimes describes as our perception of their moral goodness—and subsequently finds that the acts which he approves are those prompted by benevolence, and concludes that what we ought to do is acts prompted by benevolence.[5] Martineau, too,

---

[1] See p. 143 above.   [2] The italics are mine.
[3] i.e. an act which he ought to do.
[4] *Fundamental Principles of the Metaphysics of Morals* (Abbott's trans.), p. 37.
[5] It is, however, significant that he is unable to keep to this view, and when he comes to consider the details of what we ought to do, represents as the most virtuous

propounds the same theory in a more elaborate form. For he holds that our various desires form a sort of hierarchy in the scale of goodness and that our duty consists in following, i.e. in acting on, the higher of two desires, whenever they conflict.

The theory, however, perhaps finds most explicit expression in Richard Price:

> *Morally good* and *evil* [he says], *reasonable* and *unreasonable*, are epithets also commonly applied to actions, evidently meaning the same with *right* and *wrong*, *fit* and *unfit*.
>
> *Approving* an action is the same with discerning it to be *right*; as *assenting* to a proposition is the same with discerning it to be *true*.
>
> But *Obligation* is the term most necessary to be here considered; and to the explication of it, the best part of this chapter shall be devoted.
>
> *Obligation* to action, and *rightness* of action, are plainly coincident and identical; so far so, that we cannot form a notion of the one, without taking in the other. This may appear to any one upon considering, whether he can point out any difference between what is *right*, *meet* or *fit* to be done, and what *ought* to be done. It is not indeed plainer, that figure implies something figured, solidity resistance, or an effect a cause, than it is that *rightness* implies *oughtness* (if I may be allowed this word) or *obligatoriness*. And as easily can we conceive of figure without extension, or motion without a change of place, as that it can be *fit* for us to do an action, and yet that it may not be what we *should* do, what it is our *duty* to do, or what we are under an obligation to do.—*Right*, *fit*, *ought*, *should*, *duty*, *obligation*, convey, then, ideas necessarily including one another. From hence it follows,
>
> *First*, that virtue, *as such*, has a real obligatory power antecedently to all positive laws, and independently of all will: for obligation, we see, is involved in the very nature of it.[1]

It should be noted, however, that the second view has taken one or other of two very different forms. As Hume insisted, when we praise some action and consider it good, we do so on account of its motive. But among the motives which we think good, in addition to certain desires which we ordinarily group together as virtuous, such as the desire to repay a benefit and the desire to overcome our fear, there is one which is very different from the rest. This is what we sometimes vaguely call the sense of duty, and either consider to be the thought that the act is a duty or else consider to be the desire to do it as being a duty. And some theorists, and notably

---

act that which tends most to the general happiness, thus tacitly dropping the motive as the ground of obligation.

[1] Price, R., *Review of the Principal Questions in Morals*, ed. D. D. Raphael, pp. 104–5.

Kant, have singled out this either as the only motive which is good, or else as a motive which is pre-eminently good, and have in consequence represented what we call moral goodness, i.e. conscientiousness, as the basis of duty,[1] their view being that the character required for an act to be a duty is that of being morally good. Others, however, have concentrated attention on the other good motives, and consequently have represented virtue as the basis of duty, their view being that the character required is that of being virtuous. Of this latter view Hutcheson is a prominent exponent, and also Butler, who always takes for granted that what we ought to do is virtuous actions. And in modern times a more elaborate form of the same view is to be found in Martineau.

VIII. *Goodness and Obligation* (*continued*)

In considering the truth of the three theories set out in the preceding chapter, it seems best to consider first the difficulties which arise out of the special nature of each, and then those which are common to them all.

To the truth of the first of the three it must be allowed that there is one outstanding and indeed insuperable objection. This is simply that it fails to stand the test of instances. If we are to become convinced that what renders some act a duty is its causing something good, then when we consider some act which would cause something good, we must think not only that the act is a duty but that it is rendered a duty by its causing something good, or more accurately by the fact that it would if done cause something good. But we do not. To realize this, we must consider an instance of an act which would cause something which is indubitably good, such as an increase in that disposition which we call patience. And such an instance would be found in some act of self-restraint which we thought of as one which to some slight extent would render us more patient, and, again, in the making of some remark to another which we thought of as an act which would render him more patient. According to the theory we should not only think that we ought to do the action, but also think that what renders us bound to do it is that in doing it we should be causing something to become better. But though we shall think in the one case that we ought to perform the act of self-restraint and in the other that we

---

[1] It should be noted, however, that another view is also to be found in Kant: see p. 156 below.

ought to make the remark, we shall not in so thinking be abstracting in the one case from the fact that we shall be making *ourselves*
better and in the other from the fact that we shall be making *another*
better, and so shall not be thinking of the act as one in which we
shall be making someone or something better. We shall be thinking
of the acts as duties of different sorts just because the one will be
making *ourselves* better and the other making *someone else* better;
and we shall be thinking of the act of self-restraint as being a duty
just because it would be one of making not someone but ourselves
better, and of the making the remark as being a duty just because
it would be the making another better. And in a similar way,
when we consider whether we ought to help to make some child
better, we do not think the question irrelevant whether the child
is ours or the child of some relation, or the child of a stranger,
or, again, an orphan without relations. Yet we should think this
question irrelevant if we thought that what mattered was our
making someone better. The truth indeed appears to be that in
order to think of some change as one which *we* ought to cause, we
must think of the change as in some special way related to ourselves, even if that way consists in its affecting someone other than
ourselves. Consequently, it may be noted, we need only to consider our thought about particular instances to be able to reject
Professor Moore's refutation of Egoism, viz. his contention that
if a man's happiness is not good, he is not justified in pursuing
it, i.e. bringing it about, and if it is, everyone else has an equal
reason to pursue it.[1]

To the truth of the second of the three theories it must also be
allowed that there is an insuperable objection, although of quite
a different sort. This is, to put it shortly, that the theory (*a*) on
its positive side implies an idea which we have already seen to
be false,[2] viz. that our duty is to have a certain motive in action,
and (*b*) on its negative side implies another idea which cannot
be true, viz. that there cannot be any *action* which we ought
to do.

The theory, in representing as it does the ground of an obligation to do some action as lying in its goodness, and its goodness as
lying in the goodness of its motive, is implying the idea that the
motive of an action is part of it. But, as has been pointed out earlier,
the motive of an action, though necessary to it, is not part of it. And
once the necessary correction has been introduced into the theory,

---

[1] *Principia Ethica*, § 64.   [2] See pp. 129–35 above.

it becomes the theory not that we ought to do a certain action because it would be good (since no action would be good) but that we ought to be moved by a certain desire or a certain thought, because that desire or thought would be good, it therefore being implied that there is no action which we ought to do. No doubt, then, according to the theory, if we are moved to act by the good desire or thought, we shall do some action, viz. the action which the desire or the thought moves us to do, but our duty will consist in being moved by the desire or thought, and is irrespective of what it would move us to do, so that, to put it rather loosely, our duty does not concern what we do but only our manner or way of doing what we do.

This conclusion, it should be noticed, would have to be admitted even if we were to allow that the motive of an action is part of it. For anyone who maintains this would have to allow that in doing so he was using the term 'action' in the more inclusive sense in which we speak, for instance, of some action as generous, and not in the narrower sense in which we speak, for instance, of killing someone as an action; and he would then have to distinguish from an action in the more inclusive sense an action in the less inclusive sense, viz. that of effecting, or at least making an effort to effect, some change, since otherwise he would have nothing for the motive to be the motive of. He would then have to allow that according to the theory only acts in the more inclusive sense can be duties, so that acts in the less inclusive sense cannot.

The theory therefore substitutes for the obligation to effect something, or, alternatively, to make an effort to effect something, the obligation to be moved by some thought or desire to effect or make an effort to effect something, and thereby it leaves us with nothing which we ought to do.

We can bring home to ourselves the nature of this conclusion by noticing the forms which it takes according as the goodness of certain actions, on which the duty of doing them is represented as depending, is (a) that of virtuousness or (b) that of moral goodness. According to the former view, to have a duty we must have some virtuous desire, such as the desire to help another out of trouble, and if we have such a desire, our duty will be to be moved by this desire to act, no matter what the act be to which the desire prompts us, and whatever we do, it will not have been our duty to do it. Again, according to the latter view, to have a duty we must have the idea that there is a certain act which we ought to do, e.g. to torture a certain heretic, or alternatively to load him with kindness, and given that we have this desire, our duty will be to be moved to act by this idea, or alternatively, by the desire to do this as being an act we think a duty, and whether we do this or anything else, it will not have been our duty to do it.

The latter form of the view, moreover, involves the paradoxical, and indeed untenable, idea that the existence of moral goodness depends on the existence of an illusion. To see this we need only consider the special form which this view assumes in Kant, for *mutatis mutandis* the same consideration will apply to basing duty on moral goodness, while at the same time considering a morally good action to be that prompted by the *desire* to do the action as one the agent thinks to be a duty. According to Kant, a morally good action requires the idea that there is a duty to do it, and indeed is an action prompted solely by this idea. But also, according to Kant, this idea is false, since there are no acts which we ought to do, and our duty is only to have a certain idea as our motive. Now if it be allowed that a man in doing some action has been wholly or in part influenced by the idea that he ought to do it, to assert that his idea is mistaken is no ground for refusing to attribute complete or some moral goodness to his action, provided it be held that there is some act which it is his duty to do, and therefore that he is only mistaken about what his duty is. And, in fact, we think that the question whether some act was morally good is quite independent of whether he was right in thinking he ought to do what he did. Again, provided we think, for instance, that an inquisitor was acting conscientiously, we think his action morally good however misguided we think his idea of his duty. But it is quite a different matter to try to attribute moral goodness to an act if it be held, as it really was by Kant, that the very idea that there can be a duty to *do* something, i.e. to effect something, as distinct from a duty to have a certain motive, is a mistake. And we certainly should not continue to believe that there is such a thing as moral goodness, if we thought it a mistake to think that there is a duty to do anything whatever. Indeed, in this respect Kant is killing the goose which is to lay his golden eggs. For he is trying to convince us that we have a duty, viz. to act morally, while telling us that if we so act we shall be acting on a mistake; and to do this is impossible. Indeed, if he succeeds in persuading us that our idea that there can be actions which we ought to do is false, he will render it impossible for us to act morally, for we cannot be led to act on an idea which we know to be false, and therefore no longer have.

It will naturally be asked, 'How, if this be so, did the objection fail to escape Kant's notice?' The answer, however, does not seem hard to find. For there is in him, besides this representation of moral goodness as the basis of duty, a totally different view according to which our thoughts that particular actions of certain sorts, e.g. acts of telling the truth, are duties *are* true, and consequently he fails to see that according to him to do a morally good action is to act on an illusion. This view arises when, ceasing to be preoccupied with the goodness of conscientious action, he asks himself, 'What acts in particular ought we to do?' He is then struck with the idea that, since the character required for an act to be a duty, unlike that of an act hypothetically prescribed, cannot be deduced from that of a purpose, the only thing left for it to be deducible from is the nature of a principle of duty, which is necessarily binding on all; and realizing that only the doing of an act capable of being done by all can be binding on all, he is led to conclude that the character required for an act to be a duty is that of being capable of being done by all;[1] and he considers that the acts which we ordinarily think duties have this character. What, however, he fails to see is that *both* accounts of the basis of duty cannot be true, and therefore also that in accepting moral goodness as the basis, he is tacitly rejecting the other account of the basis according to which our thoughts that certain actions are duties are true.

It should, however, be noticed that Kant's main mistake does not lie in his account of moral goodness. Anyone would at least have to allow that this, if not true as it stands, contains an element of truth, and would be true if modified to the extent of substituting for the *thought* of the duty of doing some action the *desire* to do it as an act we think a duty. His main mistake lies in representing moral goodness as the basis of duty. The truth is that here Kant is guilty of an inversion. Whereas, in fact, to arrive at the idea that certain acts are morally good, we must already, and so independently, have the idea that there are acts which are duties, Kant is maintaining that to arrive at the latter idea we must already, and so independently, have the former.

There remains, however, to be pointed out a further objection to the second of the three theories under consideration, viz. that if

---

[1] It need hardly be pointed out that this conclusion is untrue.

it be true, there cannot be such a thing as conscientious action, whether by 'conscientious action' be understood action prompted by the thought that we ought to do the action, or action prompted by the desire to do the act as being a duty. The objection is one of which Hume had a glimpse in connexion with the second of the two forms which it assumes,[1] without, however, appreciating its full force. Hume brings forward an argument which at least proves that if we ought to do what is virtuous, our motive in doing our duty can never be what he calls the sense of duty.[2] The argument, though well known, does not seem to have been given the weight it deserves. Hume himself states it obscurely and indeed inaccurately,[3] but properly stated it is this: 'What we ought to do is virtuous actions. But the virtue of a virtuous action is that of its motive, i.e. the goodness of some desire forming its motive, such as the desire of a parent to help his child, arising from parental affection. Hence, what we ought to do is actions of which the motive would be some virtuous desire, and therefore in doing something which we ought our motive cannot be the thought that we ought to do it, for if it were, the act would not be virtuous and so not a duty.' Hume, however, in presenting the argument only states the conclusion thus: 'In short, it may be established as an undoubted maxim, *that no action can be virtuous, or morally good, unless there be in human nature some motive to produce it, distinct from the sense of its morality*', thereby implying only that the motive cannot *always* be the thought that we ought to do it but must sometimes be a virtuous desire. And this is unfortunate because if the premisses prove anything they prove that the motive can *never* be the sense of duty; and in a later passage[4] he himself gives this as the conclusion. His half-heartedness is due to his conviction that sometimes we really do do an action from the sense of duty.[5] But he fails to notice that in admitting this he is abandoning his view that we only think an act a duty if we think it would be virtuous.

Hume's argument, of course, only applies to the form of the second theory which represents virtue as the basis of obligation. But a similar argument applies to the form which bases obligation on moral goodness. For this form really implies the idea that there are two forms of the sense of duty, viz. (1) the mistaken thought that we ought to do so and so, and (2) the true thought that we

---

[1] See pp. 151–2, above.
[2] For Hume's use of the phrase, see his *Treatise*, Book III. 2, § 5.
[3] Ibid., § 1.   [4] Ibid., § 5.   [5] Ibid., § 1.

ought to have this thought as our motive, in virtue of the goodness of being so moved. And an argument similar to Hume's will establish that our motive in doing what we ought must always be the false, and can never be the true, sense of duty.

Hence on either form of the view, though we have duties and know that we have, we cannot do a duty from the sense of duty. And in this connexion it is significant that Martineau is driven to admit this when he is forced to allow that the sense of duty cannot be a spring of action.

Of special difficulties presented by the third of the three theories hardly anything need be said. For according to this view what is required for an act to be a duty is either that it would cause something good or that it would be good. For the objections to considering (a) that causing something good, and (b) that being good, can render an act a duty have already been considered, and whatever objection there may be to representing these as alternative grounds of an obligation will turn out if examined, as will appear presently,[1] to be bound up with an objection which is common to them all.

IX. *Goodness and Obligation* (*continued*)

It now remains to be considered whether there are any objections to the three theories under consideration which are common to them all. And here, to anticipate matters, it will have to be allowed that we get a surprise—the surprise of finding that they involve a mistake which is far more radical than any which we should even be inclined to suspect beforehand. The mistake is analogous to that underlying teleological theories in that it consists in resolving obligation into something else; and in particular it consists in resolving it into what has to be called ought-to-existence.

We shall be more ready to admit the existence of the mistake if we notice a certain implication, which so far has not been referred to, of the question to which these theories are intended to be the answer. As has already been pointed out,[2] the question is: 'What is the character which an act must possess for us to be morally bound to do it?', and to ask it is to imply the idea that all the acts which we are bound to do have in common a character their possession of which renders us bound to do them, and so is in effect to ask: 'What is this common character?' But, as is clear when we

¹ See pp. 158–63.   ² See p. 114, above.

reflect, the only thing which it is possible to think that an act's possession of a certain character can give rise to is its possession of some other character. Therefore, to ask: 'What is the common character the possession of which renders us bound to do the various acts which we are bound to do?' is to imply the idea that what we call our being bound to do these various acts is their possession of a certain character. It is, therefore, to imply the idea that that to which we are referring when we say of ourselves that we ought, or that we are morally bound, to do a certain action is not even in the widest sense of the term a characteristic of ourselves, as the statement suggests that it is, but a characteristic of the action. Anyone, therefore, who puts the question is implying the idea that that to which the term 'ought' refers is really a character of some action, and he is therefore resolving what is really someone's obligation to do some action into something which it is not, viz. some character of the action, i.e. thinking of it as being something which it is not.

Joseph would have denied this. For while agreeing that there is no such thing as the obligatoriness of an action, he does hold that an act's having a certain character gives rise to something which is not its having some other character, viz. our obligation to do it; and thereby he implies that it is possible to think of an act's having a certain character as giving rise to something which is not its having some other character.

Obligatoriness [he says] is not a character of actions. There is no ought-to-be-done-ness, or ought-to-be-forborne-ness. To say that an act is obligatory means that the doing it is obligatory on me. An obligatory act is like a well-remembered face; the face no doubt has characters because of which it is well remembered, but it is called well-remembered to signify not those characters, but that others remember it well. And an act is called obligatory because of some character which it has, but to signify not that character, but that we ought to do it because thereof.[1]

This position, however, must on reflection be admitted to be untenable. It is impossible to maintain that what is called my being bound to do a certain action arises from that action's having a certain character, without being committed to holding that what is so called is the action's having a certain character. And the parallel case of a well-remembered face only serves to bring this impossibility home. For it cannot be maintained that what renders

[1] *Some Problems in Ethics*, pp. 61–2.

a face well remembered is its having certain distinctive features, as distinct from our having noticed that it has them, without implying that what is called its being well remembered is a certain character of the face.

Since then anyone who puts the question to which what we called theories of obligation are intended to be the answer, is implying the idea that what is called an obligation to do some action is really the act's possession of a certain character, we must ask, in the case of any given individual who asks the question, what in particular is the character into the possession of which he is resolving obligation. At any rate we can say that it cannot be that the appropriate term for which would be that coined from the term 'obligation', viz. obligatoriness. For anyone who speaks of some action as obligatory on X would allow, as Joseph would admit, that in speaking thus he was only stating in a misleading way that X ought to do the action. No one thinks that there is such a thing as obligatoriness. And this being so, it at least seems likely that what anyone who puts the question is resolving obligation into is that for which we have to coin the term 'ought-to-existence', simply because it is difficult, if not impossible, to think of anything else into which it can be resolved.

Given this preparation, it will become easy to recognize that at any rate the three theories under consideration are resolving obligation into what for lack of a better term has been called ought-to-existence. For it is now clear (1) that in common with other theories they are resolving it into some character of an action; (2) that this character is not what if it existed would have to be called obligatoriness; and (3) that they agree in holding that for there to be an obligation to do an action, something related to the action must be good. This being so, it becomes clear that the only character which they can be resolving it into is that ought-to-existence which at least some think is possessed by anything good. To see this we need only consider what defence of these views their respective supporters could offer. A supporter of the second view, if asked: '*Why* does an action's being good render us bound to do it?', could only answer: 'Because it is involved in the very nature of goodness that whatever is good should or ought to exist.' A supporter of the first, if asked: '*Why* does an act's causing something good render us bound to do it?', could only answer: 'Because causing something good, though not itself good, and therefore not for that reason something which ought to exist, yet is something which ought to exist, as being something which causes something which is itself good and therefore ought to exist. And a supporter of the third view would have to defend it by applying these arguments respectively to acts themselves good and acts causing something good.

Confirmation of the conclusion that these theories involve the reduction of obligation to 'ought-to-exist' is to be found in statements of some of the writers referred to, in which when trying to state what is fundamental they express themselves in terms of 'ought-to-exist'. Thus Rashdall, in a passage already quoted,[1] says: 'There is no attempt here to get rid of the ultimate unanalysable "ought". The good is that which "ought to be"', and in effect he repeats this statement a little later[2] by saying: 'The fundamental idea in Morality is the idea of Value' (i.e. goodness), 'in which the idea of "ought" is implicitly contained.' Other instances are to be found in Laird. In an article in *Mind*[3] I had in effect contended that to be able to conclude from our knowledge that a certain thing would be good that we ought to do some action which would produce it, we need in addition the knowledge that what is good ought to exist, on the ground that an 'ought', if it is to be deduced, can be deduced only from another 'ought'. Laird, commenting on this contention, admits the need of this additional knowledge that what is good ought to exist, as a link between the premiss and the conclusion, and says that this link is peculiarly obvious and that he is only concerned to state it firmly and with precision.[4] Also, speaking of the question which moral inquiry has to consider, he says: 'This question is whether any given action is what it *ought to be*. In other words, moral theory is concerned with the reasons that *justify* action.'[5] Again, the language of Professor Moore's *Principia Ethica* is even more explicit. For in it we find (*a*) statements which imply the idea that the fact that something X ought to exist, if not actually identical with its goodness, is at least necessitated by it; and (*b*) others which imply the idea that the statement 'I ought to do this' is only a way of saying 'This act ought to exist'. As an instance of the former we may take: 'Whenever he [i.e. someone] thinks of "intrinsic value" or "intrinsic worth", or says that a thing "ought to exist", he has before his mind the unique object—the unique property of things—which I

---

[1] See p. 144, above.   [2] *Theory of Good and Evil*, i, p. 135.
[3] See p. 4 above.
[4] *Study in Moral Theory*, p. 25 n.   [5] Ibid. The italics are mine.

mean by "good" ',[1] and he also speaks of the question: 'What *sort of* things are good, what are the things which, whether they *are* real or not, ought to be real?'[2] As instances of the latter we may cite his speaking[3] of the question: 'What ought we to do?' or 'What ought to exist now?' and of 'the reason why a thing ought to be done or to exist now'. In addition he makes statements which imply both ideas. Thus he says:[4] 'It is plain that when we assert that a certain action is our absolute duty, we are asserting that the performance of that action at that time is unique in respect of value.' And again,[3] he implies that a thing ought to be done or to exist now only if it itself has intrinsic value or else causes something which has. Again,[3] he speaks of almost all ethical writers as having failed to distinguish whether the reason why a thing ought to be done or to exist now, is that it is itself possessed of intrinsic value, or that it is a means to what has intrinsic value. It is, therefore, abundantly clear that at least in the minds of Rashdall, Laird, and Professor Moore the 'ought' of duty is reducible to, i.e. is really, the 'ought' of 'ought-to-exist' which some at least think inseparable from whatever is good. And even in the case of Joseph, who does not use the language of 'ought-to-exist', it is difficult to see what answer he could give to the question: '*Why* does the goodness of an act give rise to the obligation to do it?', except that whatever is good should or ought to exist.

Further, since it is now clear that the three theories involve the reduction of the 'ought' of duty to the 'ought' of 'ought-to-exist' involved in the goodness of anything good, it is also clear that they are at bottom the same, in spite of what at first seem their differences,[5] and differ only about the kinds of thing which can be good. For the same reason, the appearance of queerness presented by the third theory as laying down alternative grounds of an obligation disappears, since anyone who considers the goodness of an action as a reason why it ought to exist will have to allow that its causing something good is equally a reason, as being the causing of something which ought to exist, and anyone who considers causing something good as a reason will have to allow that being good is also a reason. In addition we can now understand, as we could not otherwise, how a supporter of the first or of the second view comes to pass so easily to the third, all that is needed being that he should take into account the goodness in the one case of an action

---

[1] *Principia Ethica*, § 13.   [2] Ib., § 70.   [3] Ib., § 104.
[4] Ib., § 89.   [5] See pp. 142–52, above.

and the goodness in the other of a result, which hitherto he had ignored.

Now that the nature of the three theories is thus clear, it might seem that no comment on them is needed beyond that of pointing out that the 'ought' of obligation is not that of 'ought-to-exist', and that therefore they are resolving obligation into something which it is not. There is, however, another which may usefully be made, in case it should be thought that after all these theories are right in representing what we at least call our obligation to do some action as being the action's being something which should or ought to exist. This is simply that if this idea were true, there could be no such thing as an obligation to do some action, until the act is already done, whereas from its very nature there can only be an obligation to do an action so long as it is not done. This must be so, because, though it may at first escape our notice, only something which is can be something which ought, or ought not, to exist. To say, e.g., that a feeling of generosity which I am not having 'ought' to exist is to say nothing, just because *ex hypothesi* there is nothing here for 'being something which ought to exist' to be attributed to.

6

THE OBJECT OF A DESIRE

IF in considering what it is we desire we confine attention to such desiring as is involved in action, it is plausible to speak of a desire as necessarily a desire for the existence of something not existing. For whether we think of the thing desired as being the action or as being something which we think the act will effect, the thing desired seems essentially something not yet existing, and the existence of which must be in the future. And Cook Wilson, in an unpublished essay on *Means and End*, speaks of a desire as the desire for the existence of something not existing. Mitchell,[1] too, implies this view when he says: 'The point is that we do not desire what we already have; to use the word [sc. desire] in this sense is confusing, for we mean simply that we like it, and that is only emotion.'

This way of speaking, of course, requires an obvious correction. We need instead to say: 'A desire is necessarily a desire for the existence of something which we either know or think, i.e. think without question, to be not existing, i.e. not now existing.' (By 'think without question' here is meant Cook Wilson's 'being under the impression that', and by 'think' here will always be meant 'thinking without question', this referring to a condition in which we are not uncertain.)

This amended statement is undoubtedly plausible. It has two implications, viz. that we cannot desire something unless we know or think it (1) not to be existing, and (2) not to be existing now.

If someone who accepts it is asked: 'Existing *when* do we desire it?' he has to answer 'at once', i.e. in the immediate future—with the implication that we shall go on desiring it until we know or think it is existing. Further, if the statement is true, we cannot desire something to exist at a later moment than the present—say, in ten minutes' time—or for a period of time beginning at a later moment, e.g. we cannot desire ourselves, or another, X, to be at a certain place, or to be free from pain, ten minutes hence, or to be free from pain during tomorrow, or our family to have the means of subsistence next year or after our death. Therefore, if the state-

---

[1] *Structure and Growth of the Mind*, p. 34.

ment is true, where we are said to have these desires the desire we have must really be different, must be, e.g., the desire for the state of things to be at once such as will involve that our family will be well off after our death. And in support of this it may be urged that when we come to think the state of things to be such, owing to our thought of what we or others have done, the desire we had has gone, we are merely pleased by the thought that things are such that our family will be well off.

To this position it may be objected (a) that there really is such a desire as, e.g., our desire for our family to be well off after our death, and (b) that there really is such a desire even when we think things to be such that it will be well off, so that implication (1) of the amended statement is untrue.

Whether, however, statements (a) and (b) are true or not, there are other objections which are fatal.

The first is that 'not existing now' means not existing at this moment, and 'existing at once', or in the immediate future, will have to mean 'at the next moment'. But there is no such thing as the next moment. There is, of course, such a thing as the next portion of time, which is next to the last portion, the common limit of both being the present, but there is no moment next to the present moment. Consequently the 'desiring something to exist at once' (desiring, e.g., to be free from pain at once) part of the formula will not do.

The second is that the desire connected with the thought of something as not existing now, if there be one, will really have to be the desire of its existing now. And it seems impossible to deny that there is such a thing, though we usually call it a wish, e.g. my wish, when I have a toothache, that I were free from pain— though of course this desire is not one which can lead to action. But this desire is not the desire for the thing thought not to exist now to exist later.

The third is that even anyone who holds that we cannot desire something to exist at some future time, or for a time beginning at some moment in the future, will have to allow that we desire certain things which involve a certain duration, though he would say, and would have to say, that we desire them to exist at once, e.g. that we desire to turn our head or to hear 'God save the King'. But such a thing, since it has a duration, can neither exist now, i.e. at the present moment, nor can it exist at any moment in the future. To meet this objection, the view will have to be amended to: 'A desire is necessarily a desire for the existence in the immediate future of a process which we know or think has not yet existed.' But this statement will not hold because, if the process in the immediate future does take place, it will not be the process which did not take place before, for my turning my head, e.g., beginning at 12 o'clock will not be my previous turning my head. Strictly speaking, the desire for the thing which I think did not happen will be the wish that it had happened, as when I wish I had turned my head; and this will be different from the desire for its going to happen. The statement, therefore, requires a further amendment to: 'A desire is a desire for myself or another, X, to go through a certain process similar to one which I know or think he or I have not gone through.' But then the statement is open to the fatal objection that the desire to go through a certain process in the immediate future does *not* require the thought that I have not been through a similar process in the past. I can, e.g., desire X to be free from pain for the next five seconds, without thinking that he has been in pain for the last five seconds or for any time, as is implied where I give X a drug which I think will prevent a pain starting in him now, instead of giving him a drug which I think will cause him at once to become free from a pain which he already has been having. To meet this objection, the statement has to become: 'A desire is necessarily the desire of the existence in the immediate future of a process which I know or think will not exist in the immediate future.' This alteration is plainly a great alteration. And if it be allowed that some desires are desires for the existence in the immediate future of processes which we know or think will not exist in the immediate future, all objection seems gone to allowing the existence of desires for the existence of processes in the *not* immediate future, which we know or think will not then exist, such as the desire for our family's welfare after our death.

Implication (2) at p. 164 therefore has to go, and the formula will at least have to be: 'A desire is necessarily a desire for the existence during some time in the future of a process which we know or think will not exist during that time (the future here including the immediate future as a special case).'

Then, however, it is easy, without causing objection, to widen this formula to one which will take into account (1) desires which concern the past and the present as well as the future, and (2) desires concerning momentary states, e.g. my being at place A at 4 o'clock. We can say: 'A desire is necessarily a desire for the existence of some process during some portion of time in the past or in the future, as the case may be, or of the existence of some state at some moment in the past or in the future or at the present moment, the process or state being known or thought of as not going to exist during that time or at the moment in question, as the case may be.'

This statement retains implication (1) on p. 164 that what we desire is something which we know or think of as not existing, though we have ceased to understand not existing as not existing now.

The question, however, still remains: Is *know or think of* as not existing *at* or *during* a certain time right? And here, once more, an amendment seems required. For what, on reflection, we become forced to admit to be required if we are to desire X to have existed, to exist, or to be going to exist, is not that we know or think it not to have existed, to exist, or to be going to exist, but that we are uncertain about its existence. We therefore have to substitute for 'something which we know or think of as not having existed, not existing, or not going to exist', 'something of the existence of which in the past, the present, or the future, as the case may be, we are uncertain'.

Here, however, we seem to have reached bedrock, i.e. a position which is unquestionably true. And this seems to be the truth which underlies Cook Wilson's account of desiring as the desiring the existence of what does not exist, and of Mitchell's statement that we cannot desire what we already have—it being the truth, so to say, after which Cook Wilson and Mitchell are feeling or for which they are groping. In other words, to put the thing shortly, what they should have said is that we can only desire the existence of that of the existence of which in the past, present, or future, as the case may be, we are uncertain. No doubt the alteration is considerable, but it does leave a sort of core of truth in what they say.

Further, if this be allowed, then it cannot be true that we can desire, e.g., our family to be well off after our death, when we think without question that it *will* be well off, or, analogously, desire X to be now happy or at a place A when we think he *is* happy or at a place A, or desire X to have had a good holiday when we think he *has* had a good holiday.

In the preceding 'desiring something X' has throughout been represented as the desiring the existence of X, and the problems that have arisen have been concerned with the question 'existence when?' and the question 'Does it involve the thought or knowledge of X as existing?' But the question may be asked: 'Is this representation not misleading, if only because it is artificial to speak of thinking or apprehending something X as not existing—or even as existing?' For to think of anything as something or as not something, or to apprehend it as something or as not something, we must be thinking of it or apprehending it as something, i.e. something existing. The alternative account seems to be to represent a desire as a desire for something which I apprehend or else think of as having existed, existing, or going to exist, to have been, be, or be going to be of a certain sort, or, to put this otherwise, to have had, have, or be going to have a certain character, e.g. to represent (*a*) my desire to turn my head, as the desire for the process which I think of as that which I am going to go through, to be going to be one of turning my head, and (*b*) my desire for my family's being well off after my death, as the desire for what I think of as my family's state after my death, to be going to be one of being well off. Stated thus, a desire is not a desire for the existence of something but a desire for something *to be* (or, more fully, to have been, to be, or to be going to be, as the case may be) *so and so*. This seems a better answer, as soon as we take into account the thought (here using the word in a very wide sense) which is involved in a desire.

7

THE OBLIGATION TO KEEP
A PROMISE

IN promising, agreeing, or undertaking to do some action we seem to be creating or bringing into existence the obligation to do it, so much so that promising seems just to *be* binding ourselves, i.e. making ourselves bound, to do it, and the statement 'I ought to keep a promise', like 'I ought not to steal', seems a mere pleonasm. Once call some act a promise and all question of whether there is an obligation to do it seems to have vanished. In fact, the difference between doing something and promising to do it seems just to be that while in the one case we bring something into existence, in the other we bring into existence the obligation to bring it into existence.

Yet an obligation seems a fact of a kind which it is impossible to create or bring into existence. There are, no doubt, certain facts which we do seem able to create. If, e.g., I make someone angry, I appear to bring into existence the fact that he is angry. But the fact that I am bound to do some action seems no more one of these than does the fact that the square of three is odd.

The paradox is one which promising shares with giving and exchanging something. For, to take the case of giving only, what we call my giving X something seems to consist in substituting for an obligation on other people's part to refrain from doing anything which would prevent my having the power to use some material thing, a similar obligation on the part of me and everyone else except X to refrain from doing anything which would prevent X having the power to use it—so that it seems to consist in destroying one obligation and creating another. And for this reason giving and exchanging are just as paradoxical.

I propose to assume that we shall all allow on reflection that an obligation is a fact of a kind which it really is impossible to create or bring into existence directly. On this assumption we shall have to allow that the only way to resolve, i.e. to get rid of, the paradox is to succeed in making out that in what we call promising to do some action what we create or bring about is not really, as the term 'promising' suggests, the obligation to do the act promised but something else, our creation of which renders us bound to do the action promised. In other words, I shall assume that on reflection we shall all have to agree that what we call 'promising' to do so and so cannot really be what the term 'promising' suggests it is, viz. creating an obligation to do the action, but must be the creating something else, the creation of which gives rise to the obligation to do it, and that the problem is to find out what that something is. If we can find out what this is we shall, of course, remove the appearance of impossibility which promising presents. And in doing so we should, it may be noticed, be assimilating promising to acts of certain other kinds, our having done which we think leads to an obligation to do something else. Instances would be (1) hurting the feelings of another, which we think renders us bound to assuage them so far as we can; (2) misleading another, which we think leads to the obligation to correct the misconception; and (3) becoming the father of a family, which we think gives rise to the obligation to feed and educate it. The assimilation, however, it would seem, cannot be complete, since our immediate object in what we call promising to do some action seems to be to create, even though indirectly, the obligation to do some action, as it is not, e.g., in hurting the feelings of another.

We get into difficulties, however, as soon as we try to state what that is in what we call making a promise the production of which renders us bound to do the action which we are said to promise to do.

We never do what we should describe as promising a man X to do some action unless we have in some degree the expectation that if we do we shall produce in X the expectation that we shall do the action. Hence, the suggestion which is first likely to occur to us is that the thing for which we are looking is the expectation in the person promised that we shall do the action. But, of course, this suggestion is at least too wide. Otherwise, when, hoping to stave off the interruptions of a neighbour, I drive past him in a taxi loaded with luggage, I should be said to be promising to go away. At least the expectation, as is otherwise obvious, must be an expectation produced in a particular way, viz. by the use of language. But even so the suggestion is too wide. Otherwise an employer who, on learning that his men hesitated to put their backs into their work for fear that if they did their time rates of pay would be reduced, *argued* them into believing that he would not be such a fool as to do this, would be said to be promising not to do it. Nor—

and this is more important—is the suggestion right, if it be further limited by the condition that the language used is the expression of the thought of a resolve. If, instead, the employer said, 'I have no intention of reducing the rates', i.e. really 'I have *resolved* not to', he still would not be *promising* not to reduce them, even if his men expected that he would not change his mind and so would not, in fact, reduce the rates. And anyone in the employer's position would recognize that in saying this he was not promising. For suppose, having said this, he found he had not convinced the men, he might then, in the hope of convincing them, say: 'Well, I *promise* not to change the rates if you speed up.' And in saying this he would be aware that he was now doing something different. Moreover, if in promising we were stating that we had made a resolve, a promise would be true or false, yet while everyone would allow that a promise may be made either in good or in bad faith, no one would allow that it could be either true or false. Rather, they would insist that promising resembles asking a question or issuing an order, in that it consists not in making a statement but in doing something, in the sense in which we oppose doing to mere talking.

Further, consideration of the contrast between the employer's expressing the resolve to maintain the wage rates and his promising to do so brings to light a more important fact. The expectation, so far as it is produced, will in each case be based on quite different beliefs. In the one case it will be based on the beliefs (1) that the employer was speaking truthfully, and (2) that he is not likely to change his mind on such a matter. In the other it will be based at least in part on the belief that the employer thinks that he has bound himself simply by promising, whether he produces the expectation or not, together with the belief that since he is a comparatively moral, i.e. conscientious, being he is likely to do whatever he thinks he is bound to do. And once we realize that such expectation as is produced by a promise is of this character, we shall have to allow that any attempt to base the obligation to keep a promise on promising's being the creating of an expectation is doomed to failure. For what we have to do is to state what it is that I bring about in what is called my promising X to do some action, the thought of my bringing which about leads me or X or anyone else to think that I am bound to do the action. And this cannot be represented as the expectation in X that I shall do the action, if the expectation be one resting on the belief that I believe that, by what is called my promising, I become bound to do the action irrespectively of whether I produce the expectation that I shall do the action. For on this hypothesis X will be thinking what it is impossible for him to think, viz. that I have a certain thought which neither he nor anyone else can have.

To this we may simply add that, in fact, where I do what is called making a promise, I do not think that my obligation to do the action promised arises from my producing the expectation.

Hence, we cannot resolve the paradox by representing promising as producing an expectation. Nor do we fare better if we represent it as expressing a resolve, for even if, when we make a promise in good faith, we necessarily have resolved to do the action promised, no one on close consideration would allow that the promise is just the expression of our resolve.

What, then, are we to do? One thing is obvious. Promising requires the actual use of the word 'promise' or else of some equivalent, such as 'undertake', 'agree', 'give you my word', or 'will' in 'I *will*'. This being so, we can at least say that when I promise X to do some action, I am causing X to hear a certain noise, which has a definite meaning both to X and to me, together with the term ordinarily used for the action, in such a way that X believes that the sounds proceed from me. But then the question at once arises: 'How can my doing this give rise to an obligation to do the action?' And the answer seems to have to be: 'Only because I have already promised not to cause a noise of that kind in connexion with the phrase for some action, without going on to do the action.' And if this answer is right, what we call promising to do some action appears to be causing someone to hear in connexion with the term for the action a noise of a kind which I have promised never to use in this kind of way without going on to do the action; and, again, the reason why, when I say to X 'I promise to do so and so', I am bound to do the action is that I have previously made him a certain general promise.

Now this account of what promising is is, of course, rather odd. For 'promising' as ordinarily used means 'binding oneself', i.e. rendering oneself bound, and if the account is right, what is usually called, say, my promising to meet X in London, is, strictly speaking, not *promising* to meet him but making certain noises in virtue of which I become bound to meet him in consequence of my having previously made a certain general promise, and the real promise lies in this previous act.

Further, the most obvious objections to this account are two:

1. It seems merely fanciful to maintain that we can trace in our own mental history this general promise.
2. Even if we can make out that we have made this general promise, then, though we shall have removed the paradox of its seeming to create an obligation from what is usually called making some particular promise, we shall only have transferred the paradox to the general promise, for we shall have to allow that in making the general promise not to use a certain noise in a certain way without going on to do some action, we are *creating* the obligation not to do so; so that we are really no better off.

Here, however, two remarks may be made:

1. Even if it be true that the problem has only been transferred from one thing to another, it may still be true that the problem has to be so transferred. It may be *true* that a so-called particular promise implies a prior general promise, and if so we have to transfer the problem to get at it in its proper form. It is therefore of importance to ascertain whether what we call a particular promise really *does* imply a prior general promise.
2. The account is *not* open to what at first seems a fatal objection, viz. that it bases the obligation to keep an agreement (a promise) on a general agreement to keep agreements, and on that ground involves us in an infinite regress. For, strictly speaking, according to this account, an agreement to do a particular action is *not* an agreement, and the general agreement is not an agreement to keep our agreements, but an agreement to do what is ordinarily called keeping our agreements, i.e. not to make a certain noise in connexion with the phrase for some action without going on to do the action.

Before considering, however, whether this account can be defended, it will be well first to do something else. It is, no doubt, puzzling to be told that where we have used the language of promising, what we call the obligation to keep a promise depends on our having made a previous general promise. But, nevertheless, as things are now, we all in fact think that by using this language in connexion with the phrase for some action we do become bound to do the action.

It is, however, possible to imagine ourselves at a stage at which we do not think that by using this or any other special form of language we become so bound. And if we do this, we can ask: (1) Should we at this stage come to want at least to be *able* by using some special form of language to become bound, and (2) if we did, is there any step which we could take, by taking which we should become able?

These assertions, however, need some elucidation and defence before we can try to act on them.

Two things at least seem clear. One is that keeping some promise cannot be the first act which a man thinks himself bound to do. For if he is even to think of such a thing as promising, or to know the meaning of the term 'promising' or a synonym for it, he must already have the thought of obligation, and therefore must have already thought of other acts as duties. The second is that promises can only be made between members of a group of men—which need not consist of more than two—each of whom believes, and in acting to some extent relies on the belief, that the others are beings who not only think they have certain obligations but are likely to do what they think themselves bound to do. For promising seems to require a certain reliance by others on the belief that the man who promises is to some degree likely to carry out what he thinks he is bound to do, and others can only acquire this belief by finding that he has frequently carried out other acts he thought duties because he thought them duties. For promising, then, to be possible, there must be a group of men who think they have certain obligations to others, natural in the sense of independent of any promise, and who are, and are thought, likely to carry out what they think obligations. Instances of what they might think to be such obligations might be to refrain from affecting or dealing with the body of another and to refrain from affecting those material things with which a man has 'mixed his labour'.

It is, therefore, not nonsense to speak of the existence of such a group, and we can imagine ourselves as forming such a group, i.e. a group of men who as yet have no idea that there can be such a thing as promising, but who think they have certain duties to the others and are, and are thought, likely to act on the thought. Now imagine ourselves such a group. It is obvious that if we formed such a group, we should each soon come to realize that the success of any efforts to achieve a welfare of our own would depend not merely on the fact that the others would act, and refrain from acting, in certain ways which they thought a duty, but also on our being able to rely on the belief that they would. Otherwise we could not hope with success even to make plans for seeking our welfare, except in a very minor degree. But it would soon also become obvious to us that to devise even moderately hopeful plans we should need more. To realize that more is needed we should only have to notice that nearly all action which is of importance for our own welfare requires the co-operation of someone else, and then to consider what is required for the co-operation to be possible. Where two people co-operate, they have either the same or different ends, but the realization of their end or ends requires the realization of a common means which has in part to be brought about by the one and in part by the other, as where two walkers by their joint efforts manage to remove from their path an obstructing log, which neither could move separately. And their co-operation requires the use of language, in a wide sense of the term, whereby each comes to have some expectation that the other will do a certain action if he himself does a certain other action. Further, to a limited extent co-operation is possible if the communication between them consists in the expression of an intention, i.e., really, of a resolve. For let A and B stand for the men whose way is blocked by a log, and assume that A is a sensible or rational person, and also that A thinks B a sensible or rational person. For A to start shifting one end of the log it is enough for him to come to think, on the strength of some communication from B, not, of course, necessarily in words, that B has resolved to start shifting the other end, if he sees A starting to shift the former end. For A will then think that B, being a sensible person, is unlikely to change his mind either before A starts lifting or half-way through. But the possibility of the co-operation which depends on the expression of a resolve is very limited in range because everyone knows men's liability to change their minds. And what each of us would soon realize is that, for co-operation to be possible for us on any important scale, we should have to get into a position in which, if some other member of our group were to use certain language with reference to some action he might take, we could rely on the belief that he would, in fact, go on to do the action in consequence of having used the language, even in cases where he would have been likely to change his mind but for having used the language.

We should then begin to consider how it would be possible to get into such a position, as a condition necessary for the successful pursuit of our own welfare to a reasonable extent.

It would, of course, occur to us that some outside party could get us into the position if he could devise and set up the means of enforcing a system of penalties for using some given symbol in connexion with the term for some action without going on to do the action. For the position would then be one in which someone else by, e.g., signing a legal document, would be bringing on himself the prospect of such a heavy loss if he did not do a certain action that we could rely on his being too little of a fool not to carry out the action, even if apart from the prospect of a penalty he was anxious to avoid doing it.

Again—and I mention this to introduce what Hume has in mind[1]—it would occur to us that provided that in some unexplained way we had all acquired the belief that others would do an action with reference to which they had used certain language, we might come to think the advantage to ourselves of others continuing to think this about ourselves in particular so great that for that reason we should as sensible or rational beings always carry out such an action in consequence—to quote Hume's phrase[2]—of having subjected ourselves 'to the penalty of never being trusted again'. In this way (we should realize) we should produce the position desired for ourselves, though the possibility of our doing it would seem to be barred by what would seem the impossibility of acquiring the initial belief.

But, of course, we should realize that if the position were arrived at in either of these ways, we should not, when we had reached it, in the least be led to think that we were bound to do any action with reference to which we had used the language. We should only think doing the action wise or sensible.

We should next come to think that as we were all fairly conscientious we could attain the position if we could all somehow manage to come to think that if we used certain language in connexion with some action we thereby became bound to do the action, since then also each of us could rely on the belief that another would do the action. We should then wish we all did think this. But, unfortunately, being neither lunatics nor pragmatists, we should recognize that any attempt to attain the position in this way would fail, since our knowledge that if we all had this belief our having it would be extremely useful to ourselves would not in the least lead us to have it. And we should abandon any attempt to carry out this plan, merely regretfully wishing we had the belief, and perhaps envying any who had it.

[1] *A Treatise of Human Nature*, Bk. III, § 5.   [2] Ib., p. 522 (see Selby-Bigge).

As regards what we should, in fact, do next there seems to be little doubt, even if afterwards we could not defend our procedure from the charge of absurdity. We should say to one another: 'Obviously we all want this position to arise: let us attain it by first fixing on a certain noise or mark on paper which could be made in connexion with using the term for an action, and then agreeing or promising not to make this noise or mark in connexion with using the term for some action without going on to do the action. If we do this the trick will be done, because then, by making the noise or mark thus, we shall be bringing into existence the obligation to do the action in virtue of our general agreement or promise.' And we should, in fact, come to agree to do this because we should recognize that we should have much to gain by agreeing and nothing which we should necessarily lose, since there is no hardship in abstaining from making a certain noise, and we could keep our agreement by never making the noise.

Now it is, of course, easy to retort that to talk thus is simply to talk nonsense. In particular it is easy to urge (1) that the supposed general agreement could itself only be made by the use of special language, and that to account for our thinking we were bound by it we should have to allow that we thought we had already made another agreement which formed the reason why, when using this language in making the general agreement, we were bound to keep it, and that this thought would in turn require another similar thought, and so on; and (2) that in imagining that we in the circumstances supposed should make the general agreement, we are tacitly taking for granted that we are the beings we are now, who already think ourselves bound by any agreement.

Nevertheless, it is not clear that even if the idea stated is nonsense, it is such nonsense as all that, and that there may not after all be something in it. We all think that by what we call promising to do some action we do render ourselves bound to do it, so much so that if we are asked what we mean by 'promising', we are apt to answer that it is just binding ourselves to do it. But obviously it is impossible by any action whatever simply to create an obligation, i.e. to create it and nothing else. If we are to create an obligation, we can do it only by creating or bringing into existence something else. And, in the case of what we call promising to do some action, that by creating which we think we are creating the obligation to do the action is, strictly speaking, certain noises. Consequently we have got to account for the fact that we do think that by making certain noises we render ourselves bound to do a certain action; and consequently we must admit the reality of any thought which we must have, if we are to have, as we do have, this thought. And if we can make out that it would be simply impossible to think that the production of the noises would give rise to an obligation, unless we thought that we had already made some promise about our making such noises, then we have got to allow that in some way or other we have this thought, and that therefore there must have been some such promise, though from the nature of the case we must have made it somehow without language. And here, to emphasize the difficulty of avoiding giving this answer, it is worth while to notice two answers which certainly will not do.

First, it is of course obvious that if I merely cause the hearing of the noise 'promise' in the mind of another along with the noise ordinarily used as a symbol for some action, without my knowing, or without his knowing, what (as we should say) the noise means, I am not making a promise, nor do we think that I thereby become bound to do the action. Where I make a promise, not only must I make the noise 'promise' but I must know and the other man must know what the word means. Realizing this, we are apt to try to maintain, as a way of getting an easier solution, that the very act of using the term 'promise' in its ordinary sense in connexion with the phrase for some particular action, to someone who understands this sense, involves as something inseparable from itself an act of promising not to make such a noise in connexion with the term for any action without going on to do the action. This answer would have the advantage of saving us from having to admit the existence of a *prior* promise. But unfortunately it will not do. For the problem is to understand how it is that we think that if we make the noise 'promise' in connexion with the phrase for some action we shall thereby become bound to do the action. And to account for this thought we shall have to represent ourselves, not as thinking that by doing the action we should be making the general promise, but as thinking that we have already made it. To put this otherwise, to account for our using the term 'promise' in the ordinary sense, we must think of ourselves as thinking we have already made the general promise, and not as thinking that, in using it, we shall be, or are, making it.

Then, second, as an alternative way of easing the difficulty we may try to maintain that where we are said to promise someone that we shall do some action, we are inevitably representing ourselves to him as a being who *thinks* that by making the noise 'promise' in connexion with the term for some action he becomes bound to do the action, and that by so representing ourselves we become as much bound to do such an action as we should be if making the noise really did render us bound to do it. But if this answer were right we could not do what is called making a promise without lying, for in doing this we should inevitably be representing ourselves as thinking that by making the noise we became bound, although in fact we thought we were not.

The general conclusion which I wish to suggest, but only with the greatest hesitation, is that promising to do this or that action, in the ordinary sense of promising, can only exist among individuals between whom there has already been something which looks at first like an agreement to keep agreements, but is really an agreement not to use certain noises except in a certain way, the agreement nevertheless being one which, unlike ordinary agreements, does not require the use of language. But, of course, it would be more accurate to say that what I am suggesting is not a conclusion but rather a problem for consideration; viz. what is that something implied in the existence of agreements which looks very much like an agreement and yet, strictly speaking, cannot be an agreement?

8

EXCHANGING

EVEN exchanging one thing for another seems to involve promising. Suppose I have a spare banana, and X has a spare apple, and we meet. I realize that I should gain if it happened that I lost control of the banana and also gained control of the apple. But I want not to lose control of the banana unless somehow I do it by an act which will give me control of the apple. I may, e.g., resolve to hand over the banana, if I can be assured that if I do I shall in consequence receive the apple. But I shall not hand over the banana unless I have some confidence that if I do I shall in consequence get the apple. How am I to acquire this confidence?

In actual life I should say to X, 'I will give you this banana if you will give me that apple', and X might say to me, 'All right; if you hand over the banana I will hand you the apple'—and then I, hearing X, would be likely to hand over the banana, expecting that when I have done so X will hand over the apple.

Can we express these statements in terms of expressing a resolve?

The first will have to be: I have resolved to hand over to you this banana, if I hear you say, 'I have resolved to hand over this apple, if I find you hand over the banana.'

This implies that it is possible for me to think that it is possible for X to have resolved to hand over the apple, *if* he finds that I have handed over the banana. But though it is possible for X to resolve to hand over the apple anyhow, he cannot resolve to do it if, i.e. *only if*, I have handed over the banana. For *ex hypothesi* if X had not resolved to hand it over before, the knowledge that I have handed over the banana would not get him any nearer resolving to hand over the apple. And, again, for this reason, X cannot truthfully say 'I have resolved to hand you over the apple if I find you have handed over the banana'.

This is parallel to Hume's case, where my corn is ripe to-morrow and X's corn is ripe to-day. X cannot resolve to cut my corn to-morrow if he finds I have cut his to-day. And so I cannot say, 'I will cut your corn to-day, if you have resolved that if I do you will cut mine to-morrow.' I do not think such a resolve on X's part is possible.

I must mean: 'I bind myself to hand over the banana, provided you bind yourself, on seeing me hand it over, to hand over the apple.' And X must mean: 'Since you have bound yourself to hand over the banana provided that I bind myself to hand over the apple provided that I see you hand over the banana, I bind myself to hand over the apple provided that I see you hand over the banana.'

The difference between my act and his is that I bind myself to do some act α, provided that X binds himself to do some other act β, if he finds I do the action α, whereas X binds himself to do something β provided he finds that I do something α.

I, in binding myself thus, think that if he binds himself to do a certain action if he finds a certain condition fulfilled, he will do it if he finds the condition fulfilled.

X, in binding himself thus, thinks that as I have bound myself to do a certain action if a certain condition is fulfilled, I shall in consequence do it.

In the above cases my action comes first (handing over the banana; reaping X's corn), and X binds himself to do his action, if he finds that I have done mine.

But what about the cases where my action need not come first, and X's obligation is not conditional on knowing that I have done it? Such a case would be: 'I will fetch water for you if you will fetch bananas for me.' I make the proposal and say: 'I bind myself to fetch water for you, provided you bind yourself to fetch bananas for me.' X must mean: 'Since you have bound yourself to fetch water for me provided I bind myself to fetch bananas for you, I bind myself to fetch bananas for you.'

I in promising think that if X binds himself he *will* fetch bananas for me.

X in binding himself thinks that as I have bound myself to fetch him water if he binds himself to fetch bananas for me, if he binds himself I shall in consequence think myself bound to fetch his water, and shall in consequence fetch it.

9

THE TIME OF AN OBLIGATION

1. To express the thought that I ought to do a certain action α in the *is* form, in order to make an understandable contrast with 'I am doing α', we have to substitute either 'I am oughting to do α' or else 'I am under an obligation to do α', in both statements 'am' seeming to have the sense of the present tense.

2. It would ordinarily be said that it is a condition of my oughting or being under a moral obligation to do α, that I have not done α and that it may be that I shall not. The alternative view is that this is not true, the truth being that it is not a condition either that I shall or that I shall not, my obligation being independent of whether I shall or whether I shall not do it, and (it seems also) that it is impossible that I should have done what I am under an obligation to do.

3. The proper contrasts are between:

    (*a*) 'I shall do α'
         and 'I shall be oughting to do α'.
    (*b*) 'I am doing α'
         and 'I am oughting to do α'.
    (*c*) 'I was doing α'
         and 'I was oughting to do α'.

An action takes time. And it would be natural to say: 'I shall to-morrow from ten to eleven be under an obligation to lecture from ten to eleven,' and also: 'I was yesterday from ten to eleven under an obligation to lecture yesterday from ten to eleven,' the truth of the first statement being independent of whether I shall, and that of the second independent of whether I did—so that it may be the case that I was from ten to eleven both oughting to do α from ten to eleven and also from ten to eleven doing α from ten to eleven; and the truth of the first half of the statement being compatible with that of the second, and not requiring that I *did not* lecture from ten to eleven.

What about the contrast between, e.g. 'I am going to bed' and 'I should be going, or am *oughting* to go, to bed'?

'I am going to bed' really refers to an action, part of which is just over and part of which is to come. And with this contrasts

'I ought to go to bed, or am under an obligation to go to bed', a statement referring partly to a just past being under an obligation to go to bed during that past time, and a just future obligation to go to bed during that future time—I *am* oughting to go to bed not having the force of a present.

Alternatively, however, 'I am going to bed' may mean 'I am starting to go to bed', i.e. *beginning* a certain process, and with this contrasts 'I am under an obligation to begin the process of going to bed'; this statement being independent of whether I *am* going to bed.

The corresponding independence in the former case is the non-dependence of a past obligation to do part of the process of going to bed on my having done this, and that of a future obligation on my coming to do it.

4. The moral is that 'I am oughting, or under an obligation, to go to bed' refers to the future, meaning 'from now on I shall be under an obligation to go to bed', the obligation coinciding in time with the act, and has as its contrast 'from now on I shall be going to bed'; and that it does not require that I shall not do the action; and also, that it does not require that I have not done the action.

10

THE PSYCHOLOGY OF WILLING

THERE are many occasions on which if I were to do a certain action, although my doing it would cause a certain evil to me, it would cause a benefit to me greater than the pain. Instances would be (1) putting a drug on my tooth which would kill a nerve, and so permanently getting rid of the pain, (2) asking a dentist to take out a certain tooth. There are also occasions on which, although doing the action would cause a certain gain to me, it would bring me a greater evil later, e.g. (1) taking an extra glass of wine, or an extra helping of a certain food, (2) when I have gout, taking a drug which would stop the pain for the moment, but would make the gout worse.

In any of these cases, I may do what we should describe as considering doing it. When this happens, what will happen? No general answer is possible.

Consider the drugging the tooth case (killing the nerve). A dentist may have told me that though the pain will be sharp it will not be more than sharp, and will not last, and I may believe him and be confident that the toothache will go on if I do not put on the drug. It may happen that I shall decide without difficulty to put it on, i.e. it may not take much, if any, effort to decide. And having decided to put it on, I put it on. (This implies a distinction between deciding to put it on and putting it on.) And it might afterwards happen that, having put it on, I found the pain so very much worse than I had been led to expect, that I should say afterwards 'Putting it on was not worth it', and that if the situation were to repeat itself with another tooth, I should decide not to put the nerve-killing stuff on. And I might add that my decision would be correct or the right decision. (E.g. 'It would be the right decision not to take the pain-killing stuff in the next case, when I had on a former occasion taken the drug, thinking that I should thereby gain more than I should lose.') Suppose the situation repeated itself about the nerve-killer. I should at once conclude that to put on the nerve-killer would not bring me gain, and I should have an instinctive aversion to putting the nerve-killer on. Would there be a decision not to put the stuff on? It looks as if there would, and a decision at once. Suppose, however, that I had once put on the nerve-killer (or that someone else had for me) and afterwards I thought it had been worth while, and now thought that the situation repeated itself in the case of another tooth, and thought that if I put the stuff on, I should on balance gain. Suppose, too, that I desired to put the stuff on.

I want the iodine to be on my gum. I know that if it is to come to be on my gum, I must cause it to go from the end of a brush in my hand to my gum. I ask: 'How am I to cause it to go through this movement?' I answer: 'I must cause my hand which is holding the brush to go from where it is to a spot A. How am I to cause this?' The question is mistaken, involving an infinite process. But I may think that if I were to will this movement, my willing it would cause my hand to go from where it is to A.

Suppose I say: If I am to will this movement to exist, I must cause the willing to exist', and suppose I then ask: 'How am I to cause the willing of that movement?' I might answer: 'Well, to cause this to exist, I must will the willing of that movement, thinking this willing the willing would cause it to exist'; and this seems impossible.

I say to myself: 'How is the willing of that movement to come to exist?' (not 'How am I to cause it?'). Only by my desiring to will it, and desiring to will it more than I am averse to willing it.

I then say to myself: 'Desiring to will it, I in consequence desire to come to desire more to will it, and desiring to desire more to will it, I in consequence desire to think more of what I should gain if I should will that movement'—thinking that if I thought more of what I should gain if I willed that movement, I should in consequence come to desire more to will that movement, in the hope that in consequence I should desire to will it to a degree sufficient to make me will that movement. (Here I am presupposing that, if I come to desire to a sufficient degree to will it, I shall will that movement.)

I am then presupposing that if I *do* come to will that movement, that in consequence of which I shall come to will it is my coming to desire to a sufficient degree to will that movement; so that if I do come to will that movement, I come to will it not by doing something but by desiring something, i.e. desiring to a sufficient degree to will it. For this to happen I must will the thinking, more than I *am* thinking, of what I should gain if I willed that movement more.

Desiring to desire more the willing the change, I desire to come to think more of what would happen if I willed that movement, since I think that if I do I shall strengthen my desire to will that movement; and thinking thus I shall think more fully of what I shall gain if I do come to will this change—thinking that if I do I shall increase my desire to will the change—so that it comes about that I will the thinking of what I shall gain if I do will that movement; this really, of course, being an act of will. If, then, I do come to will the change X, there has been beforehand my willing to think more of what I shall gain if I will it, this causing an increase of my desire to will that change. There will then have been two acts of will: first, a willing to think more of what I shall gain if I will X—this due to the desire to will X—and second, a willing the change X.

11

ACTING, WILLING, DESIRING

THE question 'What is acting or doing something?' seems at first unreal, i.e. a question to which we already know the answer. For it looks as though everyone knows what doing something is and would be ready to offer instances. No one, for instance, would hesitate to say to another 'You ought to go to bed', on the ground that neither he nor the other knows the kind of thing meant by 'going to bed'. Yet, when we consider instances that would be offered, we do not find it easy to state the common character which we think they had which led us to call them actions.

If, as a preliminary, we look for help to the psychologists, from whom we naturally expect to get it, we find we fail. We find plenty of talk about reflex actions, ideo-motor actions, instinctive actions, and so on, but no discussion of what actions are. Instead, they seem to take for granted that our actions are physical processes taking place within our body, which they certainly are not.

We should at first say that to do something is to originate or to bring into existence, i.e., really, to cause, some not yet existing state either of ourselves or of someone else, or, again, of some body. But, for clearness' sake, we should go on to distinguish those actions in doing which we originated some new state directly from those in which we did this only indirectly, i.e. by originating directly some other state, by originating which we indirectly originated the final state. As instances of the former we might give moving or turning our head, and as instances of the latter, curing our toothache by swallowing aspirin, and killing another by pressing a switch which exploded a charge underneath him. If challenged, however, we should have to allow that even in instances of the former kind we did not originate directly what the instances suggest that we did, since what we did originate directly must have been some new state or states of our nerve-cells, of the nature of which we are ignorant. We should, however, insist that in doing any action we must have originated *something* directly, since otherwise we could not originate anything indirectly.

The view that to act is to originate something was maintained by Cook Wilson in a paper on *Means and End*. In the course of this paper he also maintained (1) that an action required the desire to do it, and (2) that it is important to avoid the mistake of thinking that the origination of something X is the willing of X, apparently on the ground that if it were, X would exist as soon as we willed it, and yet it usually does not. He also appeared to hold that the origination of X, though not identical with willing the origination, required it, so that when I originated a movement of my hand, this required as an antecedent my willing this origination, and this willing in turn required the desiring to originate the movement.

According to Cook Wilson, then, in considering an action we have to distinguish three things: first, the action itself, the originating something; second, the required willing to originate this; and third, the required desire to originate this. And according to him what we will and what we desire are the same, viz. the action.

Professor Macmurray, in a Symposium[1] on 'What is action?', takes substantially the same view of what an action is. He says: 'An action is not the concomitance of an intention in the mind and an occurrence in the physical world: it is the *producing* of the occurrence by the Self, the *making* of a change in the external world, the *doing* of a deed. No process which terminates in the mind, such as forming an intention, deciding to act, or willing, is either an action or a component of action.' But he goes on to add: 'In certain circumstances such a mental event or process may be followed *necessarily* by action.'

Now, so far as I can see, this account of what an action is, though plausible and having as a truth underlying it that usually in acting we do cause something, is not tenable.

Unquestionably the thing meant by 'an action' is an activity. This is so whether we speak of a man's action in moving his hand, or of a body's action such as that of the heart in pumping the blood, or that of one electron in repelling another. But though we think that some man in moving his hand, or that the sun in attracting the earth, causes a certain movement, we do not think that the man's or the sun's activity *is* or *consists in* causing the movement. And if we ask ourselves: 'Is there such an activity as originating or causing a change in something else?', we have to answer that there is not. To say this, of course, is not to say that there is no such thing as causing something, but only to say that

¹ Aristotelian Society, Supplementary Volume XVII (1938).

though the causing a change may require an activity, it is not itself an activity. If we then ask: 'What is the kind of activity required when one body causes another to move?', we have to answer that we do not know, and that when we speak of a force of attraction or of repulsion we are only expressing our knowledge that there is some activity at work, while being ignorant of what the kind of activity is. In the case, however, of a man, i.e., really, of a man's mind, the matter is different. When, e.g., we think of ourselves as having moved our hand, we are thinking of ourselves as having performed an activity of a certain kind, and, it almost goes without saying, a *mental* activity of a certain kind, an activity of whose nature we were dimly aware in doing the action and of which we can become more clearly aware by reflecting on it. And that we are aware of its special nature is shown by our unhesitatingly distinguishing it from other special mental activities such as thinking, wondering, and imagining. If we ask 'What is the word used for this special kind of activity?' the answer, it seems, has to be 'willing'. (I now think I was mistaken in suggesting that the phrase in use for it is 'setting oneself to cause'.) We also have to admit that while we know the general character of that to which we refer when we use the word 'willing', this character is *sui generis* and so incapable of being defined, i.e. of having its nature expressed in terms of the nature of other things. Even Hume virtually admits this when he says: 'By the *will*, I mean nothing but *the internal impression we feel and are conscious of, when we knowingly give rise to any new motion of our body or new perception of our mind*',[1] and then goes on to add that the impression is impossible to define. Though, however, the activity of willing is indefinable, we can distinguish it from a number of things which it is not. Thus obviously, as Locke insisted, willing is different from desiring, and again, willing is not, as some psychologists would have it, a species of something called conation of which desiring is another species. There is no such genus. Again, it is not, as Green in one passage[2] implies, a species of desiring which is desiring in another sense than that ordinary sense in which we are said to desire while hesitating to act.

In addition, plainly, willing is not resolving, nor attending to a difficult object, as James holds, nor for that matter attending to anything, nor, again, consenting to the reality of what is attended to, as James also maintains, nor, indeed, consenting to anything,

[1] Hume, *Treatise* (Selby-Bigge, p. 399).   [2] *Prolegomena*, §§ 140–2.

nor, once more, identifying ourself with some object of desire, as Green asserts in another passage.[1]

Consequently, there seems to be no resisting the conclusion that where we think of ourselves or of another as having done a certain action, the kind of activity of which we are thinking is that of willing (though we should have to add that we are thinking of our particular act of willing as having been the doing of the action in question, only because we think it caused a certain change), and that when we refer to some instance of this activity, such as our having moved our finger or given some friend a headache, we refer to it thus not because we think it was, or consisted in, the causing our finger to move or our friend's head to ache, but because we think it had a certain change of state as an effect.

If, as it seems we must, we accept this conclusion, that to act is really to will something, we then become faced by the question: 'What sort of thing is it that we will?'

Those who, like Cook Wilson, distinguish between acting and willing, answer that what we will is an action, which according to him is the originating some change. Thus Green says: 'To will an event' (i.e. presumably some change) 'as distinguished from an act is a contradiction.' And by this he seems to mean that, for instance, in the case which he takes of our paying a debt, what we will is the paying of our debt and not our creditor's coming into possession of what we owe him. Again, James and Stout, though they do not consider the question, show by their instances that they take for granted that what we will is an action. Thus James says: 'I will to write, and the act follows. I will to sneeze and it does not.'[2] And Stout illustrates a volition by a man's willing to produce an explosion by applying a lighted match to gunpowder.[3] But, unfortunately, James speaks of what he has referred to as, the act of writing which I will, as certain physiological movements, and similarly Stout speaks of, the production of an explosion which I will, as certain bodily movements. And, of course, the bodily movements to which they are referring are not actions, though they may be the effects of actions. Plainly, then, both are only doing lipservice to the idea that what we will is an action. And James, at least, drops doing even this. For immediately after making the statement just quoted, viz. 'I will to write, and the act follows. I will to sneeze and it does not', he adds: 'I will that the distant

---

[1] *Prolegomena*, § 146.   [2] James, *Psychology*, ii, p. 560.
[3] Stout, *Manual of Psychology*, iv, p. 641.

table slide over the floor towards me; it also does not.' Yet no one would say that the sliding of the table, as distinct from my sliding it, was an action.

In this connexion it is well for clearness' sake to bear two things in mind. The first is that some transitive verbs used for particular actions are also used intransitively. Thus one not only speaks of turning one's head but also says that one's head turned. And the second is that, while the phrase 'turning one's head' stands for an action and so for an activity of one's mind, yet when I say 'my head turned' I am speaking simply of a movement of my head which is a change of place and not an action. The difference is made clear by considering what is plainly a mistake made by Professor Macmurray. He says that the term 'action' is ambiguous. He says: 'It may refer either to what is done or to the doing of it. It may mean either "doing" or "deed". When we talk of "an action" we are normally referring to what is done. . . . To act is to effect a change in the external world. The deed is the change so effected.' And he emphasizes what he considers the ambiguity in order to indicate that it is doings and not deeds that he is considering. Obviously, however, there is no ambiguity whatever. When I move my hand, the movement of my hand, though an effect of my action, is not itself an action, and no one who considered the matter would say it was, any more than he would say that the death of Caesar, as distinct from his murder, was an action or even part of an action.

This difference between, e.g., my moving my hand and a movement of my hand, is one which James and Stout seem to ignore, as becomes obvious when James speaks of the sliding of a table as, like writing, an action. We find the same thing, too, in Locke. For though, e.g., he says that 'we find by experience, that, barely by willing it, we can move the parts of our bodies',[1] yet in contrasting a human with a physical action he implies that what we will is a movement of our body. Probably, if pressed, he would have said that, strictly speaking, what we will is a movement and so not an action. In addition, James and Stout seem to treat the distinction between an act of willing, or, as they prefer to call it, a volition, and what is willed, as if it were the same as the distinction between an act of willing and its effect, although they are totally different.

It should be clear from what I have just said that those who hold that what we will is an action must, to be successful, mean

[1] Locke, *Essay*, ii. 21, § 4.

by an action something which really is an action. They may, of course, maintain that what we will is a physical process, such as a movement of my hand, but if they do they are really denying that what we will is an action.

It should also now be clear that if we face the question 'What sort of thing do we will?', we have only two answers to consider: (1) that it is some change of state of some thing or person; and (2) that it is an action. If, however, we are forced to conclude, as we have been, that doing something is an act of willing, we seem forced to exclude the second answer, simply on the ground that if it were true, then whenever we think of ourselves as having done some action, we must be thinking of ourselves as having willed some action, i.e. as having willed the willing of some change X; and to think this seems impossible. By the very nature of willing, it seems, what we will must be something other than willing, so that to will the willing of a change X must be an impossibility. And if we even try to deny this, we find ourselves forced to admit that the willing of X, which (we are contending) is what we will, must in turn really be the willing the willing of something else, and so on, and thus become involved in an infinite regress. It is true that Cook Wilson, in a long unpublished discussion, tried to vindicate the analogous idea that in certain limiting cases, viz. those in which the desire moving us is not the desire of some change but the desire to cause it ourselves, as happens in playing golf or patience, what we originate is identical with our origination of something. But he never seems to me to succeed in meeting the objection that this identity must be impossible. Similarly, it seems to me, it is impossible for there to be a case in which the willing the willing of X is identical with willing X.

We are thus left with the conclusion that where we think we have done some action, e.g. have raised our arm or written a word, what we willed was some change, e.g. some movement of our arm or some movement of ink to a certain place on a piece of paper in front of us. But we have to bear in mind that the change which we willed may not have been the same as the change we think we effected. Thus, where I willed some movement of my second finger, I may at least afterwards think that the change I effected was a movement of my first finger, and, only too often, where I willed the existence of a certain word on a piece of paper, I afterwards find that what I caused was a different word. Again, in two cases of the act we call trying to thread a needle, what I willed may have been the same, though the changes I afterwards think I effected were very different, being in the one case the thread's going through the needle and in the other its passing well outside it.

Suppose now that it be allowed that so far I have been right. Then the following admissions must be made:

1. An action, i.e. a human action, instead of being the originating or causing of some change, is an activity of willing some change, this usually causing some change, and in some cases a physical change, its doing or not doing this depending on the physical conditions of which the agent is largely ignorant.

2. Sometimes, however, we have performed such an activity without, at any rate so far as we know, having caused any physical change. This has happened when, e.g., we willed a movement of our hand, at a time when it was either paralysed or numb with cold, whether we knew this or not. No doubt in such cases our activity would not ordinarily be called an action, but it is of the same sort as what we ordinarily call and think of as an action.

3. There is no reason to limit the change which it is possible to will to a movement of some part of our body, since, as James says in effect, we can just as much will the sliding of a table towards us as a movement of our hand towards our head. Indeed, we may, in fact, will this in order to convince ourselves or someone else that by doing so we shall not cause the table to slide. And it looks as though we sometimes will such things in ordinary life, as when in watching a football match we want some player's speed to increase, and will it to increase.

4. Where we have willed some movement of our body and think we have caused it, we cannot have directly caused it. For what we directly caused, if anything, must have been some change in our brain.

5. Where we think that by willing some change we effected some change in the physical world, we are implying the idea that in doing so, we are butting into, or interfering with, the physical system, just as we think of an approaching comet as effecting a breach in the order of the solar system, so long as we do not regard the comet as part of the system. This idea is, of course, inconsistent with our belief in the uniformity of nature unless we include in nature minds as well as bodies;

and in any case it is inconsistent with our belief in the conservation of energy. But so long as we think, as we do, that at any rate on some occasions we really effect something in the physical world, we must admit this. And if we knew that such effecting was impossible, we should give up acting.

We have now to face another question, viz. 'Does acting require a desire, and if it does, the desire of what?'

It is at least very difficult to avoid Aristotle's conclusion that acting requires a desire, if only for the reason he gives, viz. that διάνοια αὐτὴ οὐθὲν κινεῖ. It seems that, as Locke maintained, if we never desired something we should never do anything. But what is the desire required?

Here only one or other of two answers seems possible, viz. (1) that it is a desire of the change X which we will, and (2) that it is a desire of the willing of X. And when we try, we do not find it easy to decide between them. For on the one hand, the desire required seems to have to be the desire of X, on the ground that, if we are to will X, we must desire X. And on the other hand, it seems that it must be the desire to will X, since unless we *desired* to will X we could not will X. Indeed, just for this reason Plato seems to have gone too far in the *Gorgias* when he maintained that in acting we never desire to do what we do, but only that for the sake of which we do it. For, if acting is willing, it seems that the desire required must be a desire of the willing, even though the desire be a dependent desire, i.e. a desire depending on the desire of something else for its own sake, viz. that for the sake of which we do the action. And Plato's mistake seems to have been that of restricting desiring to desiring something for its own sake.

The two answers are, of course, radically different. For if the desire required is the desire of X, the thing desired and the thing willed will be the same, as indeed Green implies that they are when he maintains that willing is desiring in a special sense of 'desiring'. But if so, while the willing of X will require what for want of a better term we seem to have to call the thought of X, as being something involved in the desire of X, it will not require either the desire of the willing of X or, for that reason, even the thought of willing X. On the other hand, if the desire required is the desire to will X, the thing desired and the thing willed will necessarily be different, and while the willing of X will require the desire of willing X and so also the thought of willing X, it will not require the desire of X, though it will require the thought of X, as being something involved in the thought of willing X. It should, however, be noted that in the case of the latter alternative, the desire of X may in some cases be required indirectly as a condition of our desiring the willing of X.

To repeat here for clearness' sake what is central—if the desire required is the desire of X, the willing of X will not require either the desire of the willing of X or even the thought of willing X, while, if the desire required is the desire of willing X, the willing of X will not require the desire of X, though it will require the thought of X.

On consideration, however, we have to reject the idea that the desire required is the desire of X, on three grounds. First, if it were true, we should always will any change which we desired to happen, such as the sliding of the table, whether or not we thought that if we were to will it to happen we should thereby cause it to happen; and obviously we do not. Second, we occasionally will a change to happen without any desire for it to happen. This must occur, e.g., if a man ever does an act moved solely by the desire for revenge, willing, say, the movement of a switch which he is confident will result in the death of another, not from any desire for his death but solely from the desire to cause it by willing the movement. And even if there are no acts animated solely by the desire for revenge, there are certainly actions approximating to this. At all events, in the case of playing a game the desire at work must be not the desire of some change but the desire to cause it. A putter at golf, e.g., has no desire for the ball to fall into the hole; he only desires to cause it to fall in. This contention is, I think, not met by maintaining, as Cook Wilson in fact does, that the player desires the falling into the hole as caused by his action, and so desires the falling as part of, or an element in, his action. Its falling is neither a part of, nor an element in, his action; at best it is only an effect of it. And the player could only be said to desire the falling if, as he does not, he desired it to happen irrespectively of what would cause it to happen. And in this connexion it may be added that if the desire required were the desire of X, it would be impossible to do any act as one which we think would or might fulfil some obligation, since *ex hypothesi* the desire required will be a desire for a change X and not a desire to *will* a change X. Then, third, there is a consideration which comes to light if we consider more closely what it is that we will in certain cases, and more especially in those in which we describe an action as one of trying to do so and so. Suppose, e.g., I have done what we describe as having tried to jump a ditch, and so imply that beforehand I was doubtful of success. Obviously I did not will a movement of my body which I was sure would land me, say, two clear yards on the other side, since if I had thought of willing this I should have realized that willing this would not result in my getting across. I willed that movement the willing of which, if I were to will it, I thought the most likely of all the willings of movements in my power to result in my landing on the farther bank. And in this connexion it seems worth noting that what we call trying to do something is as much doing something as what we ordinarily call doing something, although the word 'trying' suggests that it is not. It is the willing a change described in the way in which I have just described what I willed in trying to jump a ditch.

It therefore seems that the desire required must be the desire of the willing of a certain change X. Yet this conclusion is exposed to two objections. The first is that if it were true, it would be impossible to will something X for the first time. For in this context we mean by a desire to will X a desire we can only have in consequence of thinking that if we were to will X, our doing so would be likely to cause something else, and ultimately something which we desire for its own sake. But we cannot desire to will something X, unless we at least have a conjecture that if we were to will X, our willing X might cause some change which we desire for its own sake. And this conjecture requires the thought that on some previous occasion we have willed X and thence concluded from what we think followed this willing of X that it may have caused something else Y. Yet ex hypothesi we cannot have willed X on this previous occasion from the desire to will X, since then we had no idea of what willing X might cause. James expresses what is really this objection, though in a misleading way, when he says: 'If, in voluntary action properly so-called' (i.e. in what is really an action), 'the act must be foreseen, it follows that no creature not endowed with divinatory power can perform an act voluntarily for the first time.'[1] The statement as it stands is, of course, absurd, because no one before acting knows what his act will be, or even that he will act. But it can be taken as an inaccurate way of expressing the thought that an act of will requires an idea of something which we may cause if we perform the act.

[1] James, Psychology, ii, p. 487.

To this objection I have to confess that I cannot see an answer. Yet I think that there must be an answer, since, however it has come about, for us as we are now an act of will does seem to require the desire of it, and so some idea of something which it might effect. I need hardly add that it is no answer to maintain that the desire immediately required by willing something X is in some cases the desire of X, and in others the desire of willing X.

The second objection is one which seems to me, though insidious, an objection which can be met. It can be stated thus: 'It is all very well to say that the desire immediately presupposed by willing X is the desire to will X. But to say this is not enough. For we often desire to will X, and yet do not, as when we hesitate to get out of bed or out of a warm bath, and when this is so, obviously something else is required, and this something can only be the willing to will X, so that after all there must be such a thing as willing to will.' But to this the reply seems clear. Though it is possible to desire to desire, as when I desire to desire the welfare of my country more than I do, it is impossible to will to will, for the reason already given. And where we hesitate to will X, what is required is not the willing to will X but either a certain increase in our desire to will X or a decrease in our aversion to doing so. Certainly, too, we often act on this idea, hoping, e.g., that by making ourselves think of the coldness of our breakfast if we stay in bed we shall reach a state of desire in which we shall will certain movements of our body. And sometimes we succeed, and when we do, we sometimes, as James puts it, suddenly find that we have got up, the explanation of our surprise apparently being that we, having been absorbed in the process of trying to stimulate our desire to get up, have not reflected on our state of desire and so have not noticed its increase.

There is also to be noticed in this connexion a mistake into which we are apt to fall which leads us to think that there must be such a thing as willing to will. We of course frequently want certain changes to happen and also want to will certain changes. But we are apt not to notice that the objects of these desires differ in respect of the conditions of their realization, and in consequence to carry the account of the process of deliberation described by Aristotle one step too far—as Aristotle did not. According to him, when we want the happening of something Z which is not an action of ours and which we think we cannot cause directly, we often look for something else Y from the happening of which the happening of Z would result, and then if necessary for something else X from the happening of which Y would result, until we come to think of something A from the happening of which X, Y, and Z would in turn result, and which we also think it in our power to cause by a certain act α. And when we have found A the process stops. We, however, are apt to carry the process one step farther, and apply to the act α, i.e. the willing of something β, the willing of which we think likely to cause A, the same process that we applied to Z, Y, X, and A, thus treating the willing of β as if it were not the willing of something (which it is), but a change which some act of willing might cause. As a result of doing this we ask 'From what act of willing would the willing of β result?', and the answer has to be 'The willing the willing of β'. But the very question is mistaken, because the willing of β is not a change like Z, Y, X, and A. The only proper question at this stage must be not 'From what *willing* would the willing of β result?' but 'From what *something* would the willing of β result?' And the proper answer must be: 'From a certain increase in our desire to will β.'

12

'OUGHT'

SUPPOSE 'I ought to will α' means 'my willing α ought to exist'. Then the only true statement would have to be: 'If I were to will a certain change α, my willing α would be something that ought to exist.'

For this statement to be true, it would have to be true either that if I were to will α my willing α would itself be something good, or that if I were to will α my willing α would be something which would cause something good and would therefore be something which ought to exist.

If, therefore, I were to *know* that if I were to will α, my willing α would be something which ought to exist, I should have to know either (1) that willing α would be itself good, and that what would be good would be something which ought to exist, or (2) that willing α would be something which would cause a thing β, that β would be itself good and therefore ought to exist, and that what would cause something which ought to exist would itself be something which ought to exist.

Accept alternative (2). And suppose that I know that if I willed α, my willing α would be something which ought to exist as causing something β which ought to exist. Suppose that then I ask myself 'How is it to come about that I will α?', i.e. 'What would have to happen from the happening of which it would follow that I willed α?' What is the answer? 'My desiring the willing of α as being something which ought to exist.'

But why is not the answer 'My desiring the willing of α, for *any* reason', and so desiring α even if I did not know that willing α would be something which should exist? Of course, if the thought that willing a certain thing α would be something which should exist necessarily aroused the desire to will α, and if the desire to will a certain something necessarily led to my willing it, then knowing that I knew that willing α ought to exist would enable me to know that I shall in fact will α, since I should know that if I am to will α, all that is required is a desire to will α, and that I shall have this desire.

Substitute for *knowing* that if I were to will α, my willing α would cause something which should exist, *thinking* the same thing, i.e. that if I were to will α, my willing α would cause β and so would cause something which should exist, then I could only *think* that if I were to will α, my willing α would be something which should exist.

Suppose, then, it were true that if I were to will a change α, my willing it would cause the change β, then willing α would be something which ought to exist. And in that case I should know that if I were to will a certain unknown change, my willing would be something that should exist, but that I could not know what this change was, and it might happen that I came to will a change α, the willing of which caused β and so did cause something which should exist, though in willing it I should think it very unlikely that I should cause β.

Substitute for 'If I were to will α, my willing α would be something which would cause something good, and so be something which should exist' 'If I were to will α, α would be something which would cause something good, and so be something which should exist'. Then, as before, I cannot know that if I were to will α, α would be something which should exist, because I cannot know that it would cause something which would be good.

Then, as a substitute, try 'If I were to will α, α would be something which I think would be likely to be something which would cause β, and so be something which should exist'.

Thus, if I am thinking that if α were to exist, α would be something which should exist, I could will α, and could will α thinking α would be something which should exist.

Then there is the same objection as before, viz. that I cannot know that if I were to will α, my willing α would be something which ought to exist; I should only know that if I were to will α I should be willing something which I *thought* should exist.

DUTY AND INTEREST

An Inaugural Lecture

DELIVERED BEFORE THE UNIVERSITY OF OXFORD

ON 29 OCTOBER 1928

DUTY AND INTEREST

You will naturally wish me to begin by giving expression to the regret occasioned by the severance of Professor Stewart's connexion with White's Chair, a connexion which has extended over thirty-one years. He brought to the service of the Chair the mind of a poet, of a mystic, and of a scholar with enthusiasm for learning and especially for the more humane studies. His writings and the variety of the subjects on which he lectured testify to the devotion with which as professor he served the University. Not everyone will go so far with him as to maintain that the real clue to the interpretation of Plato lies in the researches of modern psychologists, and that Plato is at least as important as a prophet or seer as he is as a philosopher; but all will recognize the infectious character of his admiration for Plato and the importance of his insistence that the interpretation of Plato requires a many-sided mind and a penetrating eye for the things which are unseen. Many, too, will think of that mine of information, his *Notes on the Nicomachean Ethics*, with feelings of admiration and personal gratitude. And you will naturally wish to join me in wishing Professor Stewart long continuance of what he has described as the life of practical Platonism.

I cannot refrain from also referring to Wallace and Green. No one, I think, could realize that he was, in a way, standing in their shoes without feeling humbled. To hear Wallace was an impressive experience. You felt that here was a spectator of all time and all existence telling you quietly and dispassionately about what he had seen. His literary skill and, even more, his penetration still strike me as astonishing; and when I have tried to console myself for my inability to follow Hegel's argument, I have found help in the reflection that even Wallace in interpreting him seems unable to do more than repeat what Hegel says in rather different language. Of the weightiness, earnestness, and calibre of Green it would be impertinent for me to speak. But, because it seems seldom recognized, I should like to refer to what has for long struck me as a minor but important merit of his writings. It may be very difficult to make out what Green means, and you may find yourself differing from him in almost every particular; but the more you study any particular sentence, the more you become convinced that every word of it has been weighed, and that, whether or not it be true, it expresses exactly what he meant to say. And this characteristic, I think, renders the study of Green especially valuable at a time like the present, when the most obvious feature of current books on philosophy is language so loose that it is usually difficult, and often impossible, to make out what their authors are trying to maintain.

In seeking a subject for an inaugural lecture, I have tried to find one which, without raising too technical issues, is near enough to every one to be of general interest and yet would be considered by philosophers still sufficiently controversial to deserve consideration. This subject I hope I have found in the relation between duty and interest. The topic is, of course, well worn. Nevertheless anyone who considers it closely will find that it has not the simple and straightforward character which at first sight it appears to possess.

A general but not very critical familiarity with the literature of Moral Philosophy might well lead to the remark that much of it is occupied with attempts either to prove that there is a necessary connexion between duty and interest or in certain cases even to exhibit the connexion as something self-evident. And the remark, even if not strictly accurate, plainly has some truth in it. It might be said in support that Plato's treatment of justice in the *Republic* is obviously such an attempt, and that even Aristotle in the *Ethics* tries to do the same thing, disguised and weak though his attempt may be. As modern instances, Butler and Hutcheson might be cited; and to these might be added not only Kant, in whom we should perhaps least expect to find such a proof, but also Green.

When we read the attempts referred to we naturally cannot help in a way wishing them to succeed; and we might express our wish in the form that we should all like to be able to believe that honesty is the best policy. At the same time we also cannot help feeling that somehow they are out of place, so that the real question is not so much whether they are successful, but whether they ought ever to have been made. And my object is to try to justify our feeling of dissatisfaction by considering what these attempts really amount to, and more especially what they amount to in view of the ideas which have prompted them. For this purpose, the views of Plato, Butler, and Green, may, I think, be taken as representative, and I propose to concentrate attention on them.

One preliminary remark is necessary. It must not be assumed that what are thus grouped together as attempts either to prove or to exhibit the self-evidence of a connexion between duty and interest are properly described by this phrase, or even that they are all attempts to do one and the same thing. And in particular I shall try to show that the attempts so described really consist of endeavours, based on mutually inconsistent presuppositions, to do one or another of three different things.

On a casual acquaintance with the *Republic*, we should probably say without hesitation that, apart from its general metaphysics, what it is concerned with is justice and injustice, and that, with regard to justice and injustice, its main argument is an elaborate attempt, continued to the end of the book, to show in detail that if we look below the surface and consider what just actions really consist in and also the nature of the soul, and, to a minor degree, the nature of the world in which we have to act, it will become obvious, in spite of appearance to the contrary, that it is by acting justly that we shall really gain or become happy.

Further, if we were to ask ourselves, 'What are Plato's words for right and wrong?'—and plainly the question is fair—we should have in the end to give as the true answer what at first would strike us as a paradox. We should have to allow that Plato's words for right and wrong are not to be found in such words as χρῆ or δεῖ and their contraries, as in χρῆ δίκαιον εἶναι or ὅντινα τρόπον χρῆ ζῆν, where the subject is implied by the context to be τὸν μέλλοντα μακάριον ἔσεσθαι, but in δίκαιον and ἄδικον themselves. When he says of some action that it is δίκαιον, that is his way of saying that it is right, or a duty, or an act which we are morally bound to do. When he says that it is ἄδικον, that is his way of saying that it is wrong. And in the sense in which we use the terms 'justice' and 'injustice', it is less accurate to describe what Plato is discussing as justice and injustice than as right and wrong. Our previous statement, therefore, might be put in the form that Plato is mainly occupied in the *Republic* with attempting to show it is by doing our duty, or what we are morally bound to do, that we shall become happy.

This is the account of his object which we are more particularly inclined to give if we chiefly have in mind what Socrates in the fourth Book is made to offer as the solution of the main problem. But this solution is preceded by an elaborate statement of the problem itself, put into the mouth of Glaucon and Adeimantus; and if we consider this statement closely, we find ourselves forced to make a substantial revision of this account of Plato's object. Glaucon and Adeimantus make it quite clear that whatever it is that they are asking Socrates to show about what they refer to as justice, their object in doing so is to obtain a refutation of what may be called the Sophistic theory of morality. Consequently, if we judge by what Glaucon and Adeimantus say, whatever Plato is trying to prove must be something which Plato would consider as affording a refutation of the Sophistic theory. But what is this theory as represented by Plato? It almost goes without saying that in the first instance men's attitude towards matters of right and wrong is an unquestioning one. However they have come to do so, and in particular whether their doing so is due to teaching or not, they think, and think without having any doubts, that certain actions are right and that certain others are wrong. No doubt in special cases, they may be doubtful; but, as regards some actions, they have no doubt at all, though to say this is not the same as to say that they are certain. But there comes a time when men are stirred out of this unquestioning frame of mind; and in particular the Sophists, as Plato represents them, were thus stirred by the reflection that the actions which men in ordinary life thought right, such as paying a debt, helping a friend, obeying the government, however they differed in other respects, at least agreed in bringing directly a definite loss to the agent. This reflection led them to wonder whether men were right in thinking these actions duties, i.e. whether they thought so truly. Then, having failed to find indirect advantages of these actions which would more than compensate for the direct loss, i.e. such advantages as are found in what we call prudent actions, they drew the conclusion that these actions cannot really be duties at all, and that therefore what may roughly be described as the moral convictions which they and others held in ordinary life were one gigantic mistake or illusion. Finally, they clinched this conclusion by offering something which they represented as an account of the origin of justice, but which is really an account of how they and others came to make the mistake of thinking these actions just, i.e. right.

This is the theory which on Plato's own showing he wants to refute. It is a theory about certain actions, and, on his own showing, what he has to maintain is the opposite theory about these same actions. But how, if our language is to be accurate, should these actions be referred to? Should they be referred to as *just*, i.e. right, actions, or should they be referred to as those actions which in ordinary life we *think* just, i.e. right? The difference, though at first it may seem unimportant, is really vital. In the unquestioning attitude of ordinary life we must either be *knowing* that certain actions are right or not knowing that they are right, but doing something else for which '*thinking them right*' is perhaps the least unsatisfactory phrase. There is no possibility of what might be suggested as a third alternative, viz. that our activity is one of thinking, which in instances where we are thinking truly is also one of knowing. For, as Plato realized, to think truly is not to know, and to discover that in some particular case we were thinking truly is not to discover that in doing so we were knowing. Moreover, when we are what is described as reflecting on the activity involved in our unquestioning attitude of mind, we are inevitably thinking of it as having a certain definite character, and, in so thinking of it, we must inevitably be implying either that the activity is one of knowing or that it is not. For we must think of this attitude either as one of thinking, or as one of knowing, and if we think of it as one of thinking, we imply that it is not one of knowing, and *vice versa*. In fact, however we think of the activity, we are committed one way or the other. Now the Sophists clearly implied that this unquestioning attitude is one of thinking and not one of knowing; for it would not have been sense to maintain that those actions which in ordinary life we know to be right are really not right. Their theory, then, must be expressed by saying that those actions which in ordinary life we think, and so do not know, to be right are not really right. Consequently Plato also, since he regards this as the theory to be refuted, is implying that in ordinary life we think, and do not know, that certain actions are right, and that, to this extent, he agrees with the Sophists. And for this reason, if we are to state accurately the problem which he is setting himself, we must represent it as referring not to

just actions but to those actions which he and others in ordinary
life *think* just.

It is clear then that when Plato states through the medium
of Glaucon and Adeimantus the problem which he has to solve,
he is guilty of an inaccuracy, which, though it may easily escape
notice, is important. For Glaucon and Adeimantus persistently
refer to the actions of which they ask Socrates to reconsider the
profitableness as just and unjust actions, whereas they should
have referred to them as the actions which men in ordinary
life think just and unjust.

I shall now take it as established that when we judge from
Plato's own statement of his problem, worked out as it is by
reference to the Sophists, we have to allow that he is presupposing that ordinarily we do not know but think that certain
actions are right and that he is thinking of his task as that of having to vindicate the truth of these thoughts against the Sophists'
objection. And this is what must be really meant when it is
said that Plato's object is to vindicate *morality* against the
Sophistic view of it, for here 'morality' can only be a loose
phrase for our ordinary moral thoughts or convictions.

Glaucon and Adeimantus, however, do not simply ask
Socrates to refute the Sophistic view; they ask him to do so in a
particular way, which they imply to be the only way possible,
viz. by showing that if we go deeper than the Sophists and
consider not merely the gains and losses of which they take
account, viz. gains and losses really due to the reputation for
doing what men think just and unjust, but also those which
these actions directly bring to the man's own soul, it will become
obvious that it is by doing what we think just that we shall
really gain. And so far as the rest of the *Republic* is an attempt to
satisfy this request, this must be what it is an attempt to show.

Now on a first reading of the *Republic*, it is not likely to strike
us that there is anything peculiar or unnatural about this part
of the request. Just because Plato takes for granted that this is
the only way to refute the Sophists, we are apt in reading
him to do the same, especially as our attention is likely to be
fully taken up by the effort to follow Plato's thought. But if
we can manage to consider Plato's endeavour to refute the
Sophists with detachment, what strikes us most is not his dissent
from their view concerning the comparative profitableness of the
actions which men think just and unjust—great, of course, as

his dissent is—but the identity of principle underlying the position of both. The Sophists in reaching their conclusion were presupposing that for an action to be really just, it must be advantageous; for it was solely on this ground that they concluded that what we ordinarily think just is not really just. And what in the end most strikes us is that at no stage in the *Republic* does Plato take the line, or even suggest as a possibility, that the very presupposition of the Sophists' arguments is false, and that therefore the question whether some action which men think just will be profitable to the agent has really nothing to do with the question whether it is right, so that Thrasymachus may enlarge as much as he pleases on the losses incurred by doing the actions we think just without getting any nearer to showing that it is a mere mistake to think them just. Plato, on the contrary, instead of urging that the Sophistic contention that men lose by doing what they think just is simply irrelevant to the question whether these actions are just, throughout treats this contention with the utmost seriousness; and he implies that unless the Sophists can be met on their own ground by being shown that, in spite of appearances to the contrary, these actions will really be for the good of the agent, their conclusion that men's moral convictions are mere conventions must be allowed to stand. He therefore, equally with the Sophists, is implying that it is impossible for any action to be really just, i.e. a duty, unless it is for the advantage of the agent.

This presupposition, however, as soon as we consider it, strikes us as a paradox. For though we may find ourselves quite unable to state what it is that does render an action a duty, we ordinarily think that, whatever it is, it is not conduciveness to our advantage; and we also think that though an action which is a duty may be advantageous it need not be so. And while we may not be surprised to find the presupposition in the Sophists, whose moral convictions are represented as at least shallow, we are surprised to find it in Plato, whose moral earnestness is that of a prophet. At first, no doubt, we may try to mitigate our surprise by emphasizing the superior character of the advantages which Plato had in mind. But to do this does not really help. For after all, whatever be meant by the 'superiority' of the advantages of which Plato was thinking, it is simply as advantages that Plato uses them to show that the actions from which they follow are right.

Yet the presupposition cannot simply be dismissed as obviously untrue. For one thing, any view of Plato's is entitled to respect. For another, there appear to be moments in which we find the presupposition in ourselves. There appear to be moments in which, feeling acutely the weight of our responsibilities, we say to ourselves, 'Why *should* I do all these actions, since after all it is others and not I who will gain by doing them?'.

Moreover, there at least seems to be the same presupposition in the mind of those preachers whose method of exhortation consists in appeal to rewards. When, for instance, they commend a certain mode of life on the ground that it will bring about a peace of mind which the pursuit of worldly things cannot yield, they appear to be giving a resulting gain as the reason why we ought to do certain actions, and therefore to be implying that in general it is advantageousness to ourselves which renders an action one which we are bound to do. In fact the only difference between the view of such preachers and that of the Sophists seems to be that the former, in view of their theological beliefs, think that the various actions which we think right will have certain specific rewards the existence of which the Sophists would deny. And the identity of principle underlying their view becomes obvious if the preacher goes on to maintain, as some have done, that if he were to cease to believe in heaven, he would cease to believe in right and wrong. Again, among philosophers, Plato is far from being alone in presupposing that an action, to be right, must be for the good or advantage of the agent. To go no further afield than a commentator on Plato, we may cite Cook Wilson, whose claim to respect no one in Oxford will deny, and who was, to my mind, one of the acutest of thinkers. In lecturing on the *Republic* he used to insist that when men begin to reflect on morality they not only demand, but also have the right to demand, that any action which is right must justify its claim to be right by being shown to be for their own good; and he used to maintain that Plato took the right and only way of justifying our moral convictions, by showing that the actions which we think right are for the good of the society of which we are members, and that at the same time the good of that society *is* our good, as becomes obvious when the nature of our good is properly understood.

Moreover Plato, if he has been rightly interpreted, does not stand alone among the historical philosophers in presupposing the existence of a necessary connexion between duty and interest. At least Butler, whose thoughtfulness is incontestable, is with him. In fact in this matter he seems at first sight only distinguished from Plato by going further. In a well-known passage in the eleventh *Sermon*, after stating that religion always addresses itself to self-love when reason presides in a man, he says: 'Let it be allowed, though virtue or moral rectitude does indeed consist in affection to and pursuit of what is right and good, as such; yet that when we sit down in a cool hour, we can neither justify to ourselves this or any other pursuit, till we are convinced that it will be for our happiness, or at least not contrary to it.'

Here, if we take the phrase 'justify an action to ourselves' in its natural sense of come to know that we ought to do the action by apprehending a reason why we ought to do it, we seem to have to allow that Butler is maintaining that in the last resort there is one, and only one, reason why we ought to do anything whatever, viz. the conduciveness of the action to our happiness or advantage. And if this is right, Butler is not simply presupposing but definitely asserting a necessary connexion between duty and interest, and going further than Plato by maintaining that it is actually conduciveness to the agent's interest which renders an action right.

Nevertheless, when we seriously face the view that unless an action be advantageous, it cannot really be a duty, we are forced both to abandon it and also to allow that even if it were true, it would not enable us to vindicate the truth of our ordinary moral convictions.

It is easy to see that if we persist in maintaining that an action, to be right, must be advantageous, we cannot stop short of maintaining that it is precisely advantageousness and nothing else which renders an action right. It is impossible to rest in the intermediate position that, though it is something other than advantageousness which renders an action right, nevertheless an action cannot really be right unless it be advantageous. For if it be held that an action is rendered a duty by the possession of some other characteristic, then the only chance of showing that a right action must necessarily be advantageous must consist either in showing that actions having this other characteristic must necessarily be advantageous or in showing that the very fact that we are bound to do some action, irrespectively of what renders us bound to do it, necessitates that we shall gain by doing it. But the former alternative is not possible. By 'an action' in this context must be meant an activity by which a man brings certain things about. And if the characteristic of an action which renders it right does not consist in its bringing about an advantage to the agent, which we may symbolize by 'an X', it must consist in bringing about something of a different kind, which we may symbolize by 'a Y', say, for the sake of argument, an advantage to a friend, or an improvement in someone's character. There can, however, be no means of showing that when we bring about something of one kind, e.g. a Y, we must necessarily bring about something of a different kind, e.g. an X. The nature of an action as being the bringing about a Y cannot require, i.e. necessitate, it to be also the bringing about an X, i.e. to have an X as its consequence; and whether bringing about a Y in any particular case will bring about an X will depend not only on the nature of the act as being the bringing about a Y, but also on the nature of the agent and of the special circumstances in which the act is done. It may be objected that we could avoid the necessity of having to admit this on one condition, viz. that we knew the existence of a Divine Being who would intervene, where necessary, with rewards. But this knowledge would give the required conclusion only on one condition, viz. that this knowledge was really the knowledge that the fact of being bound to do some action itself necessitated the existence of such a Being as a consequence. For if it were the knowledge of the existence of such a Being based on other grounds, it would not enable us to know that the very fact that some action was the bringing about a Y *itself* necessitated that it would also be the bringing about an X, i.e. some advantage to the agent. No doubt if we could successfully maintain not only that an action's being the bringing about a Y necessitated its being a duty, but also that an action's being a duty necessitated as a consequence the existence of a Being who would reward it, we could show that an action's being the bringing about a Y necessitated its being rewarded. But to maintain this is really to fall back on the second alternative; and this alternative will, on consideration, turn out no more tenable than the first. It cannot successfully be maintained that the very fact that some action is a duty necessitates, not that the agent will *deserve* to gain—a conclusion which it is of course easy to draw, but that he *will* gain, unless it can be shown that this very fact necessitates, as a consequence, the existence of a being who will, if necessary, reward it. And this obviously cannot be done.

No doubt Kant maintained, and thought it possible to prove, not indeed that the obligation to do *any* action, but that the obligation to do a *certain* action, involves as a consequence that men will gain by carrying out their obligations.[1] In effect he assumed that we know that one of our duties is to endeavour to advance the realization of the highest good, viz. a state of affairs in which men both act morally, i.e. do what they think right, purely from the thought that it is right, and at the same time attain the happiness which in consequence they deserve. And he maintained that from this knowledge we can conclude *first* that the realization of the highest good must be possible, i.e. that so far as we succeed in making ourselves and others more moral, we and others will become proportionately happier; and *second* that, therefore, since the realization of this consequence requires, as the cause of the world in which we have to act, a supreme intelligent will which renders the world such as to cause happiness in proportion to morality, there must be such a cause. But his argument, although it has a certain plausibility, involves an inversion. If, as he rightly implied, an action can only be a duty if we *can* do it, and if we can only even in a slight degree advance a state of affairs in which a certain degree of morality is combined with a corresponding degree of happiness, *provided* there be such a supreme cause of nature, it will be impossible to know, as he assumed that we do, that to advance this state of affairs is a duty, *until* we know that there is such a supreme cause. So far, therefore, from the connexion which he thought to exist between right action and happiness being demonstrable from our knowledge of the duty in question, knowledge of the duty, if attainable at all, will itself require independent knowledge of the connexion.

We are therefore forced to allow that in order to maintain that for an action to be right, it must be advantageous, we have to maintain that advantageousness is what renders an action right. But this is obviously something which no one is going to maintain, if he considers it seriously. For he will be involved in maintaining not only that it is a duty to do whatever is for our

[1] Kant, *Critique of Practical Reason* (Bk. II, ii. § 5) [Abbott's Translation, pp. 220–9.]

advantage, but that this is our only duty. And the fatal objection to maintaining this is simply that no one actually thinks it.

Moreover, as it is easy to see, if we were to maintain this,
our doing so, so far from helping us, would render it impossible
for us, to vindicate the truth of our ordinary moral convictions.
For wherever in ordinary life we think of some particular action
as a duty, we are not simply thinking of it as right, but also
thinking of its rightness as constituted by the possession of some
definite characteristic other than that of being advantageous to
the agent. For we think of the action as a particular action *of a
certain kind*, the nature of which is indicated by general words
contained in the phrase by which we refer to the action, e.g.
'*fulfilling* the *promise* which we made to X yesterday', or '*looking
after* our *parents*'. And we do not think of the action as right
blindly, i.e. irrespectively of the special character which we
think the act to possess; rather we think of it as being right in
virtue of possessing a particular characteristic of the kind
indicated by the phrase by which we refer to it. Thus in thinking
of our keeping our promise to X as a duty, we are thinking of the
action as rendered a duty by its being the keeping of our promise.
This is obvious because we should never, for instance, think of
using as an illustration of an action which we think right,
telling X what we think of him, or meeting him in London, even
though we thought that if we thought of these actions in certain
other aspects we should think them right. Consequently if we
were to maintain that conduciveness to the agent's advantage is
what renders an action right, we should have to allow that any
of our ordinary moral convictions, so far from being capable of
vindication, is simply a mistake, as being really the conviction
that some particular action is rendered a duty by its possession
of some characteristic which is not that of being advantageous.

The general moral is obvious. Certain arguments, which
would ordinarily be referred to as arguments designed to prove
that doing what is right will be for the good of the agent, turn
out to be attempts to prove that the actions which in ordinary
life we think right will be for the good of the agent. There is
really no need to consider in detail whether these arguments
are successful; for even if they are successful, they will do nothing
to prove what they are intended to prove, viz. that the moral
convictions of our ordinary life are true. Further the attempts
arise simply out of a presupposition which on reflection anyone

is bound to abandon, viz. that conduciveness to personal advantage is what renders an action a duty. What Plato should have said to the Sophists is: 'You may be right in maintaining that in our ordinary unquestioning frame of mind we do not know, but only think, that certain actions are right. These thoughts or convictions may or may not be true. But they cannot be false for the reason which you give. You do nothing whatever to show that they are false by urging that the actions in question are disadvantageous; and I should do nothing to show that they are true, if I were to show that these actions are after all advantageous. Your real mistake lies in presupposing throughout that advantageousness is what renders an action a duty. If you will only reflect you will abandon this presupposition altogether, and then you yourself will withdraw your arguments.'

I next propose to contend that there is also to be found both in Plato and Butler, besides this attempt to show that actions which we *think* right will be for our good, another attempt which neither of them distinguishes from it and which *is* accurately described as an attempt to prove that *right* actions will be for our good. I also propose to ask what is the idea which led them to make the attempt, and to consider whether it is tenable.

When Plato raises the question 'What is justice?' he does not mean by the question 'What do we *mean* by the terms "justice" and "just", or, in our language, "duty" and "right"?', as we might ask 'What do we *mean* by the term "optimism", or again, by the phrase "living thing"?'. And as a matter of fact if he had meant this, he would have been raising what was only verbally, and not really, a question at all, in that any attempt to ask it would have implied that the answer was already known and that therefore there was nothing to ask. He means 'What is the characteristic the possession of which by an action necessitates that the action is just, i.e. an act which it is our duty, or which we ought, to do?' In short he means 'What renders a just or right action, just or right?'

Now this question really means 'What is the characteristic common to particular just acts which renders them just?' And for anyone even to *ask* this question is to imply that he already *knows* what particular actions are just. For even to *ask* 'What is the character common to certain things?' is to imply that we already *know* what the things are of which we are wanting to find the common character. Equally, of course, any attempt to *answer* the question has the same implication. For such an attempt can only consist in considering the particular actions which we know to be just and attempting to discover what is the characteristic common to them all, the vague apprehension of which has led us to apprehend them to be just. Plato therefore, both in representing Socrates as raising with his hearers the question 'What is justice?' and also in representing them all as attempting to answer it, is implying, whether he is aware that he is doing so or not, that they all know what particular acts are, and what particular acts are not, just. If on the contrary what he had presupposed was that the members of the dialogue think, instead of knowing, that certain actions are just, his question— whether he had expressed it thus or not—would really have been, not 'What *is* justice?', but 'What do we *think* that justice is?'; or, more clearly, not 'What renders an act just?' but 'What do we think renders an act just?'. But in that case an answer, whatever its character, would have thrown no light on the question 'What is justice?'; and apart from this, he is plainly not asking 'What do we *think* that justice is?'.

As has been pointed out, however, the view which Plato attributes to the Sophists presupposes that ordinary mankind, which of course includes the members of the dialogue, only thinks and does not know that certain actions are just. Therefore, when Plato introduces this view as requiring refutation and, in doing so, represents the members of the dialogue as not questioning the presupposition, he ought in consistency to have made someone point out that in view of the acceptance of this presupposition Socrates' original question 'What is justice?' required to be amended to the question 'What do we think that justice is?'. But Plato does not do so. In the present context the significant fact is that even after he has introduced the view of the Sophists he still represents the question to be answered as being 'What is justice?', and therefore still implies that the members of the dialogue know what is just in particular. Even in making Glaucon and Adeimantus ask Socrates to refute the Sophists, what he, inconsistently, makes them ask Socrates to exhibit the nature of is not the acts which men think just but just acts. And when Plato in the fourth book goes on to give Socrates' answer, which, of course, is intended to express the truth, he in the same way represents Socrates as offering, and the others as accepting, an account of the nature of *just* acts, viz. that they consist in conferring those benefits on society which a man's nature renders him best suited to confer, and then makes Socrates argue in detail that it is *just* action which will be profitable. In doing so he is of course implying, inconsistently with the implication of his treatment of the Sophists' view, that the members of the dialogue, and therefore also mankind in ordinary life, *know* what is just in particular. For in the end the statement 'Justice is conferring certain benefits on society' can only mean that conferring these benefits is the characteristic the vague apprehension of which in certain actions leads us to know or apprehend them to be just; and the acceptance of this statement by the members of the dialogue must be understood as expressing their recognition that this characteristic is the common character of the particular acts which they already know to be just.

It therefore must be allowed that, although to do so is inconsistent with his view of the way in which the Sophistic theory has to be refuted, Plato is in the fourth book (and of course the same admission must be made about the eighth and ninth) endeavouring to prove that *just*, i.e. *right*, action, will be for the good or advantage of the agent.

Given that this is what Plato wants to prove in the fourth book, the general nature of what he conceives to be the proof is obvious. His idea is that if we start with the knowledge of what right actions consist in, viz., to put it shortly, serving the state, and then consider what the effects of these and other actions will be by taking into account not only the circumstances in which we are placed, but also the various desires of the human soul and the varying amounts of satisfaction to which the realization of these objects will give rise, it will be obvious that it is by doing what is right that, at any rate in the long run, we shall become happy.

Now a particular proof of this kind, such as Plato's, naturally provokes two comments. The first is that there is no need to consider its success in detail, since we know on general grounds that it must fail. For it can only be shown that actions characterized by being the bringing about things of one kind, in this case benefits to society, will always have as their consequence things of another kind, in this case elements of happiness in the agent, provided that we can prove, as Plato makes no attempt to do, the existence of a Being who will intervene to introduce suitable rewards where they are needed. The second is that though the establishment of this conclusion, whether with or without the help of theological arguments, would be of the greatest benefit to us, since we should all be better off if we knew it to be true, yet it differs from the establishment of the corresponding conclusion against the Sophists in that it would throw no light whatever on the question 'What is our duty in detail, and why?'. And this second comment naturally raises the question which seems to be the important one to ask in this connexion, viz. '*Why* did Plato think it important to prove that right action would benefit the agent?'.

The explanation obviously cannot be simply, or even mainly, that the combination in Plato of a desire to do what is right and of a desire to become happy led him to try to satisfy himself that by doing what is right he would be, so to say, having it both ways. The main explanation must lie in a quite different direction. There is no escaping the conclusion that when Plato sets himself to consider not what *should*, but what *actually does* as a matter of fact, lead a man to act, when he is acting deliberately, and not merely in consequence of an impulse, he answers 'The desire for some good to himself and that only'. In other words we have to allow that, according to Plato, a man pursues whatever he pursues simply as a good to himself, i.e. really as something which will give him satisfaction, or, as perhaps we ought to say, as an element in what will render him happy. In the *Republic* this view comes to light in the sixth book. He there speaks of τὸ ἀγαθόν as that which every soul pursues and for the sake of which it does all it does, divining that it is something but being perplexed and unable to grasp adequately what it is; and he goes on to say of things that are good (τὰ ἀγαθά) that while many are ready to do and to obtain and to be what only *seems* just, even if it is not, no one is content with obtaining what *seems* good, but endeavours to obtain what is *really* good. It might be objected that these statements do not bear out the view which is attributed to Plato, since Plato certainly did not mean by an ἀγαθόν a source of satisfaction or happiness to oneself. But to this the answer is that wherever Plato uses the term ἀγαθά (goods) elsewhere in the *Republic* and in other dialogues, such as the *Philebus*, the context always shows that he means by a good a good to oneself, and, this being so, he must really be meaning by an ἀγαθόν, a source of satisfaction, or perhaps, more generally, a source of happiness. The view, however, emerges most clearly in the Gorgias, where Plato, in order to show that rhetoricians and tyrants do not do what they really wish to do, maintains that in all actions alike, and even when we kill a man or despoil him of his goods, we do what we do because we think it will be better for us to do so.

Now if we grant, as we must, that Plato thought this, we can find in the admission a natural explanation of Plato's desire to prove that just action will be advantageous. For plainly he passionately wanted men to do what is right, and if he thought that it was only desire of some good to themselves which moved them in all deliberate action, it would be natural, and indeed necessary, for him to think that if men are to be induced to do what is just, the only way to induce them is to convince them that thereby they will gain or become better off.

In Butler also we are driven to find the same attempt to prove that right action will benefit the agent, and to give the same explanation. The proper interpretation of the most important part of the statement quoted from Butler is not very easy to discover. What he says is that when we sit down in a cool hour we can neither justify to ourselves the pursuit of what is *right* and *good*, as such, or any other pursuit, till we are convinced that it will be for our happiness or at least not against it. Here a puzzle arises from the fact that whereas by referring to certain of the actions which we have to justify to ourselves as the pursuit of what is *right*, he inevitably implies that we already *know* them to be right, yet by speaking of our having to justify them to ourselves, i.e. apparently to prove to ourselves that they are right, he seems to imply that we do *not* know them to be right. The interpretation given earlier evaded the puzzle by tacitly assuming that Butler was using the term 'right' loosely for what we think, and so do not know, to be right. But it may well be asked whether the assumption was justified. And if we consider the statement in reference to the *Sermons* generally, we seem bound to conclude that Butler was really maintaining two different, and indeed inconsistent, doctrines without realizing their difference, the one involving that the word 'right' is here used strictly, and the other involving that it is not. When Kant contrasts the two kinds of statement containing the word 'ought' which he designated as Categorical and Hypothetical Imperatives, he implies, although he does not expressly state, that the term 'ought' is being used in the two kinds of statement in radically different senses. In a Categorical Imperative, he implies, 'ought' has the ordinary moral sense in which it is co-extensive with 'duty', and 'morally bound'. In a Hypothetical Imperative it has the purely non-moral sense of proper in respect of being the thing which is conducive to our purpose, whether that purpose be the object of some special desire which is moving us, e.g. as when we wash in order to become clean, or whether it be our happiness, as when we make friends in order to become happy. Corresponding to these two senses of the term 'ought', there will be two senses of 'justifying a certain action', the one moral and the other not. We may mean by the phrase proving to ourselves that it is a duty to do the action, or we may mean proving to ourselves that the act is the proper one to do in respect of its being the act which will lead to the realization of our purpose.

Now if we understand Butler's word 'right' to be a loose phrase for what in ordinary life we *think* to be right, we can understand him to be using 'justify' in the moral sense of 'justify', without having to admit that he is involved in contradiction. We can understand him to be saying that in order to know that some action which we ordinarily think to be right is right, we must first prove to ourselves that it will be for our happiness, or at least not against it; and we shall then be representing him as explicitly maintaining what the Sophists and Plato, in seeking to refute them, presupposed. On the other hand if we understand Butler to be using the term 'right' strictly, we can only avoid attributing to him the self-contradictory view already referred to by understanding him to be using the term 'justify' in the non-moral sense. For while he would be involved in contradiction if he maintained that even where we knew that some action is right, we still need to prove to ourselves that we ought in the moral sense to do it, he would not be so involved, if he maintained instead that what we still need is to prove to ourselves that we ought to do it in the non-moral sense. Now the general drift of what Butler says of conscience, and especially his statement that it carries its own authority with it, implies that he considered that in ordinary life we *know* and do not *think* that certain actions are right; and if we judge by this, we must understand Butler to be here using 'right' strictly, and to be maintaining that even when we know that we morally ought to

do something, we still need to know that we ought to do it in the
non-moral sense of its being conducive to our purpose, and that
therefore, since our happiness is our purpose, we still need to
know that it will conduce to our happiness. But if we think that
this is what Butler is maintaining, we have to allow that the
explanation of his maintaining it can only be the same as that
given with regard to Plato. For if we ask 'Why, according to
Butler, when we already know that doing some action is a duty,
do we still require to know that we ought to do the action in the
non-moral sense of "ought"?', the answer can only be 'Because
otherwise we shall not do the action'. And the implication will
be that when, to use Butler's phrase, we sit down in a cool hour,
i.e. when we are not under the influence of impulses, the only
thing we desire, and therefore the only purpose we have, is our
own happiness, and that therefore we shall do whatever we do
only in order that we may become happy. The general drift of
his *Sermons*, however, and more especially his statement that it is
manifest that nothing can be of consequence to mankind or
any creature but happiness shows that Butler actually thought
this. We have therefore to attribute to Butler side by side with the
view already attributed to him, and undistinguished from it, a
view which is inconsistent with it and is really the second view
already attributed to Plato, viz. that even though we know certain
actions to be right, we must have it proved to us that they will be
for our good or happiness, since otherwise, as we act only from
desire of our own happiness, we shall not do them.

I propose now to take it as established (1) that both Plato and
Butler in a certain vein of thought are really endeavouring to
prove that right actions, in the strict sense of 'right actions', will
be for the agent's advantage; (2) that their reason for doing so
lies in the conviction that even where we know some action to
be right, we shall not do it unless we think that it will be for our
advantage; and (3) that behind this conviction lies the conviction
of which it is really a corollary, viz. the conviction that desire for
some good to oneself is the only motive of deliberate action.

But are these convictions true? For if it can be shown that they
are not, then at least Plato and Butler's reason for trying to prove
the advantageousness of right action will have disappeared.

The conviction that even where we know some action to be
right, we shall not do it unless we think we shall be the better off
for doing it, of course, strikes us as a paradox. At first no doubt we

are apt to mis-state the paradox. We are apt to say that the
conviction, implying as it does that we only act out of self-
interest, really implies that it is impossible for us to do anything
which we ought to do at all, since if we did some action out of
self-interest we could not have done anything which was a duty.
But to say this is to make the mistake of thinking that the motive
with which we do an action can possibly have something to do
with its rightness or wrongness. To be morally bound is to be
morally bound to *do* something, i.e. to bring something about;
and even if it be only from the lowest of motives that we have
brought about something which we ought to have brought about,
we have still done something which we ought to have done. The
fact that I have given *A* credit in order to spite his rival *B*, or again,
in order to secure future favours from *A*, has, as we see when we
reflect, no bearing whatever on the question whether I ought to
have given *A* credit. The real paradox inherent in the conviction
lies in its implication that there is no such thing as moral goodness.
If I gave *A* credit solely to obtain future favours, and even if I
gave him credit either thinking or knowing that I ought to do so,
but in no way directly or indirectly influenced by my either so
thinking or knowing, then even though it has to be allowed that I
did something which I was morally bound to do, it has to be
admitted that there was no moral goodness whatever about my
action. And the conviction in question is really what is ordinarily
called the doctrine that morality needs a sanction, i.e. really the
doctrine that, to stimulate a man into doing some action, it is
not merely insufficient but even useless to convince him that he is
morally bound to do it, and that, instead, we have to appeal to
his desire to become better off.

Now we are apt to smile in a superior way when in reading
Mill we find him taking for granted that morality needs a sanction,
but we cannot afford to do so when we find Butler, and still more
when we find Plato, really doing the same thing. Moreover when
Plato and Butler maintain the doctrine that lies at the back of this
conviction, viz. the doctrine that we always aim at, i.e. act from
the desire of, some good to ourselves, they are in the best of
company. Aristotle is practically only repeating the statement
quoted from the sixth book of the *Republic* when he says in the
first sentence of the *Ethics*, that every deliberate action seems to
aim at something good, and that therefore the good has rightly
been declared to be that at which all things aim. For this to

become obvious it is only necessary to consider what meaning must be attributed to the term ἀγαθόν in the early chapters of the *Ethics*. Again, to take a modern instance, Green says: 'The motive in every imputable act for which the agent is conscious on reflection that he is answerable, is a desire for personal good in some form or other. . . . It is superfluous to add good to *himself*, for anything conceived as good in such a way that the agent acts for the sake of it, must be conceived as *his own* good, though he may conceive it as his own good only on account of his interest in others, and in spite of any amount of suffering on his own part incidental to its attainment.'[1] Moreover the doctrine seems plausible enough, if we ask ourselves in a purely general way 'How are we to be led into doing something?'. For the natural answer is: 'Only by thinking of some state of affairs which it is in my power to bring about and by which I shall become better off than I am now'; and the answer implies that only in this way shall we come to desire to do an action, and that, unless we desire to do it, we shall not do it.

Nevertheless it seems difficult, and indeed in the end impossible, to think that the doctrine will stand the test of instances. It seems impossible to allow that in what would usually be called disinterested actions, whether they be good or bad, there is not at least some element of disinterestedness. It strikes us as absurd to think that in what would be called a benevolent action, we are not moved at least in part by the desire that someone else shall be better off and also by the desire to *make* him better off, even though we may also necessarily have, and be influenced by, the desire to have the satisfaction of thinking that he is better off and that we have made him so. It seems equally absurd to maintain that where we are said to treat someone maliciously, we are not moved in part by the desire of his unhappiness and also partly by the desire to *make* him unhappy. Again when we are said to be pursuing scientific studies without a practical aim, it seems mere distortion of the facts to say that we are moved solely by the desire to have the satisfaction of knowing some particular thing and not, at least in part, by the desire to know it. And we seem driven to make a similar admission when we consider actions in which we are said to have acted conscientiously.

In this connexion it should be noted that the doctrine under consideration, viz. that our motive in doing any action is desire

---

[1] *Prolegomena to Ethics*, §§ 91-2.

for some good to ourselves to which we think the action will lead, has two negative implications. The first is that the thought, or, alternatively, the knowledge, that some action is right has no influence on us in acting, i.e. that the thought, or the knowledge, that an action is a duty can neither be our motive nor even an element in our motive. The existence of this implication is obvious, since if our motive is held to be the desire for a certain good to ourselves, it is implied that the thought that the action is a duty, though present, is neither what moves us, nor an element in what moves us, to do the action. The second implication is that there is no such thing as a *desire* to do what is right, or more fully, a desire to do some action in virtue of its being a duty. The existence of this second implication is also obvious, since if such a desire were allowed to exist, there would be no reason for maintaining that when we do some action which we think to be a duty, our motive is necessarily the desire for a certain good to ourselves. The truth of the doctrine could therefore be contested in one of two alternative ways. We might either deny the truth of the former implication; or, again, we might deny the truth of the latter. The former is, of course, the line taken by Kant, at any rate in a qualified form. He maintained in effect that the mere thought that an action is a duty, apart from a desire to do what we ought to do—a desire the existence of which he refused to admit—is at any rate in certain instances the motive, or at least an element in the motive, of an action. No doubt he insisted that the existence of this fact gave rise to a problem, and a problem which only vindication of freedom of the will could resolve; but he maintained that the problem was soluble, and that therefore he was entitled to insist on this fact. Now this method of refutation has adherents and at first sight it is attractive. For it seems mere wild paradox to maintain that in no case in which we do what we think of as right, do we ever in any degree do it *because* we think it right; and to say that we do some action *because* we think it right seems to imply that the thought that it is right is our motive. Again the statement seems natural that where we are said to have acted thus, we obviously did not want to do what we did but acted against our desires or inclinations. Nevertheless we are, I think, on further reflection bound to abandon this view. For one reason, to appeal to a consideration of which the full elucidation and vindication would take too long, the view involves that where we are said to have done some action because we thought it right, though we had a motive for what we did, we had no purpose in doing it. For we really mean by our purpose in doing some action that the *desire* of which for its own sake leads us to do the action. Again, if we face the purely general question 'Can we really do anything whatever unless in some respect or other we desire to do it?' we have to answer 'No'. But if we allow this, then we have to allow that the obvious way to endeavour to meet Plato's view is to maintain the existence of a desire to do what is right. And it does not seem difficult to do so with success. For we obviously are referring to a fact when we speak of someone as possessing a sense of duty and, again, a strong sense of duty. And if we consider what we are thinking of in these individuals whom we think of as possessing it, we find we cannot exclude from it a desire to do what is a duty, as such, or for its own sake, or, more simply, a desire to do what is a duty. In fact it is hard to resist the conclusion that Kant himself would have taken this line instead of the extreme line which he did, had he not had the fixed idea that all desire is for enjoyment. But if we think this—as it seems we must—we, of course, have no need to admit the truth of Plato's reason for trying to prove that right actions must be advantageous. For if we admit the existence of a desire to do what is right, there is no longer any reason for maintaining as a general thesis that in any case in which a man knows some action to be right, he must, if he is to be led to do it, be convinced that he will gain by doing it. For we shall be able to maintain that his desire to do what is right, if strong enough, will lead him to do the action in spite of any aversion from doing it which he may feel on account of its disadvantages.

It may be objected that if we maintain the existence of a desire to do what is right, we shall become involved in an insoluble difficulty. For we shall also have to allow that we have a desire to become well off or happy, and that therefore men have two radically different desires, i.e. desires the object of which are completely incommensurable. We shall therefore be implying that in those instances—which of course must exist—in which a man has either to do what is right or to do what is for his happiness he can have no means of choosing which he shall do, since there can be no comparable characteristic of the two alternative actions which will enable him to choose to do the one rather than, or in preference to, the other. But to this objection there is an answer which, even if it be at first paradoxical, is in the end irresistible,

viz. that in connexion with such instances it is wholly inappropriate to speak of a *choice*. A choice is, no doubt, necessarily a choice
between comparable alternatives, e.g. between an afternoon's
enjoyment on the river and an afternoon's enjoyment at a cinema.
But it is purely arbitrary to maintain that wherever we have two
alternative courses of action before us we have necessarily to
choose between them. Thus a man contemplating retirement may
be offered a new post. He may, on thinking it over, be unable to resist the conclusion that it is a duty on his part to accept it and
equally convinced that if he accepts it, he will lose in happiness.
He will either accept from his desire to do what is right in spite
of his aversion from doing what will bring himself a loss of happiness, or he will refuse from his desire of happiness, in spite of his
aversion from doing what is wrong. But whichever he does,
though he will have *decided* to do what he does, he will not have
chosen to do it, i.e. chosen to do it in preference to doing the
alternative action.

For the reasons given I shall treat it as established that,
though there is to be found in Plato and Butler what is really an
attempt to prove that right action is advantageous, the question
of its success or failure can be ignored, since the attempt is based
on a fundamental mistake about actual human nature.

I next and last propose to consider what I shall contend to be
an instance of the third of what I referred to as three different
endeavours which would ordinarily be described as attempts
either to prove or to exhibit the self-evidence of a connexion
between duty and interest. This consists in what must be allowed to
be Green's attempt to make out that the very idea that a certain
action is a duty involves the idea that it will be for our interest.

Green holds, for a reason which will have to be considered,
that he is bound to give an account of the origin of the moral
ideal, i.e. really, to explain how men's thought that certain actions
are duties has arisen out of a prior state in which they had no
thought of duties at all. At the root of his explanation lies his
analysis of deliberate action. Of this analysis an outline is given
in a sentence already quoted: 'The motive in every imputable
act for which the agent is conscious on reflection that he is
answerable is a desire for personal good in some form or other.'
He draws a sharp distinction between instinctive action, the
capacity for which men share with animals, and deliberate action,
which is distinctive of human beings. And when he speaks of an

action to which praise or blame can be imputed, or of a moral action, in the sense of an act of a kind which is either morally good or morally bad, what he is thinking of is a deliberate action, i.e. an action in which we have a purpose. He expresses the fact that in such an action we have a purpose by saying that in it we have a motive, and he maintains that a motive is always a desire. At first he represents a desire for some particular thing as a good to, i.e. as something which will give satisfaction to, the agent. But later his account of a desire becomes more complicated. He represents it as implying in the agent the thought of himself as a being who is distinct from his various wants and impulses, which may be of animal origin, who may become completely satisfied by having his wants satisfied, and for whom there is in given circumstances a greatest good possible, i.e. a state in which the nearest approximation to his being completely satisfied will be attained. And he represents a desire as a desire of some particular thing as that which will be in the circumstances his greatest good, i.e. will render himself as completely satisfied as possible in the circumstances. And, in accordance with this, he represents Esau's motive in selling his birthright for a mess of pottage as being the desire of the pleasure of eating the pottage as under the circumstances his greatest good.

He is emphatic in insisting that this account of deliberate action is an account of *all* deliberate action, whether morally good or morally bad, and that therefore it raises the question 'What are the distinguishing marks of morally good and morally bad deliberate action, i.e. of virtue and vice?'. To this question his real answer is that as everyone in acting always does what he thinks will be productive of his greatest good, the distinguishing characteristic of a morally bad, i.e. vicious, action, lies in an error made by the agent about what will be for his greatest good. At first, no doubt, this interpretation seems obviously wrong. For it is glaringly inconsistent with his general descriptions of a morally good action, as when he speaks of having taken the moral ideal to be a devotion of character and life in some form or other to the perfecting of man,[1] and again of having found that the highest moral goodness was an attribute of character, in so far as it issued in acts done for the sake of their goodness.[2] Moreover he seems expressly repudiating this interpretation when he shows anxiety to remove

[1] *Prolegomena*, § 310.
[2] *Lectures on the Principles of Political Obligation*, § 2.

what he describes as the impression to which his account of conduct, whether virtuous or vicious, is likely to give rise, viz. that
this account, if true, would take away the only intelligible foundation of Ethics by reducing virtuous and vicious action to the same
motive.[1] Nevertheless, this is the interpretation required by his
account of deliberate action, an account to which he always
adheres. And later on we find what amounts to an explicit statement of the doctrine. Speaking of a man's thought of himself, and
of his thought of himself as a being capable of being satisfied, he
says: 'Hence arises the impulse which becomes the source,
according to the direction it takes, both of vice and virtue. It is
the source of vicious self-seeking and self-assertion, so far as the spirit
which is in man seeks to satisfy itself or to realize its capabilities in
modes in which, according to the law which its divine origin
imposes on it, and which is equally the law of the universe and of
human society, its self-satisfaction or self-realization is not to be
found. Such, for instance—so self-defeating—is the quest for self-
satisfaction in the life of the voluptuary. So it is again with the
man who seeks to assert himself, to realize himself, to show what
he has in him to be, in achievements which may make the world
wonder, but which in their social effects are such that the human
spirit, according to the law of its being which is a law of development in society, is not advanced but hindered by them in the
realization of its capabilities. He is living for ends of which the
divine principle that forms his self alone renders him capable, but
those ends, because in their attainment one is exalted by the
depression of others, are not in the direction in which that principle
can really fulfill the promise and potency which it contains.'[2]

Here Green is plainly contending that what renders the
voluptuary or the ambitious man vicious is that, though equally
with the virtuous man he is seeking the complete, or at least the
completest possible, satisfaction of himself, he is seeking it in a
way in which in view of man's actual nature, and in particular in
view of man's actual wants, it is not to be found. This account of
how there come to be such things as virtuous and vicious action is,
of course, not an account of how men come to have the idea that
certain actions are duties. But it at least makes clear that Green
really holds the view which eventually turns out to underlie his

---

[1] *Prolegomena*, § 115.
[2] *Prolegomena*, § 176; cf. 'The true good we shall understand in the same way. It is
an end in which the effort of a moral agent can really find rest' (§ 171).

account of this, viz. the view that in all deliberate action whatever, bad as well as good, what the agent is wanting is the good or
the satisfaction of himself.

We are now in a position to follow Green's account of the origin
of what he describes as the moral ideal, i.e. really, of the idea that
certain actions are duties. This is given in a later chapter entitled
The Origin and Development of the Moral Ideal. Its essence is contained in a short paragraph. Having pointed out that a human being
obviously has a disinterested interest in the good of others, he
goes on to say: 'The conception of a moral law, in its strict
philosophical form, is no doubt an analogical adaptation of the
notion of law in the more primary sense—the notion of it as a command enforced by a political superior, or by some power to which
obedience is habitually rendered by those to whom the command is
addressed. But there is an idea which equally underlies the
conception both of moral duty and of legal right; which is prior,
so to speak, to the distinction between them; which must have
been at work in the minds of men before they could be capable of
recognizing any kind of action as one that *ought* to be done, whether
because it is enjoined by law or authoritative custom, or because,
though not thus enjoined, a man owes it to himself or to his
neighbour or to God. This is the idea of an absolute and a common
good; a good common to the person conceiving it with others,
and good for him and them, whether at any moment it answers
their likings or no. As affected by such an idea, a man's attitude
to his likes and dislikes will be one of which, in his inward converse, the "Thou shalt" or "Thou must" of command is the natural
expression, though of law, in the sense either of the command of
a political superior or of a self-imposed rule of life, he may as yet
have no definite conception.'[1] An adequate consideration of the
meaning of this passage would require much comment. More
especially we should have to ask 'What is meant by "a common
good"?', and even whether the phrase does not really involve a
contradiction in terms. But without going into details it is possible
to say that Green at least means that if a man is to think of some
action as a duty, he must think of it as conducive to the realization
of something which is at once the good of a society of which he is a
member and his own good. It is, he implies, neither enough to
think of that to which the act is conducive as the good of the
whole body, nor enough to think of it as his own good. He must think

[1] *Prolegomena*, § 202.

of it as at once both. And if we allow, as we must, that this is what Green means, the real nature of his thought becomes obvious. He sees perfectly well that no one will come to think of some action as a duty by simply thinking of it as conducive to his own personal interest. He considers, whether rightly or wrongly, that on the contrary we shall not think of an action as a duty unless we think of it as part of a plan of action devised for members of a society as conducive to the good of the whole body. But also thinking that we only desire anything as being for our own good, and that in consequence we only think of an action as one which we ought to do, in virtue of thinking that it will be conducive to our own good, he holds that, in order to think of some action as a duty, we must not only think of it as conducive to the good of the whole but must also think of that good as our good. In other words, by holding that underlying any thought of some action as a duty there is the thought of the good of the whole as our good, he thinks himself able to reconcile two apparently inconsistent positions (1) that in coming to think of some action as a duty we are determined solely by the consideration of what will be for the public good; and (2) that, nevertheless, we must be thinking of the action as for our own good, since otherwise we should not be thinking of it as a duty. And he really implies that while we arrive at the character in detail of the acts which we think duties by thinking of these actions as conducive to the public good, we arrive at their character as duties by thinking of them as for our good, or, more accurately, as for our greatest good.

His view, therefore, implies that we cannot even raise the question whether a right action will be for the advantage of the agent, since the connexion is really self-evident. For according to him it is only if we think of some action as for our own good that we shall think of it as a duty at all. We may of course question whether some particular action is a duty by questioning whether it will really be for our good, but once we imply that some action is a duty, as we do by referring to it as a duty, we imply that we have already thought of it as for our good.

Here it may be pointed out that this doctrine of Green's is very different from that of Plato in the fourth book of the *Republic*, at any rate if Plato has been rightly interpreted. They have no doubt an important implication in common, viz. that in all deliberate action we are moved by the desire of our own good.

But there the identity ends. For while Green is maintaining that the very thought that some action is right involves the thought that it will be for our good, with the implication that the rightness of a right act depends on its advantageousness and that this dependence is self-evident, Plato is allowing that even if a right act be advantageous, its rightness is independent of its advantageousness, so that its advantageousness, if it be advantageous, requires to be proved.

But if we allow, as we must, that Green has been rightly interpreted, it is not difficult to see that his view is fundamentally mistaken. He is in effect offering as the explanation of our having come to think certain actions duties, the real or supposed facts (1) that we think of these actions as conducive to the good of the society of which we are members, and (2) that we think of the good of that whole as our good. And he implies that the thought to be explained and the thoughts which explain it are related as conclusion and premises. According to him, the thinking that a certain action is a duty is really the concluding that it is a duty in virtue of its being, as we think, for the good of the whole and of that good's being, as we think, our greatest good, and therefore the thinking that the action is a duty requires as its explanation the prior existence of the thoughts which form the premises of the argument. And the view really amounts to resolving the idea of duty into the idea of conduciveness to our advantage, or, in other words, resolving the moral 'ought' into the non-moral 'ought' in the sense in which it means conducive to our purpose, on the supposition that our purpose is always our greatest good or advantage. For it is only if the 'ought' in the conclusion that we ought to do these actions is understood in the non-moral sense that the conclusion can be plausibly represented as following from the premises.

If, however, we allow this, we ought to go on to ask how Green was led to make such a fundamental mistake.

Although in the *Prolegomena* he freely uses the terms 'Ethics' and 'Moral Theory', and although he obviously regards the *Prolegomena* as including an exposition, at any rate in outline, of his own moral theory, it is difficult to make out what he means by these phrases. Probably, if asked, he would have said that by 'a moral theory' he meant an account of what in the last resort renders an action a duty. Probably he would have also said that the principal object of the *Prolegomena* was to advance a moral theory.

But the Introduction makes it clear that Green considers that before he can even begin to advance a moral theory, he has to execute a preliminary task. He feels that he has first to vindicate the very existence of the subject-matter with which he proposes to deal. It is of course only possible to propound a theory of duty, or, more fully, a theory of the basis of duty, to someone who admits that there are such things as duties. For anyone who denies this will inevitably go on to contend that there is nothing about which to form a theory. And Green finds himself confronted by a school of contemporary thinkers, who, influenced by the growth of physical science, contend that for a *theory* of ethics there should be substituted a *science* of ethics. Ostensibly the contention is that whereas up to the present a special method of treatment of the subject of duty, designated 'philosophical', has been considered appropriate, the proper method is to treat duty as a fact belonging to the physical world and therefore by the same method as that by which we study other physical facts. But if we look below the surface, we find that the contention is quite different. To limit the contention to what is necessary for our purpose, it is really the contention that the fact to be considered and explained, i.e. have the reason for it exhibited, is not the fact that it is our duty to do certain actions but the fact that we have come to think so. This fact, it is implied, requires explanation, because obviously at an earlier stage of our lives we had no such thought at all; and in any case we are in the last resort descended from men who had no such idea, and, ultimately, from animals. And the only kind of explanation possible must be scientific, i.e. physical. We have to show how the original nature of ourselves or our ancestors taken in conjunction with our environment results in, and so accounts for, our having this conviction, just as the present state of the earth and of the stars has to be shown by science to result from, and to be accounted for, by their state at an earlier time. Further it is really implied that our present thought that certain actions are duties is false, since any suggested physical explanation, say by reference to sympathy as an element in man's original nature, would only explain at best how we come to make the mistake of thinking these actions duties. It is implied, therefore, that if Ethics is to be the name for a real subject it must have as its subject-matter not duties, since there are no such things, but our false convictions that there are duties; and that its business must be to give a scientific explanation of our coming to have them, and so to state the origin of the *idea* of duty. And Green, finding this view pervading the atmosphere round him, naturally thinks that he must first demolish this view of the 'scientific' moralists before he can proceed to develop a moral theory, i.e. a theory about duty, at all.

Now there are two fundamentally different ways in which anyone who wanted to destroy this view might proceed. He might agree with the 'scientific' moralists that our possession of moral convictions requires accounting for by some prior state or activity, either of ourselves or of certain other things or beings, but insist that that prior state or activity must be non-physical. Or, alternatively, he might go further by denying that our possession of moral convictions, along with our possession of certain other things such as the ideas of space, of time, and of cause, can be accounted for by any preceding state or activity whether physical or not, and maintaining that it requires for its explanation the pre-existence in us of the capacity for having or forming these convictions, a capacity of the existence of which our previous states or activities afford no indication whatever. And if he took the latter line, he could go on to add, that in the case of any state or activity which can only be accounted for in this way, i.e. by allowing its existence to require a pre-existing corresponding capacity, the process through which the subject of the state has gone can only be understood by, so to say, reading it backwards, and not, as the scientist would like to read it, forwards. For he could say that where this kind of explanation is necessary, it is only possible to discover all that existed in the earlier stage by the help of our knowledge of the states and activities at the later stage, since the existence of the corresponding capacities at the earlier stage could be discovered only at the later stage through our knowledge of the states and activities then attained.

Of these two possible ways of meeting the 'scientific' moralists it is obvious that Green adopts the former and less drastic. In this respect his attitude towards his opponents resembles that of Plato towards the Sophists in that he agrees with them in principle but differs on a matter, though no doubt an important matter, of detail. And so far as the *Prolegomena to Ethics* is what it is called, viz. *prolegomena* to Ethics and not an ethics, it is an endeavour to meet the 'scientific' moralists on their own ground by allowing that our moral convictions must have as their explanation some prior state or activity, but trying to show that this prior state or activity must be non-physical in character.

Green's own explanation really falls into two parts, of which one has already been stated. He offers as the proximate explanation of our conviction that some action is a duty our possession of the thought that the action will be for the good of the whole, together with that of the thought that the good of the whole is our good. But he contends in effect that this latter thought presupposes the thought of ourselves as beings capable of having a good or being satisfied, and that in turn the existence of this thought in ourselves requires explanation. Consequently he implies that the complete explanation of our moral convictions requires the explanation of the existence of this thought. And, in its barest outline his explanation of the latter is as follows: What would ordinarily be described as a man's possession of animal wants and impulses, such as the want of food and hunger, may, and perhaps does, admit of a physical explanation. But no such explanation is possible of a man's thought of himself as capable of a good, a thought which is implied not merely in any moral conviction but also in any deliberate action. The existence of this thought in a man implies that he is a self-conscious being, who in virtue of his self-consciousness is able to distinguish himself from his various wants, and think of himself as a being who may become satisfied and whose satisfaction is distinct from the satisfaction of any particular want. And, this being so, the presence of this thought can be explained only by supposing that the eternal self-conscious subject of the world has reproduced itself in man, i.e. really has caused man to have the nature of a self. Consequently its presence in man cannot possibly be the result of any physical process in the world of nature, but, on the contrary, implies the operation of a non-physical cause working *ab extra*.

Now there is really no need for us to consider whether this explanation of the thought of ourselves as capable of a good is successful. For it is only introduced in order to supply part of the basis of his proximate explanation of our moral convictions, and if this proximate explanation is not in fact successful, it does not matter whether the proffered explanation of part of its basis is successful. If our conviction that we ought to do a certain action does not in fact arise from our thought that the action will conduce to the good of society which is also our good, then of course it does not matter whether Green succeeds in explaining something implied by this thought, viz. the thought of ourselves as beings capable of a good. For in that case even a successful explanation of the latter will not help him to explain the former. There is, however, no way of escaping the admission that what I have called Green's *proximate* explanation, i.e. account of the origin, of our moral convictions fails. It must in the end be allowed that in offering this explanation Green is really substituting for his opponents' physical explanation, which, it is hardly necessary to point out, is absurd on the face of it, what may in contrast be called in a very restricted and special sense a 'rational' explanation. If this explanation did explain our moral convictions then, of course, he would have explained them; but it does not, and, as I propose to contend, no 'rational' explanation, in the special sense intended, is possible.

These statements, of course, require both elucidation and vindication. When in ordinary life we ask 'What is the origin, or what is the explanation, of a man X's having a certain idea, say the idea that Y is unscrupulous?', and again when we ask what is in fact the same question, viz. 'How did X get the idea?', we are presupposing that the idea for the origin of which we are seeking was acquired by a process of reasoning, and are really asking what were the thoughts from which as premises X obtained the idea as a conclusion. We think, and think rightly, of X's having the idea as requiring explanation by reference to his past because we are thinking of the idea as one at which he has arrived, as we say, by an inference; and the explanation for which we are looking can in a special sense be called rational, because we think it consists in the prior existence of certain *thoughts* together with the exercise of the capacity of *reasoning* on the part of X. And when Green is looking for the origin of our idea that certain actions are duties, what he must really be doing, though of course without realizing it, is looking for the thoughts from which as premises we conclude that these actions are duties; and for that reason he can be said to be looking for a rational explanation of them in the sense explained. And if only it had been true, that we do sometimes think of the good of some society as our good, and that, when we think so and also think that some action will be for the good of that society, we conclude that the action is one which we are morally bound to do, Green's account of the origin of our moral convictions would have been successful. But unfortunately it is not true.

The broad fact is that on the one hand Green is really trying to show that we deduce the idea that some action is a duty from ideas which do not involve the idea of duty, and that on the other hand any such attempt must from its very nature fail. There is, of course, no difficulty in allowing that if we already think some *given* action a duty, we may go on to think in consequence that some other given action is a duty. If we think that we ought to do our day's work, then if we realize that the work cannot be done without getting up early, we shall think it a duty to get up early. There is, again, no difficulty in allowing that if we think that a given *kind* of action is a duty, we may in consequence go on to think of some given action as a duty. If we think it a duty to abstain from hurting people's feelings, then if we think that telling a man what we think of him would be hurting his feelings, we shall think we ought to abstain from telling him. But what cannot be done is to conclude that some action is a duty from thoughts *neither of which* is the thought that some action or kind of action is a duty. Aristotle was right on a fundamental matter when he pointed out the impossibility of a μετάβασις εἰς ἄλλο γένος, and not the least important case of this impossibility is to be found in the impossibility of deducing a conclusion which contains the term 'duty', from premises which do not. It is not merely that Green fails to give a successful rational explanation, in the sense explained, of our idea that certain actions are duties. Any one must fail. For he will be attempting to find the premises from which we arrive at a thought which is in fact not arrived at by an argument at all. And I would suggest as a prominent instance of the fallacy involved the attempt which is often made nowadays (as e.g. I think it is by Professor Moore and Professor Laird) to maintain a view which implies that we deduce the rightness of certain actions from our knowledge of what is *good* taken in conjunction with our knowledge of our powers of action and of existing circumstances.

The question, of course, arises. 'What line ought Green to have taken against his opponents?'. The answer is surely that he ought to have abandoned any attempt to offer a rational explanation of our moral convictions, in the sense of 'rational' explained, i.e. to represent them as attained by some process of reasoning; and that, instead, he ought to have taken the more drastic line of opposition by maintaining that they imply for their explanation the prior existence of the corresponding capacity on our part, which only becomes actualized given the appropriate stimulus.

As a clue to explaining what is meant, it is worth pointing out that it may well be questioned whether in any case whatever in which we do come to have a thought by way of inference, the thoughts which we must already have in order to draw the conclusion do *by themselves* explain our coming to have the thought. For to come to have the thought, besides having to have the thoughts which are to be its premises, we must, as we say, draw the conclusion from them; and this drawing the inference, i.e. this activity of inferring, implies the prior existence in us of something not actual, and therefore not discoverable by any activity of self-consciousness, viz. the capacity of reasoning, or, in other words, intelligence. Therefore it may rightly be said that even to account for our having a thought which we are said to acquire inferentially, we have to presuppose the pre-existence in us of a certain capacity, and therefore to allow that the explanation of the thought does not lie solely in any preceding state or activity. In an analogous way, it may, I think, rightly be contended that what Green ought to have maintained is that our possession of moral convictions cannot be explained in terms of any past state or activity of ours in which we had no such convictions, but requires us to presuppose the prior existence in ourselves of a certain capacity, viz. the capacity of having them. Two not unimportant additions may be made. First it may be said that Green himself takes a similar view with regard to our thought of ourselves as capable of a good. For he urges in effect that, to account for this thought, we have to allow that prior to having it we were selves, i.e. beings capable of self-consciousness, though he spoils the effect of this contention by going on to imply that this capacity can, and indeed must, be generated in us *ab extra*. The second addition is more important. It may fairly be said that if Green had maintained that what is required to explain our moral convictions is the prior existence of the corresponding capacity on our part, he would have maintained an explanation of them, which, unlike that offered by the 'scientific' moralists, in no way implied them to be false. For, on this view, the nature of the pre-existing capacity which we think presupposed by our possession of moral convictions will depend entirely on what we think the intrinsic nature of what are here called our moral convictions. As Plato saw, we can only discover what our capacities are through our apprehension of their actualizations. And if as the result of considering our so-called moral convictions in themselves, we consider them to be really the *knowledge* that certain actions are right, we shall have to maintain the existence in us of the capacity of *knowing* what is right. If on the other hand we consider them to be really the *thought* or *conviction* that the actions are right, then we shall have to maintain the existence in us of the capacity of *thinking* or *being convinced* that they are right, which as such may be either true or false. Consequently if Green had taken this line, he could have gone on to maintain that the need to account for our so-called convictions in no way implies them to be false, and that if anyone is anxious to discover whether they are true, he will find no light whatever thrown on this question by considering the question which the 'scientific' moralists think all-important, viz. 'What is required to account for them?'.

I am only too conscious of the length of my argument. My sole defence is that it is impossible to consider one issue without considering others. But I think it possible to sum up most of what I have been contending for by a reference to Kant. His moral philosophy is of course open to many obvious criticisms. Nevertheless he always strikes me as having, far more than any other philosopher, the root of the matter in him. More especially, he seems to me to steer completely clear of those views which I have been maintaining to be errors, and indeed to insist that they are errors. He will have nothing to do either with the idea that the rightness of an action depends on its being for our own good, or with the idea that we think of it as so depending, or with the idea that desire for our own good is our only motive. And it is, I think, for this reason that in spite of his obvious mistakes he retains so close a hold on his readers.

INDEX